DEATH
AND INSTITUTIONS

Death and Culture

*Editors: Ruth Penfold-Mounce, University of York, UK,
Kate Woodthorpe, University of Bath, UK and
Erica Borgstrom, The Open University, UK*

Mortality is a research theme in evidence across multiple disciplines,
but one that is not always explicitly acknowledged. This series provides
an outlet for a social science and cross-disciplinary exploration of all
aspects of mortality. The aim of the series is to create a forum for the
publication of sociologically relevant research that approaches death from
a cultural perspective, supported by evidence and framed by theoretical
engagement. The series advances cross-disciplinary, international and
social discussions about death and culture.

Also available in the series:

Find out more at:
bristoluniversitypress.co.uk/death-and-culture

DEATH AND INSTITUTIONS

Processes, Places and the Past

Edited by
Kate Woodthorpe, Helen Frisby
and Bethan Michael-Fox

BRISTOL
UNIVERSITY
PRESS

First published in Great Britain in 2025 by

Bristol University Press
University of Bristol
1–9 Old Park Hill
Bristol
BS2 8BB
UK
t: +44 (0)117 374 6645
e: bup-info@bristol.ac.uk

Details of international sales and distribution partners are available at bristoluniversitypress.co.uk

© Bristol University Press 2025

British Library Cataloguing in Publication Data
A catalogue record for this book is available from the British Library

ISBN 978-1-5292-3666-8 hardcover
ISBN 978-1-5292-3667-5 ePub
ISBN 978-1-5292-3668-2 ePdf

The right of Kate Woodthorpe, Helen Frisby and Bethan Michael-Fox to be identified as editors
of this work has been asserted by them in accordance with the Copyright, Designs and Patents
Act 1988.

Cover design: Liam Roberts Design
Front cover image: Stocksy/Rene de Haan
Bristol University Press uses environmentally responsible print partners.
Printed and bound in Great Britain by CPI Group (UK) Ltd, Croydon, CR0 4YY

FSC
www.fsc.org
MIX
Paper | Supporting
responsible forestry
FSC® C013604

This collection is dedicated to the chapter authors, who have worked so diligently to get this book to fruition. We thank you for your time, energy and commitment.

Contents

Series Editors' Preface

Erica Borgstrom, Ruth Penfold-Mounce and Kate Woodthorpe

Studying death can tell us an incredible amount about life. More specifically, it can illuminate a seemingly endless evolving relationship between humans and mortality. From sense-making and rituals around dying to how deceased persons are disposed of and even interwoven within human/non-human grief as ecologies shift, studying death not only deepens our understanding about loss and endings, but also of societies and culture. By attending to these matters, this book series seeks to shine a light on the cultural and social dimensions of death, exploring the wider contexts in which it is experienced, (re)presented and understood.

At a time when recognizing the differences inherent in these broader sociocultural contexts has never been more important, the series adopts a broad use of the term 'culture' to enable us to bring together a rich multidisciplinary set of monographs and edited collections. We appreciate that the concept of culture has long been debated in several disciplines, most notably within anthropology, as well as contested in terms of how to optimally study 'culture'. While this series will acknowledge this, we do not seek to replicate some of these wider theoretical and epistemological debates. Rather, we want to open out 'culture' to include anthropological, sociological, historical and philosophical perspectives as well as drawing on media and culture studies, art and literature. By adopting such an open position to what culture is and how it can be known, we welcome both the sharing of new empirical work within the series as well as theorizing about how engagements with death (re)shape understandings of what culture is, how it operates, and what the future of culture(s) may be.

As social scientists spanning anthropology, sociology, criminology and cultural studies, and supported by an international editorial board that includes experts in death, dying and the dead, our default position when thinking about death is typically two-fold. First, that death and dying are inherently social; that is, they are not only about biological or material processes and endings. Second, by attending to and foregrounding 'the social' when it comes to death, issues of culture and cultural practices necessarily organically come to the fore. Such is the importance of culture to death, that the topic does not 'fit' neatly into one discipline over another. It is a truly interdisciplinary issue that affects everyone who has lived, is living, or will live in the future; all life on the planet; and Earth itself.

This series launched in 2018 with Emerald Publishing, but relocated in 2021 to Bristol University Press. The series represents a commitment to empirically building our collective understandings about death and culture across time and places, in monographs and edited collections. As editors, we want to take this moment to thank existing and previous editors and authors, the presses we work with, and the wider academic and professional communities that facilitate the flourishing of studies of death and culture. It is only through this collective endeavour that books like this can be made, read and built upon, and we are excited to see the series grow. We welcome enquiries about future volumes, and hope that you enjoy reading this book.

About this book

This collection explores one of the most central themes within the end of life, that of the influence of institutions and processes of institutionalization. As the editors of the collection indicate in their introduction, much of work in this area to date has focused on managing dying or landscapes associated with death. This collection extends this to explore these and other places and processes associated with death, over time, across countries, and virtually.

Originating from the Centre for Death and Society 2022 annual conference on the same theme, the editors have succeeded in bringing together an eclectic array of chapters with authors from differing national contexts, disciplines and career stages. They show the enduring influence of institutions and institutionalizing processes over the end of life, and how these operate to amplify or suppress varying types of knowledge. As the editors note, at a time when there is growing recognition of the legacy of colonialism on – and the need for inclusivity in – death studies, there is much to be explored in this area to ensure that all voices, and all knowledges, can be heard.

List of Figures and Tables

Figures

Table

Notes on Contributors

Chao Fang is Lecturer in Sociology at the University of Liverpool, UK, and Visiting Research Fellow at the Centre for Death and Society at the University of Bath, UK. Chao's research interests focus on loss, death, dying and bereavement, exploring their intersections with culture. He has published widely on end-of-life care, ageing, loneliness and chronic illness. A particularly notable aspect of his research is the keen emphasis on understanding and disseminating insights into human existential needs, both through interdisciplinary research and public engagements.

Helen Frisby obtained her doctorate on Victorian funeral customs from the University of Leeds, UK, in 2009, and is Visiting Research Fellow at the Centre for Death and Society, University of Bath, UK. She continues to research, publish and speak widely on the history and folklore of death, dying and bereavement, including appearances on the History Channel and BBC Radio. Other research, conducted with the University of Bristol, investigates the tools, techniques and wider informal occupational culture of frontline cemetery staff. Helen is a council member and trustee of The Folklore Society, and former secretary of the Association for the Study of Death and Society. Helen is presently Researcher Development Manager at University of the West of England Bristol, with particular expertise in academic writing, qualitative research methods and postgraduate researcher wellbeing.

Hajar Ghorbani is an Iranian PhD student of anthropology and the Killam Scholar at the University of Alberta, Canada, specializing in death and modernity in Iran and the Middle East. She has published widely in this area and edited *The Social Studies of Death in Iran* (2020), the first book of its kind to be published on the subject of death studies in Iran. In her doctoral project, she has been studying *Dead Bodies' Agency and Western Politics*.

Devaleena Kundu is Assistant Professor at the School of Liberal Studies, UPES, Dehradun, India. In her research, Devaleena navigates the domains of death studies, gothic horror and cultural criminology. Her latest article, entitled 'Negotiating transgression, deathlessness, and senescence in Mary

Shelley's *The Mortal Immortal*' (2023) was published in *Victoriographies*. She is currently co-editing the focus issue, 'Dead Women and Gendered Death in Visual Culture' for MAI: Feminism and Visual Culture.

Bethan Michael-Fox teaches and researches in the School of English and Creative Writing at The Open University. Her research and publications focus on the representation of death in popular culture. Before relocating to Cornwall, Bethan was a senior lecturer in the School of Education and English at the University of Bedfordshire. She is Managing Editor for the academic journal *Mortality* and Social Media Manager for the Open Access journal *Revenant: Critical and Creative Studies of the Supernatural*. She is co-founder and co-host of *The Death Studies Podcast*.

Lee Moerman is Professor of Accounting at the University of Wollongong, Australia. Her research focuses on the impact of accounting practice and the disclosure of information for stewardship reasons or economic decision-making. This research is particularly concerned with how accounting embeds particular notions of accountability in complex economic and sociopolitical relationships in areas such as toxic products, the deathcare industry and postcolonial relations.

Dan O'Brien is Visiting Research Fellow at the Centre for Death and Society, University of Bath, UK, and an Associate Fellow of the Royal Historical Society. His research focuses on the undertaking trade and the organization of funerals in 18th-century England. He also seeks to understand how the undertakers and their goods were perceived by society, by analysing how death and dying were presented in the popular culture of the period. He has chapters awaiting publication which focus on the organization and execution of funerals in 18th-century England. These include an account of the development of early undertaking businesses in the fashionable city of Bath, and a study of funerary imagery in late 18th-century funeral trade ephemera.

Linda Pentikäinen is a doctoral student at the University of Helsinki, Finland, working in the Digital Death: Transforming History, Rituals and Afterlife (DiDe) research consortium. Her disciplinary background is in social psychology. Linda's research interests include digital and social media, grief influencers and gendered mourning.

Sally Raudon is Economic and Social Research Council Postdoctoral Research Fellow in the Department of Social Anthropology at St John's College, University of Cambridge, UK. A social anthropologist, Sally's research interests are death and the body, urban and political anthropology, massed graves, citizens and the state, and memorialization. She has published on death rituals; the Crown, sovereignty and constitutional reform in settler societies; and austerity in Europe. Previously Sally was an affiliated lecturer and postdoctoral research and teaching associate in social anthropology at Cambridge, a research fellow at the University of Auckland, and a teaching fellow at Te Herenga Waka Victoria University of Wellington.

Johanna Sumiala is Professor of Media and Communication, University of Helsinki, Finland and Visiting Senior Fellow at the London School of Economics and Political Science, UK, and Visiting Professor at the Centre for Death and Society at the University of Bath, UK. She has published widely on media anthropology and digital death studies. In recent years her research has focused on social media rituals, mediated victimhood, suffering and the study of digital afterlife and immortality. Her latest book is titled *Mediated Death* (Polity, 2021). Currently she leads the international research consortium Digital Death: Transforming History, Rituals and Afterlife.

Lindsay Udall is Historical Archaeologist and Visiting Research Fellow at the Centre for Death and Society, University of Bath, UK. Her previous work as the Research Officer at Arnos Vale Cemetery subsequently became the subject of her Arts and Humanities Research Council-funded PhD. Before her research life in cemeteries, Lindsay had a career in cartography, architectural history and the conservation of historic buildings and monuments. Her research interests lie in cemeteries and burial grounds, genealogical research methods, cremation and crematoria, network theory, medical history, and the history of antiquarianism.

Sandra van der Laan is Professor of Accounting at the University of Sydney Business School, Australia. Her research examines the role of accounting in organizations and society, with particular emphasis on the (in)visibilities created by the taken-for-granted nature of accounting. This allows a focus on questions of accountability in diverse settings, such as microfinance and the deathcare industry.

Renske Visser is Postdoctoral Researcher at the University of Oulu, Finland, researching children's beliefs around dying and death. She is co-host of *The Death Studies Podcast* and writes reviews on books about death, dying and the dead on her blog *Dead Good Reading*. Renske is interested in how place and space shape dying and end-of-life experiences, and has previously conducted research on homemaking in later life, ageing in secure forensic environments and cancer care in prison. Renske is co-editor of the edited volume *Difficult Death, Dying and the Dead in Media and Culture* (Palgrave Macmillan, 2023).

Anna Wilde has an MA in Death, Culture and Religion and is currently completing her PhD on the Death Positive Movement at the University of Birmingham, UK. Her research interests include death, implicit religion and digital religion. She is a director of a Community Interest Company, CEDAR (Community Education in Death Awareness and Resources) Education, and is Digital Manager at Caring for God's Acre, a charity which supports the environmental and built heritage of burial grounds in the UK.

Rhona Winnington is Senior Lecturer in Adult Nursing at the University of the West of Scotland, Dumfries, UK. Her research focuses on patient choice related to death, dying and end-of-life care within the context of institutional power. She has a specific focus on assisted dying and the experiences and impact of such legislation on individuals, families, clinicians and communities beyond the right-to-die narrative.

Kate Woodthorpe is Reader in Sociology at the University of Bath, UK where she is co-director of the Centre for Death and Society. Kate's research has centred around funeral practices, costs and families, and she has advised the UK government on these issues over the last decade. She is a Churchill Fellow, a previous editor of *Mortality*, and is a series editor for the Death and Culture series, in which this collection belongs.

Shelby Zimmerman received her PhD in Modern Irish History from Trinity College Dublin in 2024. Her thesis examined the medicalization of death in the South Dublin Union workhouse from 1872 to 1920, centering on the role the institution played in Dublin's medical landscape. Shelby's research interests include the history of medicine, institutions, welfare, poverty, and death in the 19th and early 20th centuries. She was previously an early career researcher in the Trinity Long Room Hub Arts and Humanities Research Institute.

Acknowledgements

Thank you to Georgina Robinson for her help in organizing our thoughts, to Emily Ross and Anna Richardson from Bristol University Press for their help in the drafting process, and to series editors Ruth Penfold-Mounce and Erica Borgstrom for supporting our proposal for this collection in the first place.

Thank you to the Centre for Death and Society community, who continue to share, inspire, contribute to and support the Centre's activities.

Introduction

Kate Woodthorpe, Helen Frisby and Bethan Michael-Fox

Institutions and processes of institutionalization have been an area of prime concern for social science, cultural and humanities scholars across all disciplines and cultures since time immemorial. Some of the most well-known theories and theorists have stemmed from their influence, such as Goffman's work on the impact of institutions on behaviour (1959), or Foucault's (1977) work on surveillance. The power of economic structures as institutions has also led to significant explorations of the relationships between the self, mortality and what it is to be human (Baudrillard, 1993; Han, 2021).

The influence of institutions in the study of death and dying has been profound, including work on how they routinize and control the experience of dying (James and Field, 1992; Lawton, 2000; Seymour and Clark, 2018); how they can contribute to the concealment of death behind closed doors (Ariès, 1976; Mellor and Shilling, 1993); on processes of institutionalization and how these affect dying and post-death experiences (Gorer, 1965); the rise and fall of beliefs and value systems (Walter, 2020); the growth of new sectors and their attendant processes (Parsons, 2018); or on the management and location of the dead (Kenney, 2023). A considerable amount of this work has been highly critical, or at least full of warnings, about the potentially stifling nature of institutions and institutionalizing processes, the mis/overuse of power, the overreach of practitioners, a lack of individual agentic choice, and so on. Much of it has, as a result, positioned institutions in opposition to individuals, reflecting enduring debates in sociological writing about structure and agency.

But are institutions and processes of institutionalization all bad? Are they just, as Foucault would have had it, about discipline, control and power? And how are they faring in a post-disciplinary world, a so-called 'hypermodern' age (Lipovetsky, 2005), in which individual self-expression and self-fulfilment are privileged? Certainly, experiences of dying and bereavement today are still largely shaped by institutions; be those structures of belief (religion; value systems), organizations (healthcare; cemeteries and crematoria) or

1

relationships (families and wider social networks). Within these institutions, as Jacobsen (2019) points out, there is much to celebrate with how contemporary death is handled, with greater visibility, increasing diversity in ritual, community-based approaches, and the expansion of the academic study of death itself, to name a few. As this collection will show, beyond power and surveillance, institutions and institutionalizing processes enable the effective management of change; empower people and communities; establish boundaries and parameters in which people can operate; uphold social justice; ensure clarity and consistency, transparency and accountability; provide resource distribution; and facilitate relationships between people, communities and landscapes. Indeed, for most of us, personal experience speaks to the fact that institutions and institutionalizing processes remain integral to culture as the forces and foundations on which people live their lives and die, creating a sense of stability and offering structures for meaning at some of the hardest times of life.

To date, this potential has not been fully explored within the field of death studies. Many of the existing tropes about dying, death and bereavement focus either on individuals or on institutions and institutionalizing processes as inhibiting or disempowering individuals. Little exists on their enabling functions, on the transparency that they can evoke, and the significance of culture as an intangible mediator of relationships between processes, place, the past and their perceptions, and – of course – the people within them.

It is to this relational interplay that this volume speaks. The collection comes from a conference of the same theme, organized in 2022 by the Centre for Death and Society (CDAS) at the University of Bath, UK. Such was the volume of abstracts submitted and the success of the conference that we realized we had identified a topic which resonated across the death studies field. In keeping with the ethos of CDAS as an inclusive and interdisciplinary research centre, in selecting a set of chapters for this volume we sought to include authors and topics that spanned the globe, disciplines, periods of time, settings and author career stages, from doctoral students through to professors. The chapters here cover a range of international contexts including the United Kingdom, United States, China, New Zealand and Iran, exploring Irish workhouses, prisons in the United Kingdom, cemeteries in Tehran, and a range of spaces that represent complex cross-cultural exchanges from the sale and movement of body parts to the discussion of grief in online contexts. We regret that we have not been able to source a more global spread of chapters, noting the absence of chapters from the African continent in particular. Much needed calls to decentre and decolonize death studies (Tripathi, 2021; Taylor, 2023) include recognition that death studies has lost sight of its privilege and the importance of inequity, inequality, discrimination, heritage and legacies (Puri, 2021). Ensuring a truly rich and diverse range of perspectives is central to the project to decolonize death studies, a project in which we must all be engaged through reflection and action. We see this edited collection therefore as an instigator of conversations – rather than a definitive collection – about the role of institutions and institutionalizing processes, and we hope that in producing this book we are opening up opportunities for others to take forward this discussion, in their own words and in their own time. We will do what we can to honour this commitment beyond this book's publication.

When selecting topics and chapters for this collection we were faced with a considerable task: institutions and processes of institutionalization permeate, shape or contextualize almost every – if not *every* – facet of dying, death and bereavement. Contained in this volume are 12 original chapters from authors around the world spanning history, sociology, English literature, archaeology, anthropology, gerontology and accounting. They are broadly organized around four themes in the order of process, place, the past and perceptions. Contributing to the theme of 'process' Chapter 1 by Fang explores how, in the establishment of palliative care in contemporary China, there exists an interplay between traditional collectivism and emerging individualism, shaping the perception, experience and institutionalization of a 'good death'. Chapter 2 by Moerman and van der Laan provides an overview of the 'legal' market for human body parts in its institutional context, including tracing the sources and uses of body parts as well as the relationships that exist between various market participants. Chapter 3 by Winnington, written by the author while living in New Zealand, examines the implementation of assisted dying in Aotearoa, New Zealand in 2021, exploring how socially constructed values of an assisted death can produce a contentious discourse of secrecy, stigma and judgement for not only users, but family/ *whānau*, friends and providers of this legal medical service.

Building on 'process', Chapters 4, 5 and 6 explore the theme of 'place'. Examining the experience of dying in prison, Chapter 4 by Visser explores the tensions around staff's role in providing custody or care, and the significance of recognizing the humanity of those that nearing the end of their life and facing death in a prison setting. Reflecting on the impact of COVID-19 on the institutional management of New York City's dead, in Chapter 5 Raudon reviews the history of cremation in the United States and the ways in which social change occurs both in normal times and times of crisis. Chapter 6 by Ghorbani examines the politicization of Tehran's Behesht-e Zahra cemetery as a municipality that is governed by a mayor, who upholds religious nationalist ideology and manages potential dissent.

Turning to the past, in Chapter 7 O'Brien examines the role and purpose of children in London funerals in the 18th century. In Chapter 8, Udall critically reflects on the establishment of the British garden cemetery in the 19th century alongside the emergence of civic societies (later museums), exploring their similarities as spaces of heritage, genealogy and aesthetic design. Zimmerman, in Chapter 9, examines death in the context of the 19th-century workhouse in Ireland, and questions whether workhouse staff sought to reduce institutional mortality or contributed to the workhouse's stigma in the public consciousness as an institution associated with death.

Returning to the present day, the final three chapters examine perceptions of death via visual media. In Chapter 10, drawing on empirical research with those who self-identify as death positive, Wilde assesses the ethos of the Order of the Good Death and queries whether it is establishing a new institutional movement. Chapter 11 by Kundu and Michael-Fox examines the (re)presentation of immortality on screen and in literature, using four contemporary examples as spaces through which anxieties about the medical and political institutionalization of death are depicted. Finally, Chapter 12 by Sumiala and Pentikäinen examines the emergence of Instagram deathstyle gurus, who constitute a new institutional logic of mourning.

In sum, this is an eclectic and diverse array of chapters that has 'something for everyone'. We hope you enjoy reading them. You may also wish to engage with a dedicated podcast episode available at www.thedeathstudies podcast.com, which offers you the chance to hear summaries of each chapter as well as discussion of the book's themes by the editors.

References

Ariès, P. (1976) *Western Attitudes Toward Death: From the Middle Ages to the Present*. Translated by P.M. Ranum. London and New York: Marion Boyars.

Baudrillard, J. (1993) *Symbolic Exchange and Death*. London: SAGE.

Foucault, M. (1977) *Discipline and Punish: The Birth of the Prison*. New York: Pantheon Books.

Goffman, E. (1959) *The Presentation of Self in Everyday Life*. Garden City: Doubleday.

Gorer, G. (1965) *Death, Grief and Mourning in Contemporary Britain*. London: The Cresset Press.

Han, B.-C. (2021) *Capitalism and the Death Drive*. Translated by D. Steuer. Cambridge: Polity.

Jacobsen, M.H. (2019) 'Thought for the times on the death taboo: trivialization, tivolization, and re-domestication in the age of spectacular death', in Teodorescu, A. and Jacobsen, M.H. (eds) *Death in Contemporary Popular Culture*. London: Routledge, pp 15–37.

James, N. and Field, D. (1992) 'The routinization of hospice: charisma and bureaucratization', *Social Science and Medicine*, 34(12): 1363–1375.

Kenney, F.L. (2023) '"A prison for the dead": Hart Island and spatial histories of marginalization', in Coleclough, S., Michael-Fox, B. and Visser, R. (eds) *Difficult Death, Dying and the Dead in Media and Culture*. Basingstoke: Palgrave Macmillan, pp 149–160.

Lawton, J. (2000) *The Dying Process: Patients' Experiences of Palliative Care.* London: Routledge.

Lipovetsky, G. (2005) *Hypermodern Times.* Cambridge: Polity Press.

Mellor, P.A. and Shilling, C. (1993) 'Modernity, self-identity and the sequestration of death', *Sociology*, 27(3): 411–431.

Parsons, B. (2018) *The Evolution of the British Funeral Industry in the 20th Century: From Undertaker to Funeral Director.* London: Emerald.

Puri, J. (2021) 'The forgotten lives of sociology of death: remembering Du Bois, Martineau and Wells', *The American Sociologist*, 52: 638–655.

Seymour, J. and Clark, D. (2018) 'The Liverpool care pathway for the dying patient: a critical analysis of its rise, demise and legacy in England', *Wellcome Open Research*, 3: 1–25.

Taylor, F. (2023) Interview on *The Death Studies Podcast* hosted by Michael-Fox, B. and Visser, R. Published 1 November 2023. Available at: www.thedeathstudiespodcast.com [accessed 15 March 2024].

Tripathi, K. (2021) Interview on *The Death Studies Podcast* hosted by Michael-Fox, B. and Visser, R. Published 21 October 2021. Available at: www.thedeathstudiespodcast.com [accessed 15 March 2024].

Walter, T. (2020) *Death in the Modern World.* London: SAGE.

Culture as an Institution: Assessing Quality of Death in China

Chao Fang

Introduction

The complexity of the quality of death, as perceived by dying patients and witnessed by others, is multifaceted (Patrick et al, 2001). It encompasses not only the 'quality of death' but also the 'quality of life' – illustrating how one can experience a 'good' or 'bad' death and how to live meaningfully before death, as well as the process of coping with bereavement for family members after death (Patrick et al, 2003). Understanding the quality of death is crucial for all who are directly and indirectly involved in the process of dying (Sallnow et al, 2022). These individuals include not only patients, family and care practitioners, but also policy makers and researchers who support dying patients beyond an individual level, through policies, practical guidelines and education programmes. While dying can be a deeply personal and subjective experience, the approach to death and the support surrounding it are also influenced by institutional factors (Walter, 2020). In other words, the process of dying, and more significantly, dying well, is profoundly guided and regulated within an institutionalized context that encompasses societal values, disciplinary expertise and care practices. Traditionally in China, death and dying have long been monitored by family-centred Confucian doctrines, by which dying patients, especially those from older generations, are closely cared for by family members to practise filial piety and wider family-centric values (Fang, 2020). With modernization in China since the mid-20th century, care for the dying has increasingly been dominated by clinical practices that emphasize 'cure' and 'extension of life' without adequately acknowledging the dying person's own interests (Walter, 2020). Family-centred values have also played a significant role in the traditional care model, as families often adopt medicalization (and even over-treatment) as a means of demonstrating their support for the dying family member, but predominantly from a collective perspective to emphasize family solidarity (Cheng, 2018). Meanwhile, more individualized end-of-life care models have also been observed, with an emphasis on the dying person's own wishes and preferences, particularly among those who are younger and/ or have higher educational backgrounds (Fang, 2022).

In the context of a rapidly changing nation where traditions and collective conformity increasingly compete and intersect with modernization and individualism, this chapter examines death and institutions to critically assess how evolving sociocultural norms contribute to the conceptual understanding of QoD in China (Yan, 2010). As China's living standards and life expectancy continue to rise, the concept of a good death has gained significant practical and policy interest in recent years (Fu and Glasdam, 2022). Notably, since the second half of the 2010s, the central Chinese government has developed a series of policies to shape the overall direction of palliative care. For example, the 'Outline of the Plan for "Healthy China 2030"', introduced by the State Council in 2016, highlights palliative care as a key component in the development of lifelong healthcare infrastructures, especially for older people and those living with co-morbidities. Integrated and community-based care lies at the heart of this initiative and has also significantly influenced subsequent policies (Lu et al, 2018). In the following year, the National Health and Family Planning Commission (2017a), now called the National Health Commission, launched the first pilot scheme across a geographically and socioeconomically diverse mixture of five sites in China to explore possible pathways and models to introduce institution–community integrated care for those approaching the end of life. At the time of writing, the pilot scheme has entered its third round, covering 185 cities and districts (National Health Commission, 2023).

These moves demonstrate the central government's drive to further palliative care provision and to provide improved training to community healthcare facilities, while encouraging localized interpretations and implementation. Despite these, significant barriers persist and, with public awareness of palliative care very low, a dearth of adequate funding, professional practice standards and education poses fundamental threats to its expansion within the public health system and throughout the country (Hu and Feng, 2016). In 2017 the National Guideline on Palliative Care (trial) was released, mainly serving as a clinical practice manual focusing on subjects like pain management and dietary considerations, with a brief reference to 'humanistic' assistance for overall socioemotional requirements and emotional support (for example, for grief) (National Health and Family Planning Commission, 2017b). These directives on medical and holistic care are overly broad and lack specificity, however, and as a result, it is increasingly being argued that a standardized approach is needed for palliative care policy to not only tackle the intricacies of palliative care but also inform practice in different social and healthcare settings (Lu et al, 2018). Such a pursuit of standardization reflects the aforementioned policy shift, as policy makers seek to explore applicable palliative care models that can address end-of-life needs across a vast country containing significant social and demographic differences, and many healthcare variations. The focus on standardization also parallels the devolution of palliative care from specialized hospitals to primary care and communities, as a means of more cost-effectively utilizing the limited healthcare resources nationwide.

The concept of a 'good death' has been widely considered the ultimate aim of end-of-life care, encompassing autonomy, dignity, comfort and preparedness at its core (Clark, 2002). Yet, due to its subjective and intricate nature, a 'good death' can be challenging to fully comprehend and address in practical terms when people are dying. The international development of 'Quality of Death' (QoD) as a clinical framework has aimed to provide an objective assessment of a good death (Patrick et al, 2001). Tools have been created across different countries to quantify the fundamental elements of QoD frameworks, thereby constituting a positive dying experience across diverse medical and social contexts (Hales et al, 2010). Initially rooted in Western care environments, QoD assessment tools like the Quality of Dying in Long-Term Care Scale and Quality of Dying and Death strongly emphasize individual preferences and needs. Researchers and practitioners from more collectivist cultures have also adapted these tools, as seen in the Good Death Scale in Taiwan and Good Death Inventory in Japan, to better encompass cultural nuances surrounding death, interpersonal relations and family values (Yao et al, 2007; Miyashita et al, 2008). The significance of culture in palliative care assessments becomes even more evident within such QoD frameworks as person-centredness takes a more prominent role (Bhadelia et al, 2022). In this context, the process of dying is understood to be a deeply (inter)personal encounter, and cultural influences are expressed through the individual experiences of both dying patients and those offering support.

With the rapid expansion of palliative care across China, it is thus becoming increasingly essential to develop standardized criteria that reflect its own fast-evolving sociocultural background. However, data suggests that only approximately 280,000 people can access palliative care in China, out of a population of over 1.4 billion (Jing, 2021). Despite the extremely limited provision, the care quality varies significantly with more medical and social resources concentrated in urban and economically developed areas (Cheng and Chen, 2021). This is crucial for assessing QoD consistently and further enhancing support for a dignified end-of-life experience, given the complexity (Patrick et al, 2001). By considering culture as an institution, in this chapter I aim to provide a conceptual foundation for a more sensitive and timely understanding of QoD in contemporary China. This includes exploring how the process of death, both as a medical and social/familial event, is negotiated by all those involved. While there exist studies on the Chinese concept of 'good death' (Fu and Glasdam, 2022), the understanding of QoD as an evaluation tool remains inadequate. This chapter therefore addresses this knowledge gap by drawing upon a range of resources, including my own research, existing academic literature, and governmental policy and legislation, to explore the potential of developing a consistent lens to understand and support a good death in the unique Chinese context.

Culture as an institution

Culture is an institution that encompasses beliefs, values, traditions, behaviours and ways of thinking shared by a particular group of people within a society (Fang, 2018). The founding father of sociology, Émile Durkheim, likened society to an 'organic analogy'. In this analogy, diverse societal domains – encompassing family, education, policies, public health systems and many others – function like human organs, operating autonomously yet interconnectedly, thereby upholding society's stability and sustainability (Alexander et al, 2004). Individuals both conform to and compose these social structures, ultimately underpinning society's functionality and solidarity. Culture in this context can be overarching, encompassing customs and principles shared by an entire country or region. It may also apply to small social units such as workplaces and local communities. Regardless of its scale, cultural norms provide a basis for individuals to seek meaning to explain experiences and to affirm a sense of security and belonging within various contexts (Berger, 2011).

Individuals, as social beings, are not however confined to adhering to cultural values and norms without critical interpretation. Instead, the connection between individuals and society, where culture exerts significant influence, is characterized by a dialectical relationship (Giddens, 1984) whereby social structures and individual actions are not distinct entities; rather, they shape each other in a reciprocal manner. On the one hand, structures provide the framework within which individuals act, influencing and restricting those actions. At the same time, individual actions possess the potential to perpetuate, alter or challenge these very structures. This duality is particularly evident in the context of death and dying, where cultural discourses on what constitutes a 'good death' and the sociofamilial mechanisms supporting it are often (and increasingly) negotiated by both individuals and society (Fang, 2018). Across the globe, research has illuminated the *agentic* nature through which individuals, such as dying patients, their families and medical staff, adopt, adapt and even reject distinct sociocultural aspects of each society (Klass and Steffen, 2017). In doing so, they craft their own scripts to achieve a 'good death' (Long, 2004).

The dualistic nature of cultural influence on death and dying is further underscored by individuals' reflexivity. That is, individuals not only reflect on their actions within their unique context but also question and adjust their actions in response to changing circumstances (Fang, 2018). The practice of reflexivity in matters of mortality closely resonates with the paradoxes of late modernity (Bauman, 2000), which is characterized by fluidity and fragmentation – existing in a state of perpetual change and uncertainty. Within this paradoxical realm, the very structures that once offered a sense of stability (for example, religion, familism), especially when confronting significant challenges like death and dying, have become less prominent and persuasive. This reflexive interaction with cultural influences can be particularly vivid in settings where traditional and individualistic norms coexist and intertwine, as evidenced by the case of Japan (Valentine, 2009; Long 2004). In a similar vein, China finds itself amidst a substantial societal transformation. As a result, the cultural paradigms in China that were once widely shared and highly esteemed regarding what constitutes a 'good death' face increasing scrutiny and challenges. Perhaps most crucially, the cultural discourses that were formerly upheld as a benchmark for understanding death and dying could inevitably lose their ability to adequately evaluate QoD in the fast-changing contexts of China.

Capturing Quality of Death in competing discourses within China

QoD is a multifaceted and complex construct encompassing elements of communal beliefs, familial principles and medical conventions. In-depth analysis in this field has delineated a spectrum of pivotal dimensions for evaluating QoD. These dimensions include not only structural components, such as the framework of governance, but also the adequacy and diversity of care provision, the calibre and safety of medical practices along with considerations of fairness and accessibility in healthcare services, as well as individual attributes (Bhadelia et al, 2022). Among these attributes are factors like preserving one's dignity, embracing preparedness, exercising autonomy, nurturing relational bonds and comprehending the profound essence of life's meaning (Hales et al, 2010).

Enhancing the conceptual discourse on QoD, while current evaluation methods are valuable, the focus should also be on understanding the essential needs that underline a 'good death' across different dimensions of palliative care. My research on sociopolitical approaches to end-of-life care in England and Japan has highlighted the interconnectedness of individual, relational and existential needs at the core of the end-of-life experience, reflecting a universal desire for comprehensive and consistent palliative care, irrespective of cultural differences (Fang and Tanaka, 2022). Embracing this perspective, grounded in these fundamental needs, can be highly advantageous for both researchers and practitioners, particularly when dealing with the intricate nature of QoD measurements within cultural contexts that are rapidly evolving and diversifying in terms of values, traditions and regulations related to death and dying. As such, this needs-based approach can provide a useful lens for cultivating more culturally nuanced understandings about how to understand and evaluate QoD in the Chinese contexts.

In the following discussion, I will commence by presenting evidence collated from diverse sources, encompassing existing academic research and government documentation. This compilation will serve to paint a dynamic and rapidly evolving panorama of the factors that constitute a meaningful death within Chinese contexts. Subsequently, I will shed further light onto how to capture the complexities inherent more adequately in the experience of death and dying in China. This will involve a clarification of the key culturally informed considerations that underpin palliative care.

Traditional culture as an institution

While no formal assessments of QoD have been developed specifically for the Chinese context, cultural expectations regarding how to achieve a positive end of life have existed for a long time. China's predominant characteristics include its collectivist and relational nature, with a strong emphasis on prioritizing social conformity (Yan, 2010). The enduring influence of collectivism and familism has contributed to a cultural environment that places a significant value on the pursuit of social harmony among individuals and groups. This emphasis on harmony is also evident in experiences related to death and dying (Fang, 2020).

In traditional Chinese culture, death transcends individual significance; it is often seen as a collective endeavour and, at times, a profound testament to the entire family, kin group and even local community (Fang, 2018). The influence of Confucianism, a philosophical ideology defining relationships among individuals, families and the state over a span of 2,000 years, has nurtured a culture emphasizing social harmony. This has given rise to hierarchical structures in social and family contexts, wherein individuals adhere to prescribed roles for mutual support and a sense of belonging within their networks (Bedford and Hwang, 2003). Chinese identity frequently revolves around group membership and the pursuit of harmony, achieved by prioritizing others' needs and the authority of groups. Within this context, death in China signifies not only the physical loss of a valuable member but also a process of family lineage continuation and reconstruction. Death can also present an opportunity or challenge to demonstrate interpersonal connectedness and collective solidarity as a means of upholding the family's reputation (Qi, 2017).

My research has portrayed the traditional spectrum of death and dying experiences within contemporary Chinese society (Fang, 2020). By engaging in conversations with 31 bereaved individuals from diverse sociodemographic backgrounds in China, I uncovered a recurring theme: the longing for harmony significantly shaped views on a 'good' death. This harmony around dying was seen especially through narratives focused on reciprocity and family bonds. Nearly all of my participants stressed family involvement in the dying person's final stages, including caregiving and decisions, interactions, especially with younger generations. For example, a 90-year-old mentioned how interactions with children and grandchildren during his wife's dying gave meaning to her death. This intergenerational focus was mirrored by many of the participants, as well as in other existing research (Fang, 2020; He and van Heugten, 2020), showing the cultural significance of filial piety – a Confucian principle of familial bonds and reciprocal obligations.

Family support also plays a pivotal role in offering vital spiritual reassurance to individuals approaching the end of their lives in China. It may not be widely known that traditions surrounding spirituality shifted significantly following the Cultural Revolution in the 1960s and 1970s, when socialist doctrines were introduced to replace conventional discourses – such as those regarding death and dying – focused on supernatural beliefs and religious practices (Fang, 2020). Research highlights that, instead of relying on traditional religious discourses, spiritual significance can often be derived from connections, relationships and introspection about fulfilled responsibilities and obligations (Jiang et al, 2023). These findings confirm the enduring spiritual value deeply rooted in interdependence. For many, the aspiration to maintain faith within the family, both during life and after death, can provide inner strength and comfort as they confront imminent mortality (Li et al, 2021). Furthermore, the aforementioned cultural significance of filial piety is likely to foster support from younger family members, facilitating the dying person's transition into becoming an 'ancestor' – integral components of the family's entity – receiving ongoing offerings and providing blessings to the lineage, even after physical death through ancestor veneration (Fang, 2018).

The importance of involving families in matters related to death cuts across generations and various circumstances of dying. In my research on the implications of losing an only child (with one child families the norm, governed by the One Child Policy), a key finding has emerged. Even in cases of sudden and premature death, which might not align with societal norms on good death, the active involvement of family members in caregiving, planning and decision-making play a significant role in shaping how people perceive and understand an individual's death and dying (Fang, 2022). The longing for family support is also expressed by terminally ill patients themselves, with research indicating that most prefer their families to be actively engaged in decision-making to ensure their best interests (Ivo et al, 2012). Yet, there are instances where individuals nearing death worry about too much family involvement. For example, data indicates that the family can conceal a diagnosis during the early stages of a person's dying to create a more peaceful environment (Ivo et al, 2012). However, this approach can potentially clash with the dying individual's desire for control and simply knowing the truth. Another example highlighting this tension is over-treatment, where a dying person's quality of life may suffer due to cultural pressures from social expectations to provide aggressive treatments. These actions stem from the desire to uphold filial piety and strengthen family bonds and display these to others, even if they go against the dying person's wishes and best interests during their final moments (Gu et al, 2016).

Assessing traditional needs for Quality of Death

While the enduring values surrounding death and dying continue to wield influence in China, there exist numerous avenues through which to approach people's traditional end-of-life needs. Hence, my intention is not to put forth particular assessment tools or approaches, but rather to elucidate overarching principles that can guide the assessment of QoD across diverse contexts.

The significance of one's individual needs for comfort and dignity at the end of life remains unaltered by sociocultural variations. Yet, in the context of assessing these needs at an individual level in China, it is necessary to view the task through the lens of traditional parameters woven around ideals of social harmony and familism. Put differently, it becomes crucial to not only recognize individual needs, but also to discern the manner in which they are supported/overlooked, within the rich matrix of relationships that envelop principles of reciprocity and solidarity, both within the family nucleus and extending beyond. In China, the course of treatments and pivotal decision-making during the final stages of one's life is often shaped by family, often driven by what close family members perceive as best for the dying person and what is best for the family unit as a whole (Huang et al, 2018). Similarly, the pursuit of autonomy and dignity at the end of life within the Chinese context encompasses a dimension that is inherently relational. Here, individual agency when nearing the end of life is often collaboratively negotiated and upheld through family bonds and a sense of interdependency with others (Gu et al, 2016). Therefore, in addition to the existing measurements that concentrate on individual physical and psychological needs, such as symptom management and place of death, assessing the individual dimension of QoD in China should also include the intersection of individual and family needs. An example of this could be the degree to which the family is involved in the medical care to ensure the comprehensive fulfilment of the dying person's physical and emotional requirements (Bhadelia et al, 2022).

The cultural significance of social harmony should also factor into assessments of QoD and needs, particularly in terms of how individuals cope with profound and often unexplainable pain when dying. Existing measurement tools have highlighted religious and spiritual needs as life draws to a close, including aspects like access to spiritual care and support from faith communities (Bhadelia et al, 2022). While this is undoubtedly valuable, evaluating the support for the existential needs of Chinese individuals at the end of life must also consider the cultural implications of being tied to spiritual and family values, as well as the influence of atheism (stemming from the influence of socialism and the Cultural Revolution). The Chinese Government estimates indicate that around 200 million Chinese citizens are associated with officially recognized religions, but the majority still align with atheism (State Council, 2018). While it is important to cater to the needs of dying people with specific faiths, providing broader support for existential meaning becomes an essential component of comprehensive care to ensure QoD (Fang and Tanaka, 2022). Once again, when faced with suffering and the approach of death, the existential needs within the Chinese context may encompass not just concerns about vulnerability, pain and the inevitability of death, but also a deeper desire to address their existence, often as relational/family-centric beings. For instance, culturally sensitive approaches to alleviate the existential pain of helplessness might involve the presence of family and the assurance of ongoing mutual support between the dying patient and their loved ones. Dealing with feelings of meaninglessness could be effectively managed by upholding strong beliefs in family connections and maintaining a social presence both before and after death (for example, through ancestor veneration). As a result, future assessments of QoD in China should pose questions that capture the cultural understanding of family and social harmony. This approach would help capture how individuals find existential meaning and retain their identity as relational beings – often centred around family and interdependence – during and beyond the dying process.

The significance of familism and social harmony warrants thorough exploration through the lens of family members' experiences and interactions with care professionals. In a culture like China's, where individuals are predominantly perceived as integral parts of their families, ensuring a high QoD requires understanding how the needs of family members are acknowledged and supported (Yan, 2010). This emphasis on family involvement emphasizes the importance of assessing the extent of family involvement in QoD evaluations. This pertains not just to the dying person's view of their family involvement at the end of life, but also to the family members themselves who seek to provide support and share the burdens of the dying. Furthermore, this assessment should extend its focus beyond the end of life per se and may involve exploring if/how follow-up support, such as bereavement support, is extended to family members to mitigate the impact of loss on the family's structure and function. Recognizing the continuum of support for family members can also contribute to a more comprehensive assessment of the wellbeing of the dying person. This is crucial since they often wish to ensure their passing does not undermine their family (Fang, 2018). Considering the integral role care professionals play in the caregiving process, their level of engagement should also factor into QoD evaluations. They act as intermediaries between patients and their families, and thus their understanding of traditional family values' significance in care is essential. Research indicates that physicians in China are often faced with ethical dilemmas, caught between respecting family members' desire to shield patients from the truth of health conditions and honouring the patient's right to make decisions about prognosis and palliative treatment (Hahne et al, 2022). Therefore, inquiries should encompass their understanding of how to minimize conflicts between these potentially opposing perspectives.

Individualization as a competing cultural institution

Culture holds significant power in shaping individual experiences and expectations. Just like in other parts of the world, culture in China is also constantly evolving, reflecting the increasingly diverse relationships that individuals cultivate within their families, the medical field and broader social discourses. The rapid improvement in quality of life and the transformation of family dynamics due to urbanization have progressively challenged traditional values concerning what constitutes a 'good death' (Fang, 2018). This is particularly evident in the growing emphasis on individual rights, independence and freedom (Yan, 2010). This shift is notably characterized by the increasing focus on individualization in the comprehension and negotiation of dying and achieving a good death.

The rise of individualization within Chinese culture can be attributed to a confluence of factors. Most significantly, the remarkable socioeconomic growth following the 'open-up' reforms of the late 1970s has provided individuals with more resources to achieve sociofinancial independence and focus on personal aspects of life (Yan, 2010). This has marked a noticeable shift in cultural narratives from a collectivist mindset to a more individualistic one, where individual identity holds more significance in comparison to conformity with collective family and social norms (Fu and Glasdam, 2022). The recognition of individuality is also accompanied by a gradual acceptance of socioethnic diversity (though not without controversy). Moreover, the recalibration of socialist principles has loosened the grip of entrenched traditions. With fewer established norms to rely on, individuals are compelled to carve their own paths, fostering an environment conducive to self-expression and personal exploration (Yan, 2010). This multifaceted transformation is steering Chinese society towards a new era where the tapestry of individuality is interwoven with the fabric of collective culture.

The significance of individualism has not yet been a central focus in studies concerning the establishment of palliative care in China, particularly within English-language literature. Nevertheless, an increasing body of observations has emphasized the importance of honouring individuality (Fu and Glasdam, 2022). This trend aligns with my research, which has documented individuals' efforts to assert their control and maintain their distinct personalities throughout the processes of death, dying and bereavement, even though this subgroup (often those in younger generations) constitutes a relatively smaller portion of those I have engaged with (Fang, 2018, 2020, 2022). The slowly growing uptake of advance care planning or advance directives is another sign of this changing picture of seeking an individual voice when preparing for dying. Among the low level of knowledge and awareness of such individualized approaches to managing dying, many individuals and families have indicated that, with sufficient education and support, they are receptive to advance care planning or advance directives (Zhang et al, 2021). Public debates on the 'rights to die' were further ignited in 2022 when Shenzhen became the first major city in China to pass legislation that honours the living wills of critically ill patients, allowing them to refuse excessive life-sustaining treatments (while euthanasia and assisted dying remain illegal) (Shenzhen Municipal People's Congress, 2022). Although this is currently regional legislation and at the time of writing is little practised, this development has laid the legal groundwork for dying individuals' wishes to be at least considered, if not given precedence, in decision-making regarding end-of-life and palliative care.

The pursuit of a more individualized approach to dying has been met with resistance, however, particularly in terms of the long-standing cultural emphasis on family and social harmony. Researchers indicate that there is a mixed picture at present in China, with both coexistence and, at times, competition, between the wishes of dying patients and their personal best interests (over-treatment and choice, for example) and the collective objectives imposed by the family (such as prolonging life at any cost for the family's sake) (Ivo et al, 2012; Huang et al, 2018). Cultural sensitivity is often emphasized in being able to understand the complexity of promoting individualistic care for the dying in a collectivist Chinese culture (Fu and Glasdam, 2022). At times this can manifest itself in individuals expressing their health and end-of-life care preferences in indirect and informal manners, such as commenting on the death of others (Cheng, 2018). This indirect expression is deeply rooted in the Chinese culture on family determination and harmony (by seeing death as a taboo) (Fang, 2018). Therefore, further actions have been called to clarify and support doctors' and nurses' knowledge, beliefs, confidence and their scope of practice for facilitating recognition and communication between patients and their family on finding a shared (at least a compromised) ground for honouring the individual agency of the dying patients (Zhang et al, 2021).

The conflicting demands between 'individualized' and 'collective' approaches to dying are particularly pronounced at an intergenerational level. In line with studies on Japanese attitudes towards death (Valentine, 2009), in China higher socioeducational levels and younger ages strongly indicate preferences for more individualized approaches to death (Fang, 2020). My research has revealed that the viewpoints of bereaved Chinese individuals vary significantly across generations within families following the death of a loved one. A small yet noticeable number of participants who were either already socioeconomically independent or in the process of seeking to become so (such as pursuing a university degree) expressed their wishes for dying in a manner characteristic to themselves and their deceased loved ones (Fang, 2018). For example, one bereaved granddaughter expressed her regret about her grandmother's over-medicalization prior to death and as such hoped that she would die in a more peaceful way. The increasing demand for more individualized approaches to dying, particularly within this demographic group, is partially attributed to the rapid improvement in living standards. This improvement has provided younger generations with greater capacity to focus on their own needs and subsequently adopt Western individualistic ideologies (Yan, 2010). The socialist reforms in the third quarter of the 20th century have also contributed to the cultural acceptance of individualism in matters of death and dying. This is especially so for those who came of age after the late 1970s, who have little to draw upon from traditional cultural values, such as religion, collectivism and altruism, which were significantly eroded due to the introduction of socialist doctrines (Fang, 2020). As a result, the perception of what constitutes a 'good death' may differ among individuals and generations in China.

Existential needs have become more fluid in various forms of longing for meaning, as a result of expanding individualism. The traditional approaches to existential needs in the process of dying in China are already no longer strictly 'conventional' due to the diminished influence of religious and spiritual ideologies caused by the socialist reforms (Fang, 2020). People embracing individualized values for death and dying often face even more significant dilemmas – they may discover limited resources available to replace the traditional support from family members and communities, and consequently have to rely (at least partially) on individualized methods to seek meaning in the face of the fundamental challenges of death and suffering. As Bauman (2000) found when examining mental health in postmodern society, feelings of frustration and existential anxiety stemming from insecurity and confusion may arise from the increasingly diversified and fluid social norms and values. Evidence from my research has suggested that the focus on individual-centred values could empower both dying individuals and their close others to identify profoundly meaningful avenues for themselves (such as personalized rituals, memory-making) (Fang, 2018). However, they might also be vulnerable to the lack of structured guidance and readily available resources to alleviate their intricate existential anguish. Hence, external and professional support (for example, therapy, mental health assistance) holds particular significance in addressing existential needs in palliative and end-of-life care within the progressively individualized Chinese context.

Accessing individualized needs for accessing Quality of Death

Existing QoD measurements, primarily originating from Western countries, have predominantly emphasized individualistic aspects in the experience of death and dying, notably comfort, autonomy and dignity (Hales et al, 2010). While it remains important to capture individual satisfaction with treatment, care, communication and understanding across diverse care settings in China, there is also a necessity to evaluate individualized needs within a society that is still largely traditional compared to Western societies. It is evident that asserting control over one's own dying process is often not a straightforward task without encountering cultural resistance from family and other traditional values (for example, prolonging life to demonstrate filial piety) (Fu and Glasdam, 2022). Therefore, when appraising QoD in China, it is imperative to not only capture how individuals nearing the end of life and their support networks perceive individual needs (such as whether they view dignity as primarily individual matters or family affairs), but also to gain insights into how individuals navigate the diverse and sometimes conflicting cultural narratives concerning traditionally collectivist and increasingly individualistic values in approaching death. In doing so, a more comprehensive understanding and assessment of individual needs can be achieved within the intersections of these traditionally collective and progressively individualistic cultural paradigms in the care of those at the end of life.

The increasing cultural emphasis on individualistic values and norms does not preclude the importance of addressing relational needs in end-of-life and palliative care. Rather, the traditional and new individualistic approaches to death are not separated but closely interwoven in real life and practice (Cheng, 2018). As mentioned earlier, contemporary Chinese deathways are often defined by a mixture of conforming to family and social harmony while seeking to assert individual agency (Fang, 2020; Li et al, 2021; Zhang et al, 2021). Traditionally, Chinese people tend to identify themselves as individuals through interdependence with family members and, more generally, affirmation from others (Bedford and Hwang, 2003). Therefore, meeting one's relational needs may contribute to the pursuit of individualistic objectives when facing death and managing the process of dying. For instance, family members and/or health professionals may be willing to support the dying patient in making decisions for themselves, such as determining their own treatment for life-sustaining or palliative care. Consequently, future research on QoD should not only assess the degree of hindrance that relational needs can pose to individualized needs when dying but also how family involvement and external support can *enable* individual agency in addressing wishes and preferences.

To facilitate a need-based perspective on QoD in an increasingly diverse and individualized Chinese society, it is imperative to develop the means of comprehending individuals' existential needs when dying. In this context, the dying person is more likely to be perceived as an individual embodying unique biography and multifaceted needs (Fang and Tanaka, 2022). When evaluating one's QoD, the focus should therefore extend beyond medical aspects to encompass the broader spectrum of their existential concerns, including their spiritual beliefs, cultural values and personal aspirations across the lifespan (Clark, 2002). This holistic approach not only acknowledges the evolving cultural landscape of China, where traditional collectivism coexists with emerging individualism, but also upholds the dignity and agency of the dying person as they navigate their final journey. As a result, questions posed during the assessment can explore whether the care provided to the dying person adheres to a one-size-fits-all model or adopts a more personalized, need-based approach. Such inquiries can shed light on how the individual, their family and their support network are engaged in identifying and addressing their unique existential needs and overall holistic wellbeing. By adopting this approach, it becomes possible to ensure that QoD reflects not only the fragmented dimensions (for example, medical aspects) but also the deeply personal and culturally significant facets of the dying person's journey. This could contribute to a more compassionate and comprehensive approach to end-of-life care in China.

Relational autonomy: a culturally sensitive approach to Quality of Death

Taking culture as an overarching social institution that both shapes and is shaped by individuals, this chapter presents a complex and evolving picture of how a 'good death' is perceived in contemporary Chinese society. It reveals that the notion of a 'good death' is far from being a singular, universally accepted concept; instead, it is influenced by a dynamic interplay between collectivist and individualistic beliefs and values. To capture this dynamism effectively, the concept of 'relational autonomy' proves valuable in understanding the experiences and identifying the needs of individuals in the process of dying. By viewing the dying person as both autonomous *and* relational, the concept of relational autonomy emphasizes the importance of comprehending capacity to make decisions within the rich matrix of familial, professional (healthcare practitioners) and wider societal relationships (Walter and Ross, 2014). For instance, inclusive decision-making, balancing individual and collective preferences, and mediated understanding and care planning may contribute to more harmonious and person-centred end-of-life care. This perspective aligns well with contemporary Chinese culture, where traditional collectivist values and increasingly prevalent Western individualistic beliefs intersect and integrate. Through this culturally sensitive lens, we can understand better the interdependence between personal choices and social connections (Gómez-Vírseda et al, 2020). This complex interplay also underscores the central role of communication and education in end-of-life care in China, where family support and the authority of healthcare professionals perform pivotal functions.

Effectively addressing these multifaceted cultural dynamics and objectively evaluating QoD within such contexts requires a systematic approach. Recognizing the multidimensional and interconnected needs (individual, relational and existential) is key to embracing person-centred care in the Chinese context, ensuring that end-of-life experiences align with the diverse cultural and relational values that define what constitutes a 'good death' (Fang and Tanaka, 2022). As future work on QoD in China unfolds, it is imperative to incorporate more cultural elements into QoD assessment frameworks. These elements must encompass the competing cultural narratives and diverse values that influence perceptions of a good death in Chinese society. Furthermore, to refine the conceptual framework of QoD and inform quantitative measurements in the future, research through in-depth conversations with individuals, their families and healthcare providers will be indispensable. These conversations can provide valuable insights into the nuances of cultural beliefs and their impact on end-of-life care decisions. By taking this culturally sensitive and person-centred approach, it will be possible to move towards a more comprehensive understanding of what constitutes a 'good death' in China and, in turn, enhance the quality of end-of-life care for all individuals.

References

Alexander, J., Eyerman, R., Giesen, B., Smelser, N.J. and Sztompka, P. (2004) *Cultural Trauma and Collective Identity*. Berkeley: University of California Press.

Bauman, Z. (2000) *Liquid Modernity*. Cambridge: Polity Press.

Bedford, O. and Hwang, K. (2003) 'Guilt and shame in Chinese culture: a cross-cultural framework from the perspective of morality and identity', *Journal for the Theory of Social Behaviour*, 33(2): 127–144.

Berger, P.L. (2011) *The Sacred Canopy: Elements of a Sociological Theory of Religion*. New York: Open Road Media.

Bhadelia, A., Oldfield, L., Cruz, J., Singh, R. and Finkelstein, E. (2022) 'Identifying core domains to assess the "quality of death": a scoping review', *Journal of Pain and Symptom Management*, 63(4): e365–e386.

Cheng, G. and Chen, C. (2021) 'End-of-life needs of dying patients and their families in mainland China: a systematic review', *OMEGA – Journal of Death and Dying*, 86(3): 1019–1045.

Cheng, H. (2018) 'Advance care planning in Chinese seniors: cultural perspectives', *Journal of Palliative Care*, 33(4): 242–246.

Clark, D. (2002) 'Between hope and acceptance: the medicalisation of dying', *BMJ*, 324(7342): 905–907.

Fang, C. (2018) *Bereavement and Motivation in Three Contrasting Cultures: Britain, Japan and China*. Doctoral thesis, University of Bath.

Fang, C. (2020) 'Exploring social constructions of bereaved people's identity in mainland China: a qualitative approach', *Mortality*, 25(4): 402–417.

Fang, C. (2022) 'Dynamics of Chinese Shidu parents' vulnerability in old age: a qualitative study', *Journal of Population Ageing*, 15: 99–119.

Fang, C. and Tanaka, M. (2022) 'An exploration of person-centred approach in end-of-life care policies in England and Japan', *BMC Palliative Care*, 21(1): Article 68.

Fu, C. and Glasdam, S. (2022) 'The "good death" in mainland China: a scoping review', *International Journal of Nursing Studies Advances*, 4: 100069.

Giddens, A. (1984) *The Constitution of Society: Outline of the Theory of Structuration*. Cambridge: Polity Press.

Gómez-Vírseda, C., de Maeseneer, Y. and Gastmans, C. (2020) 'Relational autonomy in end-of-life care ethics: a contextualized approach to real-life complexities', *BMC Medical Ethics*, 21(1): Article 50.

Gu, X., Chen, M., Liu, M., Zhang, Z. and Cheng, W. (2016) 'End-of-life decision-making of terminally ill cancer patients in a tertiary cancer center in Shanghai, China', *Supportive Care in Cancer: Official Journal of the Multinational Association of Supportive Care in Cancer*, 24(5): 2209–2215.

Hahne, J., Wang, X., Liu, R., Zhong, Y., Chen, X., Liu, X., et al (2022) 'Chinese physicians' perceptions of palliative care integration for advanced cancer patients: a qualitative analysis at a tertiary hospital in Changsha, China', *BMC Medical Ethics*, 23(1): Article 17.

Hales, S., Zimmermann, C. and Rodin, G. (2010) 'Review: the quality of dying and death: a systematic review of measures', *Palliative Medicine*, 24(2): 127–144.

He, L. and van Heugten, K. (2020) 'Chinese migrant workers' care experiences: a model of the mediating roles of filial piety', *Qualitative Health Research*, 30(11): 1749–1761.

Huang, H., Zeng, T., Mao, J. and Liu, X.H. (2018) 'The understanding of death in terminally ill cancer patients in China: an initial study', *Cambridge Quarterly of Healthcare Ethics*, 27(3): 421–430.

Hu, K. and Feng, D. (2016) 'Barriers in palliative care in China', *Lancet*, 387(10025): 1272.

Ivo, K., Younsuck, K., Ho, Y., Sang-Yeon, S., Seog, H.D., Hyunah, B., et al (2012) 'A survey of the perspectives of patients who are seriously ill regarding end-of-life decisions in some medical institutions of Korea, China and Japan', *Journal of Medical Ethics*, 38(5): 310–316.

Jiang, X., Lu, W., Luo, H., Yang, J., Chen, M., Wang, J., et al (2023) 'Spirituality and attitudes toward death among older adults in rural and urban China: a cross-sectional study', *Journal of Religion and Health*, 62(5): 3070–3094.

Jing, J. (2021) 'Suffering in the dying process as the core of terminal care', *Journal of Minzu University of China (Philosophy and Social Sciences Edition)*, 48(3): 121–129. https://doi.org/10.15970/j.cnki.1005-8575.2021.03.014

Klass, D. and Steffen, E. (eds) (2017) *Continuing Bonds in Bereavement: New Directions for Research and Practice*. London: Routledge.

Li, T., Pei, X., Chen, X. and Zhang, S. (2021) 'Identifying end-of-life preferences among Chinese patients with cancer using the heart to heart card game', *The American Journal of Hospice and Palliative Care*, 38(1): 62–67.

Long, S. (2004) 'Cultural scripts for a good death in Japan and the United States: similarities and differences', *Social Science and Medicine*, 58(5): 913–928.

Lu, Y., Gu, Y. and Yu, W. (2018) 'Hospice and palliative care in China: development and challenges', *Asia-Pacific Journal of Oncology Nursing*, 5(1): 26–32.

Miyashita, M., Morita, T., Sato, K., Hirai, K., Shima, Y. and Uchitomi, Y. (2008) 'Good death inventory: a measure for evaluating good death from the bereaved family member's perspective', *Journal of Pain and Symptom Management*, 35(5): 486–498.

National Health Commission (2023) 'Notice on implementing the third round of pilot programmes of palliative care'. Available at: http://www.nhc.gov.cn/lljks/tggg/202307/df326ed6049249c7bf823df1395c9b4f.shtml [accessed 1 August 2023].

National Health and Family Planning Commission (2017a) 'Notice on implementing pilot programmes of palliative care'. Available at: http://wsjkw.sc.gov.cn/scwsjkw/sclljk/2017/10/27/6d9318ad60734956b77e5483131ffe6c.shtml [accessed 1 August 2023].

National Health and Family Planning Commission (2017b) 'The national guideline on palliative care (trial)'. Available at: http://www.nhc.gov.cn/yzygj/s3593/201702/3ec857f8c4a244e69b233ce2f5f270b3.shtml [accessed 1 August 2023].

Patrick, D., Engelberg, R. and Curtis, J. (2001) 'Evaluating the quality of dying and death', *Journal of Pain and Symptom Management*, 22(3): 717–726.

Patrick, D., Curtis, J., Engelberg, R., Nielsen, E. and McCown, E. (2003) 'Measuring and improving the quality of dying and death', *Annals of Internal Medicine*, 139: 410–415.

Qi, X. (2017) 'Reconstructing the concept of face in cultural sociology: in Goffman's footsteps, following the Chinese case', *The Journal of Chinese Sociology*, 4: Article 19.

Sallnow, L., Smith, R., Ahmedzai, S., Bhadelia, A., Chamberlain, C., Cong, Y., et al (2022) 'Report of the Lancet Commission on the value of death: bringing death back into life', *Lancet*, 399(10327): 837–884.

Shenzhen Municipal People's Congress (2022) *Regulations on the Administration of Medical Institutions*. Available at: http://www.szrd.gov.cn/rdlv/chwgg/content/post_826158.html [accessed 1 August 2023].

State Council (2018) *The Policy and Practice in China that Ensures Freedom of Religious Belief*. Available at: https://www.gov.cn/xinwen/2018-04/03/content_5279419.htm [accessed 1 August 2023].

State Council (2016) *The Outline of the Plan for 'Healthy China 2030'*. Available at: https://www.gov.cn/zhengce/2016-10/25/content_5124174.htm [accessed 1 August 2023].

Valentine, C. (2009) 'Negotiating a loved one's dying in contemporary Japanese society', *Mortality*, 14(1): 34–52.

Walter, T. (2020) *Death in the Modern World*. London: SAGE.

Walter, J. and Ross, L. (2014) 'Relational autonomy: moving beyond the limits of isolated individualism', *Pediatrics*, 133(1): S16–S23.

Yan, Y. (2010) 'The Chinese path to individualization', *The British Journal of Sociology*, 61(3): 489–512.

Yao, C., Hu, W., Lai, Y., Cheng, S., Chen, C. and Chiu, T. (2007) 'Does dying at home influence the good death of terminal cancer patients?', *Journal of Pain and Symptom Management*, 34(5): 497–504.

Zhang, X., Jeong, S.Y. and Chan, S. (2021) 'Advance care planning for older people in mainland China: an integrative literature review', *International Journal of Older People Nursing*, 16(6): e12409.

2

The Market for Human Body Parts: Institutions, Intermediaries and Regulation

Lee Moerman and Sandra van der Laan

Introduction

The body has long been exploited as a commercial and marketable product, for example, sex workers, athletes and surrogate mothers all engage in market transactions (Nelkin and Andrews, 1998). To engage in these markets, participants must subsume their inherent human characteristics to relative economic values or price in exchange – 'wombs are rented; sperm is sold; and finally human organs "harvested"' (Harrison, 2006: 115). The individual becomes an entrepreneurial subject, *homo economicus* that has present value in the future benefits derived from its constituent parts (Kenny, 2015; Chiapello, 2017). This economic object that 'can be bartered, sold or stolen in divisible and alienable parts' traverses both time and space and raises questions of accountability (Scheper-Hughes, 2001: 1). In other words, humans in market exchange are economically productive agents (Kenny, 2015).

Medical and scientific advancements have escalated, driving an insatiable need for human tissue for research, education and transplantation. While many are already familiar with biological products from living donors, such as kidneys for transplant or gametes (reproductive cells) for assisted reproductive technologies, the harvesting of human tissue from cadavers is less well understood. While cadavers[1] provide organs for transplant, they also provide other body parts and tissues used as allografts. An allograft is defined as tissue that is transferred 'between genetically nonidentical members of the same species, although of a compatible blood type' (Corfield, 2021: np). For example, bones, tendons and ligaments are used in orthopaedic and dental procedures; heart valves and blood vessels are used in coronary surgery; skin is used to treat severe burns; and corneas to restore vision. Additionally, bone or tissue can be further processed into value-added products such as demineralized bone matrix (Maia Research, 2021).[2]

In this chapter we distinguish between the cadaver used for scientific purposes, such as research or education, and that used for harvesting human body tissue. We make a further distinction between organ[3] donation under strict state-regulated schemes and other cadaveric donations used for allografts. With demand exceeding supply, a global market for allografts has created a space for intermediaries or third-party 'brokers' to manage the relationship between the cadaver and the consumer. In this market, the institutional practice of bringing together the actors involved in the supply and demand of body parts obscures non-economic relationships and complex accountabilities. Consistent with the increasing diffusion of neoliberalism in Western societies, markets subsume spheres of life and activities that were previously 'governed by other tables of value' to mere economic practices (Brown, 2015: 21). It is in this context that we explore these relationships, consider the prevailing regulatory structures, and identify the sites for financial value creation.

Allografts are a sought-after consumer product resulting in a growing and global market. The value proposition resides in the economization of cadavers and their constituent parts so that they can be bought and sold through a network of bespoke, highly specialized intermediaries. These intermediaries function by procuring cadavers, processing tissue and supplying various products. In a global economy, the market for allografts operates beyond the reach of national regulation or oversight providing opportunities for jurisdictional arbitrage and/or exploitation (Lock, 2001). To counter this, the World Health Organization in 2010 developed principles and guidance for local regulators with the intention of providing 'an orderly, ethical and acceptable framework for the acquisition and transplantation of human cells, tissues and organs for therapeutic purposes' (World Health Organization, 2010: 1). Therefore, the legal trade in body parts raises both ethical issues and questions of accountability, especially when the ultimate use of 'donating one's body to science' is connected to commercial exchange in a relatively opaque market.

In the following section we briefly trace the history of the transforming a cadaver into a commodity. As characteristic of a neoliberal rationality that frames and measures every aspect of life and death by 'economic terms and metrics', the body parts and allograft market is a paradigm example of how economic practices penetrate non-economic domains of life through seemingly innocuous market practices (Brown, 2015: 10). We contribute by describing the institutions key to the allograft market and highlight the various relationships and reflect on the complex institutional accountabilities that arise.

Background

While the market for allografts is relatively new, there is a long history of body brokering. For example, in 18th-century Britain, cadavers were in demand for the burgeoning scientific interest in anatomy. Interestingly, while using cadavers for dissection was legal, the practice of procuring cadavers slipped into the trade of illegal bodysnatching to satisfy demand (Mitchell et al, 2011; Moerman and van der Laan, 2022). At around the same time in the United States, the practices of slavery allowed anatomists access, for a fee, to the cadavers of enslaved people (Berry, 2017). The work of the early anatomists resulted in the practice of transferring organs and other body tissue to extend or improve the quality of life. Organ transplantation is a well-established practice with the first successful heart transplant in 1967 making headlines around the world and the first successful kidney transplant a little more than a decade earlier (Brink and Hassoulas, 2009). Transplantation of other tissue has an even longer history but is less well known. For example, skin grafting has been practised since the times of the Egyptian Empire (~1500 BC) (see Kohlhauser et al, 2021) with interest in blood transplantation being noted around the 18th century (see Shelley, 2010). By the early 1930s, medical innovation saw blood transfusions, corneal grafts and tissue transplantation become common practice (Hamilton, 2012).

Since then, modern medicine has developed to a point where a distinction is made between solid organs and other body tissue. Solid organs include liver, kidney, pancreas, heart and lung, and are generally subject to nationally regulated organ donation programmes (Black et al, 2018). In some cases, certain organs, for example kidneys, can be harvested from a living donor. While early efforts at organ transplantation were not always successful, significant progress has been made to a point where all major organ transplants enjoy very high success rates. This is partly attributable to the growing acceptance of the concept of brain death, which allows organs to be harvested while the circulatory system remains intact; as well as the significant advances in anti-rejection medication (Harrison, 2006; Black et al, 2018).

The primary source of cadavers for research and education purposes is from individuals donating their body to science through quite restrictive university programmes (Wingfield, 2018). Similarly, solid organs for transplant are largely sourced through national programmes that are also tightly regulated.[4] Allografts, on the other hand, are procured for medical procedures through intermediaries known colloquially as body brokers and/or tissue banks.

Estimates of the size of the allograft market vary enormously, for example, the bone graft and substitutes[5] market was estimated at US$3.3 billion globally in 2022 (Precision Business Insights, 2022) and the soft tissue market at US$4.3 billion in 2021 (Transparency Market Research, 2021). Nonetheless, the entire market is estimated at approximately US$800 million

(MarketWatch, 2023). The largest and most developed allograft market exists in the United States with a number of entities operating listed on the stock exchange. Given increasing demand, one thing analysts agree on is that this market will experience substantial growth over the next few years (Maia Research, 2021). The following sections outline the process of commodifying human body tissue to create allografts that can be traded as marketable products and create value for various market participants.

The global market for allografts

The supply of allografts begins with whole-body donations through intermediaries known as body brokers. Figure 2.1 represents a typical, albeit simplified, structure for whole-body donations.

The transformation from whole-body donation to a marketable commodity occurs in a typical institutional environment characterized by several key market features including institutions and intermediaries that broker complex relationships; a reliance on private property rights; the forces of supply and demand; and absent, or limited, regulation.

Intermediaries: body brokers and tissue banks

Two distinct organizations accept whole-body donations. University programmes procure cadavers for the specific purpose of research and education. On the other hand, non-transplant anatomical donation organizations (NADOs; colloquially referred to as body brokers) exist to

Figure 2.1: Market structure for whole-body donations

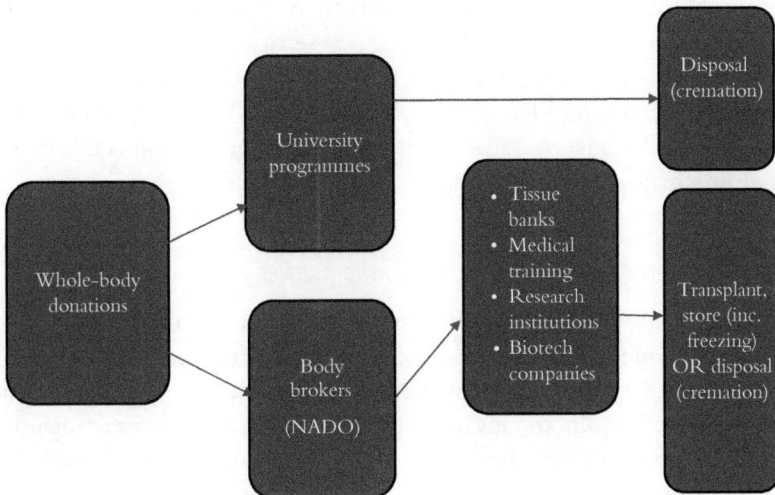

supply research and education as well as providing tissue for downstream processing by tissue banks.[6] These body brokers can be not-for-profit or for-profit entities and may be the commercial arm of governments or universities or operate as a tissue bank as well. These and other commercial relationships are often obscured by the presence of complex and intricate business structures. For example, in the United States the listed company Science Care operates both as a body broker accepting whole-body donations and as a tissue bank.

While stringent criteria for whole-body donations exist, even well-regarded body brokers have been tarnished by revelations that they have mishandled, inappropriately disposed of or 'on sold' body parts (Ling, 2004). One high-profile case reported that between 1998 and 2003, the director of the University of California, Los Angeles' Willed Body Program inappropriately sold 496 cadavers donated for research and education purposes to a subsidiary of Johnson & Johnson for a total of US$704,600 (Ling, 2004: 532).

Investigative journalists from Reuters (Grow and Shiffman, 2017) have also provided insight into the mysterious business of body brokering. For example, a 2017 exposé in the United States identified a lack of regulation and poor ethical practices from operators. They also present evidence that poorly regulated body brokers profit from exploiting vulnerable relatives unable to pay for a 'decent' funeral. Body brokers often secure cadavers by offering free cremation and appealing to a sense of generosity or altruism through the donation of the 'body to science'.

The prices charged by body brokers are generally not publicly advertised. However, information on the indicative price for some body parts in the United States was obtained by Grow and Shiffman following their investigation in 2017 (see Table 2.1).

Tissue banks procure body parts from body brokers to collect process, preserve, store and transport allografts. These tissue banks also operate as for-profit, not-for-profit, government-sponsored or private entities. For example, in the United Kingdom, NHS Blood and Tissue (see nhsbt.nhs. uk) is part of the government's National Health Service and is the United Kingdom's major supplier of human tissue for transplant.

Shifting property rights from the self to the market

One of the hallmarks of a market economy is a reliance on privatization as an efficient mode of allocating resources. According to a neoliberal ideology, the granting of private property rights is key to the exclusivity and profit motive needed to encourage market actors. While questions regarding the private ownership of one's body has risen in several jurisdictions, it is generally accepted that there are no property rights in a corpse.[7] This general

Table 2.1: Typical price for body parts from body brokers in the United States, 2017

Body part	Typical price (US$)
Whole body	$5,000
Torso (intact)	$2,100
Torso (eviscerated)	$2,000
Leg	$1,300
Brain	$750
Head	$500
Knee	$450
Shoulder (with collarbone)	$400
Cervical spine	$300
Forearm (with hand and elbow)	$250
Hand	$250
Foot	$200

Source: Adapted from Grow and Shiffman (2017)

principle, referred to as *corpus nullius in bonis*, literally translates to 'this body belongs to no one' and has its roots in English law (Madoff, 2016). In the case of *Williams* v *Williams* (1882)[8] it was established that 'a man [*sic*] cannot by will dispose of his dead body. If there can be no property in a dead body it is impossible that by will or any other instrument a body can be disposed of'. However, in the period between death and disposition some form of rights exist in terms of custodianship in most, if not all, jurisdictions. Upon death, there are generally protocols around 'claims' and the responsibility to dispose of a corpse in a legal manner. However, these legal aspects are often overshadowed by cultural and social norms. Therefore, 'the corpse suffers from categorical ambiguity ... marked by competing claims of custodianship. ... The competition is widely understood as a battle between death and living people reluctant to relinquish their ties with the person embodied in the corpse' (Hernigou, 2015: 577).

These ambiguities are threefold. First, who or what has the rights to the corpse after death? Second, who or what has the rights to the tissue or body parts once alienated? Third, who or what deserve to be compensated for any 'work and skill' performed on the tissue or the sale of allografts,[9] as long as the tissue was lawfully acquired (Edelman, 2015)?

Further complicating the property right conundrum are two important contextual considerations. First, the body donation regime and 'the medical rhetoric of scarcities, gifts, altruism and life-saving ... that allow us to think in fresh and uninhibited ways about the bodies of those presumed dead ... or presumed to be "donors" engaged in presumed acts of altruism' (Scheper-Hughes, 2001: 34–35). Often, the families and relatives' consent to whole-body donation in the belief that 'they are giving the gift of life' rather than supplying a commercial enterprise with raw material (Katches et al, 2000: np). Second, the social acceptance of life-saving or life-improving allografts combined with the medical jargon that accompanies such procedures disguises the provenance of the human tissue. The corpse is transformed to a cadaver which allows it to be alienated and sold as designated tissue or allograft. For example, in the three-page consent form from Science Care (2020), a leading body broker and tissue bank in the United States, it states:

> Science Care, in its sole discretion, will designate and provide any part or all of the Donated Tissue ('**Designated Tissue**') to Clients. Science Care may be compensated by Clients for providing the Designated Tissue. These Clients may be for-profit or non-profit and may use the Designated Tissue for Permitted Purposes. Clients may be within or located outside of the United States. (Clause 6, p 11, original emphasis)

Any opposition to the commodification of the corpse, whether on legal or moral grounds, belies the reality of a burgeoning market for human tissue. '[M]oney changes hands at numerous points in the chain of distribution from tissue source to ultimate consumer' and the debate has shifted from ownership and property rights to '*who* is entitled to share in the financial returns' (Mahoney, 2000: 165, original emphasis).

Supply and demand

The assignment of value in markets is fundamentally determined by the forces of supply and demand. Therefore, the ability to control either function creates value for market actors. However, in the case of the allograft market, actors need to be conceptualized differently. Transformation of a person (cadaver) from its human category to a commercialized object through the alienation of the body and its parts becomes a site of economic value. This economic value is achieved by the altruism of the body donor and the 'work and skill' required to convert the cadaver to saleable products used in medical procedures.

Developments in medical science and procedures to preserve or increase the quality of life have driven the demand for allografts (Harrison, 2006). Since human tissue is a scarce resource, allografts often go to their most valuable use, such as using human skin as the 'gold standard' to manage severe burns. While this use of human skin can be life-saving, donors might be surprised to learn that their skin may end up going to its most profitable use, for example, in being sold to a tissue bank and then 'processed' for use 'in vanity procedures such as penis–widening or lip enhancement' (Pirnay et al, 2012: 490).

Additionally, increases in technology to preserve and improvements in the ability to store allografts has led to a proliferation in tissue 'banking' for such purposes. 'Tissue banking is responsible for introducing a radical and dehumanizing claim: it seeks custodianship of the corpse in order to dismantle it into exchangeable and transplantable parts' (Hernigou, 2015: 577). Body brokers and tissue banks as market intermediaries have come to regulate supply and demand by acquiring rights to the cadaver and play an important role in institutionalizing value creation.

Limited regulation

Increasing global demand for allografts and the opportunities for exploitation led to the promulgation of the 'Guiding Principles on Human Cell, Tissue and Organ Transplantation' by the World Health Organization in 2010. These guiding principles cover both consent and payment for allografts, however they are not legally binding. In terms of consent, Guiding Principle 1 states: 'Cells, tissues and organs may be removed from the bodies of deceased persons for the purpose of transplantation if: (a) any consent required by law is obtained, and (b) there is no reason to believe that the deceased person objected to such removal' (World Health Organization, 2010: 2).

Guidelines around procuring organs and tissue for transplantation for financial compensation are clear. Guiding Principle 5 states:

> Cells, tissues and organs should only be donated freely, without any monetary payment or other reward of monetary value. Purchasing, or offering to purchase, cells, tissues or organs for transplantation, or their sale by living persons or by the next of kin for deceased persons, should be banned.
>
> The prohibition on sale or purchase of cells, tissues and organs does not preclude reimbursing reasonable and verifiable expenses incurred by the donor, including loss of income, or paying the costs of recovering, processing, preserving and supplying human cells, tissues or organs for transplantation. (World Health Organization, 2010: 5)

The commentary unequivocally states that exploitation of the vulnerable is at the heart of the World Health Organization's reasoning.

> Payment for cells, tissues and organs is likely to take unfair advantage of the poorest and most vulnerable groups, undermines altruistic donation, and leads to profiteering and human trafficking. Such

payment conveys the idea that some persons lack dignity, that they are mere objects to be used by others. ... National law should ensure that any gifts or rewards are not, in fact, disguised forms of payment for donated cells, tissues or organs. Incentives in the form of 'rewards' with monetary value that can be transferred to third parties are not different from monetary payment. (World Health Organization, 2010: 5)

And further:

While the worst abuses involve living organ donors, dangers also arise when payments for cells, tissues and organs are made to next of kin of deceased persons, to vendors or brokers, or to institutions (such as mortuaries) having charge of dead bodies. Financial returns to such parties should be forbidden. (World Health Organization, 2010: 5)

However, while it is illegal in most jurisdictions to sell cadavers, formal regulation has not kept pace with the trade in allografts.[10] Body brokers and tissue banks charge a 'processing fee' to customers to avoid scrutiny and further regulation driven by accusations of selling body parts (Smith, 2005: np). Nevertheless, a comparison of the fees charged between a not-for-profit public entity and a private for-profit tissue bank in the United States found the for-profit entity charged approximately twice as much for the same service, demonstrating the opportunity for value creation (Champney et al, 2019: 321).

Creating value

Realizing the value in allografts is dependent on determining the point at which the human body is commodified into its constituent and marketable parts. The harvesting of organs for donation occurs when the donor is diagnosed as 'brain dead'[11] and treated with the care and dignity of a 'patient'. This complex hybrid 'brain-dead patient-cadaver' represents both a person and a cadaver. They 'act as moral touchstones, especially in matters of life and death' (Lock, 2001: 41). It is no surprise, perhaps, that the widespread acceptance of the diagnosing of brain death[12] coincided with the development of transplant technologies and the need for 'uncompromised' organs. Additionally, the discourse of altruistic organ donation is dominated by phrases such as 'the gift of life'. Any concept of economic value to the organ recipient is rendered incalculable.

In contrast, for those donating their body after death to a body broker or tissue bank it is an entirely different story. Unlike brain-dead patient organ donors, the point of death is uncomplicated, and the corpse becomes the property of the body broker or tissue bank with any economic benefits attached. While this practice also uses the discourse of gifting life, the donated corpses become the designated tissue found in anatomical specimen catalogues. Economic value is created by transforming altruism into allografts for a lucrative market. The proliferation and marketability of body parts is associated with the ever-increasing atomization of the medicalized body (Sharp, 2000); new meanings for the 'moment of death' required for transplantation (Lock, 2001); and the relationships between institutions, body brokers[13] and tissue banks, the future donor, the corpse, and a range of recipients.

Accountability

This budding trade in body parts raises both ethical issues and questions of accountability, especially where human rights, legal rights and profit coalesce in an environment that is inconsistent, incomplete and ill-defined.

> As regard for the dead declines, the cost of body disposal rises, and the profits to be had in the body-parts marketplace soar, [corpse] abuse is likely to become less a bizarre anomaly and more a fact of life. Although putting body parts to use after the original owners no longer need them may be economically rational, final accounting should allow for the social cost of lost humanity that often accompanies the advance of rational behavior. (Whitten, 2005: 149)

The corpse has both a symbolic and instrumental value that technical societies convert into commodities (Bogard, 2008). This business of death exists where the focus on the accrual of profits subsumes the rights of citizens. When only those commodities that are productive for the economy are foregrounded through market values, issues of justice and equity take a back seat, which has implications for accountability. Brown (2015) refers to this loss of the common or public good in market-oriented ways of thinking about human capital, in our case, future allografts for the body parts market.

In this context we use the term 'necroaccountability' to understand the responsibility to give or make an account that exists between the various parties in the body parts market (Moerman and van der Laan, 2022). Necro comes from the Greek *nekros* meaning corpse and this focus provides an opportunity for alternative framing of the exploitation of the corpse and an understanding of how it relates to organizational, institutional and social relations. It is characterized by an accountability relationship with and for the dead. This relationship is additionally complex as it invokes an accountability for the next of kin or those responsible for the corpse disposition through whole-body donation. In particular, when conceived as human capital or living productive assets, more difficult questions as to how the various institutions, regulatory bodies and intermediaries discharge accountability arise. While there is ethical legitimacy and some form of accountability when an informed individual consents to donate their body to science, this relationship becomes indistinct when the product of the donation results in a purpose not envisaged (that is, used for allografts) and accruing profit to a commercial entity. In the absence of coherent regulation, does necroaccountability dissipate when the corpse is dismembered and distributed?

Conclusion

In this chapter we have outlined the emergence of the market in body parts. This has allowed us to provide an overview of the market and demonstrate that, despite regulation in most jurisdictions forbidding the sale of human corpses and body parts, a vibrant and largely unregulated market exists. Intermediaries such as body brokers and tissue banks mediate the relationships between suppliers and consumers and create value by performing 'work and skill' and charge a processing fee to remove, preserve, store and value-add.

Neoliberal rationality is a useful paradigm to understand the institutionalization of this allograft market that extends into aspects of life and death previously not imagined. Neoliberalism legitimates the shift from the rights of the human to the property rights required for corpses to become capital in the never-ending transformation of society into a market model (Trabsky, 2022). This market in body parts raises both ethical issues and questions of accountability. A new form of accountability, necroaccountability, has been offered as a way to describe the unique accountability (and increasingly institutionalized) relationship that exists between cadaver, next of kin, intermediaries, medical professionals and consumers. This is especially the case in situations where whole-body donors altruistically donate what they believe is 'the gift of life' rather than the price of doing business in medical procedures.

Notes

[1] The cadaver is a human corpse that is used in scientific or medical processes.

[2] Demineralized bone matrix (DBM) is the outcome of a process of using an acidic solution to remove mineral components, while leaving much of the proteinaceous components native to bone. DBM products come in various forms to suit the variety of applications such as sponges, strips, injectable putty, paste, and paste infused with bone chips (Zhang et al, 2019).

[3] We recognize that there is an illegal or unregulated market for organs. However, that is beyond the scope of this chapter.

[4] This regulation has led to a global black market for solid organs.

[5] This figure would include substitutes made from animal bones.

[6] In some instances, universities also enter the market as consumers.

[7] See Quigley (2018) for a detailed analysis.

[8]   *Williams* v *Williams* (1882) 20 Ch.D. 659.

[9]   For example, processes to store the tissue and ensure that it does not deteriorate.

[10] There are some tissues that can be sold legally, such as blood, plasma, gametes, breast milk, and so on, and, in some cases, even skin. These tissues are all naturally replenishable.

[11] Today's society is familiar with the concept of 'brain death', but many would be surprised to learn that this is a relatively recent concept. The first widely accepted definition of brain death was first documented by a committee from Harvard Medical School in 1968 (Paul and George, 2020). This definition was a 'diagnosis' of brain death with diagnostic tools, such as the absence of electroencephalographic (EEG) activity, rather than the previously accepted idea that biological death is a gradual process and irreversible (circulatory death).

[12] While the concept of brain death has been widely accepted since the 1970s, the diagnosis protocols varied between jurisdictions and remained inconsistent until the World Health Organization ratified a definition of brain death in 2014 (see Paul and George, 2020).

[13] Body brokers are also known as non-transplant anatomical donation organizations (NADOs) and not subject to as much, if any, regulatory scrutiny (Grow and Shiffman, 2017). This distinction is important as NADOs recover tissue that is not intended for transplantation but for research and education, most often from whole-body donations (AATB, 2021).

References

Berry, D. (2017) *The Price for Their Pound of Flesh: The Value of the Enslaved, from Womb to Grave, in the Building of a Nation.* Boston, MA: Beacon Press.

Black, C., Termanini, K., Aguirre, O., Hawksworth, J. and Sosin, M. (2018) 'Solid organ transplantation in the 21st century', *Annals of Translational Medicine*, 6(20): 409.

Bogard, W. (2008) 'Empire of the living dead', *Mortality*, 13(2): 187–200.

Brink, J. and Hassoulas, J. (2009) 'The first human heart transplant and further advances in cardiac transplantation at Groote Schuur Hospital and the University of Cape Town – with reference to the operation. A human cardiac transplant: an interim report of a successful operation performed at Groote Schuur Hospital, Cape Town', *Cardiovascular Journal of Africa*, 20(1): 31–35.

Brown, W. (2015) *Undoing the Demos: Neoliberalism's Stealth Revolution.* Brooklyn, New York: Zone Books.

Champney, T., Hildebrandt, S., Gareth Jones, D. and Winkelmann, A. (2019) 'Bodies r us: ethical views on the commercialization of the dead in medical education and research', *Anatomical Sciences Education*, 12(3): 317–325.

Chiapello, E. (2017) 'Critical accounting research and neoliberalism', *Critical Perspectives on Accounting*, 43: 47–64.

Corfield, J. (2021) 'Allograft', in *Encyclopedia Britannica*. Available at: https://www.britannica.com/science/allograft [accessed 25 September 2021].

Edelman, J. (2015) 'Property rights to our bodies and their products', *University of Western Australia Law Review*, 39(2): 47–70.

Grow, B. and Shiffman, J. (2017) *Cashing in on the Donated Dead: The Body Trade*. Reuters Investigates. Available at: https://www.reuters.com/investigates/section/usa-bodies/ [accessed 30 September 2021].

Hamilton, D. (2012) *A History of Organ Transplantation: Ancient Legends to Modern Practice*. Pittsburgh: University of Pittsburgh Press.

Harrison, T. (2006) 'Six frontiers of the market: commodifying human body parts', in Laxer, G. and Soron, D. (eds) *Not for Sale: Decommodifying Public Life*. Toronto: University of Toronto Press, pp 111–126.

Hernigou, P. (2015) 'Bone transplantation and tissue engineering, part III: allografts, bone grafting and bone banking in the twentieth century', *International Orthopaedics*, 39: 577–587.

Katches, M., Heisel, W. and Campbell, R. (2000) 'The body brokers: part 1 – assembly line: donors don't realize they are fuelling a lucrative business'. Available at: http://www.lifeissues.net/writers/kat/org_01bodybrokerspart1.html [accessed 30 September 2021].

Kenny, K. (2015) 'The biopolitics of global health: life and death in neoliberal time', *Journal of Sociology*, 51(1): 9–27.

Kohlhauser, M., Luze, H., Nischwitz, P. and Kamolz, L. (2021) 'Historical evolution of skin grafting: a journey through time', *Medicina*, 57(4): 348.

Ling, A. (2004) 'Recent developments in health law: UCLA willed body program comes under scrutiny as companies sued for the purchase of body parts', *Journal of Law, Medicine and Ethics*, 32(3): 532–534.

Lock, M. (2001) *Twice Dead: Organ Transplants and the Reinvention of Death*. Berkeley: University of California Press.

Madoff, R.D. (2016) 'The law of the American dead', *Savannah Law Review*, 3(1): 1–14.

Mahoney, J.D. (2000) 'The market for human tissue', *Virginia Law Review*, 86: 163–223.

Maia Research (2021) *Global Allograft Market Development Strategy Pre and Post COVID-19, by Corporate Strategy Analysis, Landscape, Type, Application, and Leading 20 Countries*. Hong Kong: Maia Research.

MarketWatch (2023) *Press Release*. Available at: https://www.marketwatch.com/press-release/global-allograft-market-2023-latest-report-driving-growth-through-an-economic-downturn-by-2030 [accessed 14 April 2023].

Mitchell, P., Boston, C., Chamberlain, A., Chaplin, S., Chauhan, V., Evans, J., et al (2011) 'The study of anatomy in England from 1700 to the early 20th century', *Journal of Anatomy*, 219(2): 91–99.

Moerman, L. and van der Laan, S. (2022) 'Accounting for and accounts of death: past, present and future possibilities', *Accounting History*, 27(1): 6–23.

Nelkin, D. and Andrews, L. (1998) 'Whose body is it anyway? Disputes over body tissue in a biotechnology age', *The Lancet*, 351(9095): 53–57.

Paul, S. and George, M. (2020) 'Evolution of the concepts of brain death and brain stem death', *Amrita Journal of Medicine*, 16: 43–49.

Pirnay, J.P., Vanderkelen, A., Ectors, N., Delloye, C., Dufrane, D., Baudoux, E., et al (2012) 'Beware of the commercialization of human cells and tissues: situation in the European Union', *Cell and Tissue Banking*, 13(3): 487–498.

Precision Business Insights (2022) *Press Release*. Available at: https://precis ionbusinessinsights.com/press-release/bone-substitute-and-allograft-bone-market-growth/ [accessed 14 April 2023].

Quigley, M. (2018) *Self-Ownership, Property Rights, and the Human Body: A Legal and Philosophical Analysis*. Cambridge: Cambridge University Press.

Scheper-Hughes, N. (2001) 'Bodies for sale – whole or in parts', *Body and Society*, 7(2–3): 1–8.

Science Care (2020) *Standards and Commitments Guide*. Science Care. Available at: https://www.sciencecare.com/medical-researchers/complia nce-safety [accessed 9 October 2021].

Sharp, L.A. (2000) 'The commodification of the body and its parts', *Annual Review of Anthropology*, 29: 287–328.

Shelley, L. (2010) *Human Trafficking: A Global Perspective*. Cambridge: Cambridge University Press.

Smith, A. (2005) 'Tissue from corpses in strong demand: market for allografts keeps growing, outpacing supply', *CNN/Money*, 5 October. Available at: https://money.cnn.com/2005/10/04/news/midcaps/allograft/index. htm [accessed 20 October 2024].

Trabsky, M. (2022) 'The neoliberal rationality of voluntary assisted dying', in Fleming, D.J. and Carter, D.J. (eds) *Voluntary Assisted Dying: Law? Health? Justice?* Canberra: ANU Press, pp 95–111.

Transparency Market Research (2021) *Soft Tissue Market*. Available at: https://www.transparencymarketresearch.com/soft-tissue-market.html [accessed 14 April 2023].

Whitten, D. (2005) 'Corpse abuse and the body-parts market', *The Journal of the Economic and Business Historical Society*, 23(1): 140–152.

Wingfield, H.A. (2018) 'Body donation today', *Clinical Anatomy*, 31: 86–89.

World Health Organization (2010) *WHO Guiding Principles on Human Cell, Tissue and Organ Transplantation*. Available at: https://tsanz.com.au/storage/ documents/WHOGuidingPrinciplesonHumanCellTissueandOraganTran splantation.pdf [accessed 9 October 2021].

Zhang, H., Yang, L., Yang, X.G., Wang, F., Feng, J.T., Hua, K.C., et al (2019) 'Demineralized bone matrix carriers and their clinical applications: an overview', *Orthopaedic Surgery*, 11(5): 725–737.

3

Secrecy, Judgement and Stigma: Assisted Dying in Aotearoa New Zealand

Rhona Winnington

Introduction

On 7 November 2021, the End of Life Choice Act (2019) became a legal directive across Aotearoa New Zealand (NZ) offering an assisted dying (AD) service for those who meet the eligibility criteria. Such uncharted waters regarding death and dying for NZ and its bicultural society brings with it the unknown and unknowable of how individuals, family/*whānau* and clinicians will respond when AD services are requested and implemented. This chapter considers how socially constructed values of an assisted death can produce a contentious discourse of secrecy, stigma and judgement for both users and providers of this legal medical service, thus, presenting problematic and possibly unexpected consequences in delivering this liberation of the self to control life's end. First, it deals with terminology and AD, as the legal right to end human life is ascribed many terminologies globally. This chapter uses AD to include variables across prescribed procedures, which, for the purpose of clarity when reading this chapter, includes assisted suicide, voluntary euthanasia, active euthanasia, medical assistance in dying, voluntary AD and physician assisted suicide but not passive euthanasia. AD is used as it is the terminology used in the End of Life Choice Act (2019) in NZ.

The premise of this chapter stems from experiences specific to NZ. However, when considering other countries that engage with AD, as of June 2023, the following are being referred to: Australia, Belgium, Canada, Colombia, Luxembourg, the Netherlands, Spain, Switzerland, the United States (states of California, Colorado, District of Columbia, Hawaii, Montana, Maine, New Jersey, New Mexico, Oregon, Vermont and

Washington). Although, it must be noted that actual services may differ across these countries and states at this time. In terms of the NZ context, located in the South Pacific Ocean the country is a bicultural nation comprising of Māori and non-Māori populations (Devos et al, 2020). While it is argued that NZ has a multicultural population, *Te Tiriti ō Waitangi* (1840) focuses on the partnership between Māori and the British Crown (Waitangi Tribunal, 2016). As such, the richness of Māori culture, beliefs, customs and traditions are interwoven into the tapestry of everyday life in this country.

When considering Māori culture in relation to healthcare delivery and decision-making, it is depicted through a narrative in inequalities and inequities in access to, and receipt of, adequate resources for wellbeing (Goodyear-Smith and Ashton, 2019; Hobbs et al, 2019), demonstrated through Māori life expectancy being ten years less than their European counterparts (Wilson et al, 2019). Yet, through these inequities in practice, the concept of *whānau* for Māori remains a supportive mechanism. *Whānau* can simply mean family, however, often comprises multiple generations of extended family members, friends, community members, pastors, *Kaumātua* (tribal elders) and *Pākeke* (senior adults), and others significant to an individual (Masters-Awatere et al, 2019), all of whom can be involved in decision-making. Furthermore, Māori values and beliefs such as *whanaungatanga* (developing and maintain ties/relationships within communities) are strong forces through which both Māori and non-Māori live their lives. Such inclusivity of community is important to note as it is essential to Māori (Durie, 1994; Moeke-Maxwell et al, 2020), given the secularity of the AD legislation in NZ.

The context of assisted dying

The right to choose to end human life at a time and place of one's choosing has become a legal option in a number of countries globally (Mroz et al, 2021). Such legislation brings to the fore the right-to-choice/right-to-die narratives that have dominated contemporary rights discourses (Winnington, 2016; Fontalis et al, 2018) for those seeking what they consider to be a dignified and 'good death' (Hendry et al, 2012). Legalization of AD, however, produces discomfort for many individuals and nations alike, while simultaneously supporting those who seek control over their demise (Hendry et al, 2012). AD is a divisive service (Jaye et al, 2019), often polarizing opinions, creating subjective discourses and exposing individualized positionality in relation to it. Yet it offers, for those who seek it, perceived personal agency at a life point that is often physically and emotionally challenging.

Consideration of the impact of AD services beyond the rights of the individual has, however, been somewhat limited globally when drawing up legislation. Yet, unexpected social consequences result from poorly constructed legal processes often reaching far beyond the right-to-die narrative. As such, the self-centric choice to die leaves a lasting legacy for those on the periphery of the legislation.

In NZ, the End of Life Choice Act (2019), hereafter referred to as the Act, became a legal medical service on 7 November 2021. The Act details individual eligibility criteria and assessment of competence which are easy to navigate. However, the usual assumption of competence to receive healthcare services (MCNZ, 2021) is not applicable to seeking an assisted death in NZ. For an AD competence must be proven by two or three medical practitioners (End of Life Choice Act, 2019). Furthermore, some aspects of eligibility are subjective, for example, what is considered to be unbearable suffering (End of Life Choice Act, 2019). What is significant with this legislation, however, is the burden of expectation placed upon individuals interested in AD, as *they* must be the initiators of AD conversations, rather than clinicians instigating an open and honest discussion of what services are available. This contrasts with Western Australia, for example, where clinicians under Division Four, Section 10.3 (VADA, 2019) can freely discuss AD providing they simultaneously offer all other forms of available treatment, including palliative care. Moreover, there is an assumption in NZ that individuals either already know about the service or have the ability and means to access online information, given open discussion is prohibited. As such, family and *whānau* are not able to request information on behalf of individuals in NZ nor use an activated enduring power of attorney to request AD. Nor can advanced directives be used to request an assisted death, which contrasts with the Netherlands, for example, where advanced euthanasia directives are permitted (Miller et al, 2018), even if the latter raises ethical concerns.[1] Family and *whānau*[2] are further restricted as they cannot be advised by clinicians if an individual is seeking information on, undergoing assessment for, or actually going to use AD, as the responsibility for including them sits solely with the individual concerned. The necessity for such safeguards is clear and expected, as a means to halt coercive practices such as the risk of elder or financial abuse (Storey, 2020), yet simultaneously sits juxtaposed with the culturally embedded *whānau* narrative that drives the nation.

Moreover, there are two further significant aspects of the Act that have the potential to influence societal engagement with and reaction to AD. These are that an assisted death will not be noted on death certificates, and that there is a blanket ban on any media reporting of service use (End of Life Choice Act, 2019). The recording of assisted deaths is a controversial point, with Belgium and the Netherlands clearly identifying the use of such services, whereas in Canada it is generally acknowledged in some respect on a death certificate but there are inconsistencies across the country, and in the United States it is omitted entirely (Brown et al, 2018).

As such, the Act positions individuals in isolation having to initiate conversations regarding a subject matter that is often polarizing in social opinion (Jaye et al, 2021), while family and *whānau* are excluded from all discussions unless invited by the enquiring individual. What is more, with clinicians bound by the legislation to not initiate AD discourse or promote it as an option for fear of consequences, the Act upholds a narrative of obscuration, denying open discourse and subsequently open support for all involved in service delivery.

The self, autonomy and medical power

The introduction of AD as a legal medical service can be a confronting shift in contemporary dying practices, often provoking discomfort in that death could be preferable to a poor quality of life defined by unbearable suffering (Shrestha et al, 2019). The decision to actively choose death over life can be considered an unnatural action, thus, violating the currently prescribed social norms of death and dying practices in the 21st century (Winnington, 2016). Yet, for some, AD is considered to simply be a formal version of passive euthanasia or palliative sedation therapy (Seale et al, 2015) and a common, if unspoken, reality in end-of-life care practices (Ezekiel and Joffe, 2003). Often referenced as patients being 'kept comfortable' or being given 'tender loving care', this appears more palatable than actively choosing the date and time of one's own death.

An assisted death is, however, more than a shift of terminology and legislative change. It can become an opportunity for self-control and identity when often these principles have been lost through institutionalized healthcare processes focused on saving lives. Theoretically, AD legislation allows individuals to exercise personal agency and control at life's end, albeit within the context of a specific eligibility criteria, giving an impression of individualism and choice, thus fulfilling the desire of the subjective self. Such positioning can be perceived as individualist, one's right, or even narcissistic, with value clearly placed upon the worth of the individual by the individual (Winnington, 2016). Yet, the reality of individual control is negated through the stringent, and conservative construct, of the End of Life Choice Act (2019) in NZ, as the Act simultaneously offers individual choice regarding death, while containing and constraining that perceived freedom. As such, the inextricably linked duality of structures and agency (Giddens, 2009) as an epistemological problem creates a framework for a relationship between intentional human actions and a legal medical service to occur. Thus, the perception that death can be shaped by individualistic choice to suit the self is challenging, as the structure surrounding this life choice is problematic in its construction.

AD, therefore, presents the notion that control over the demise of the self is possible where the service is legally available, yet, accessing an assisted death remains within the control of the medicalization of care (Szasz, 2002). An individual can choose to access AD and, indeed, must initiate such conversations in NZ, but the final decision as to whether such a legal death can occur sits with the medical practitioners assessing eligibility, not the individual, family or *whānau*. The positioning of the self as being autonomous in decision-making is not as clear-cut as it initially appears. The service is portrayed as giving authentic autonomy to individuals (Szasz, 2002) yet remains under the jurisdiction and control of medicine and law, which are external to the self. This situation, according to Szasz (2002), leads to a positioning of pseudo-autonomy in relation to controlling one's death. As such, this situation becomes problematic in presenting the possibility of self-control over death, but simultaneously constrains the individual through rules, regulations and being at the mercy of a clinician being willing to deliver a 'bureaucratized medical killing' (Szasz, 2002: 94).

Furthermore, this dichotomous duality does not take into consideration the wider societal impact an assisted death may bring. Specifically, the layers of secrecy and legislative constraints within in the End of Life Choice Act (2019) paint a problematic picture of a legal medical service being challenging to navigate for all concerned, including family, *whānau* and the wider population. As such, this leaves individuals isolated in accessing an assisted death, with family and *whānau* automatically excluded from AD conversations, while clinicians are prevented from engaging in open discourse, thus, supporting the enigma of what an assisted death actually is. This results from the structural dominance of both governmental instruction and the associated legal obligations of the End of Life Choice Act (2019), with law superseding medical power in this instance to preclude populist experiences and opinions being shared. As such, this presents a dichotomous positioning of the populist vote supporting AD legislation but simultaneously prevented from open engagement through institutional power houses.

Secrecy: the problem with assisted dying legislation in New Zealand

The legal and narrative construction of the End of Life Choice Act (2019) depicts an Act whereby concealment and secrecy abound. While secrecy has a known presence in human interactions (Beidelman, 1993), shaping social relations and organizations, the multi-layered secrecy of AD in the NZ context presents a challenging issue for all involved in service use and delivery, but also culturally and socially. Specifically, this institutional control of the service through the legislative narrative brings to the fore the notable lack of accountability for service provision and use. The Ministry of Health NZ has set up a division – the Support and Consultations for End-of-Life in New Zealand to oversee the ongoing implementation of the Act, usage and review at the end of 2024. Yet, this too is a closed and faceless group, with reporting of AD usage only annually, with no visibility of what is occurring on a regular basis for the general population, thus continuing not only the narrative of secrecy but also the sequestering of death from mainstream society discourse.

Western societies are already accomplished at sequestering death and dying from social view (Walter, 1991; Mellor, 1992; Mellor and Shilling, 1993; Winnington, 2016), and the AD legislation simply continues such behaviours. In Simmel and Bellman's (1984) view, secrecy suggests that there is an alternative social construct in which we can live and, as such, is a means for controlling information today (Marx and Muschert, 2009). Medics are already agents of social control (Szasz, 1970) replacing religion as the overseers of dying, with the End of Life Choice Act (2019) further layering conformity with this newly constructed paradigm of perceived choice (Hart, 2012). Yet, the concern arises that secret information can become a transactional commodity due to the lack of knowledge of the broader community. As such, the legislation exerts power over all involved in the AD transaction through not realizing the constraints of the law, thus, becoming subjects of an unexpected and invisible mechanism of social control.

Considering the potential for coercive practices to occur in relation to persuading individuals to seek an assisted death, it can easily be argued that such secrecy regarding AD has the potential to be ethically positioned as a preventative safeguard (End of Life Choice Act, 2019). It must be asked, however, whether the protective needs of a minority outstrip the need for societal transparency when moving towards the actualization of self-centric demands of humans today. Or, indeed, whether such secrecy aligns with the notion of *whānau* as an active supporting agent for those of Māori descent, thus not supporting the principles of *Te Tiriti ō Waitangi* (see earlier section on the NZ context for an explanation of this term) in relation to healthcare provision (Bergham et al, 2017). As such, the individual seeking an assisted death becomes the product of the governmental power enacted through the legislation, which constrains individualism enforcing a concealed, almost underhanded, encounter, when AD is a legal option, while AD is portrayed as an act of individualized empowerment. Yet, this discourse of secrecy becomes problematic as it is unlikely to succeed in being the safeguard for misuse that it is intended to address, as secrecy can often lead to dishonest behaviours whereby those who have a specific intent will find ways around the legislation. While consideration may not have been given to this potential outcome, the idea of hidden institutional power remains explicit, given the duality of visible legislative limitations alongside what is considered a legal medical service.

The decision, however, by the NZ government to produce legislation with so many pockets of concealment regarding accessing, delivering and reporting of the AD service, may not only be aligned to protecting the vulnerable from coercion, but may be in response to overseas experiences regarding privacy issues (Fujioka et al, 2019), or indeed the suicide tourism discourse that is prevalent at this time (Carrigan, 2023; Testoni and Arnau, 2023). With reporting banned on the use of AD in NZ, this may support the right to privacy of individuals seeking to die but it could also be questioned as to why it is necessary when AD is a legal option. The situation suggests that the polarizing opinions of advocates and opponents to AD have played a significant role in the construct of the legislation. Yet this secrecy produces a narrative of the unknown and unknowable unless directly involved in the process, further obscuring the modern death into the hidden enclaves of Western cultural practices (Winnington, 2016). It appears, therefore, that while the advent of individual choice at life's end has come to fruition, it simultaneously supports the ongoing discomfort with openly discussing the inevitability of death. Thus, the unknown and unknowable are problematic discourses for the public generally, and *whānau* specifically, as the Act has created a situation whereby the lack of accessibility to knowledge regarding AD continues to impact societal views on the service, leading to the emerging narrative of stigma and judgement for all who participate in AD.

Judgement and stigma: social consequences of assisted dying

The contemporary shift towards achieving greater autonomy and self-determination over 'natural' life events places individuals who seek an assisted death as being othered by simply considering death as preferable to life. Yet, this does not just apply to service users, but to those who are involved in service delivery also. While being 'othered' often applies to categorization through race, gender or religious affiliations perhaps (Veenstra, 2011), involvement with purposefully ending life appears to 'other' through producing judgement and labels that break down the socially constructed norm of valuing life over death (Winnington and MacLeod, 2020).

Judgement, or to be judged by others, is a fear of many in contemporary society for a broad variety of reasons (Achterbergh et al, 2020; Arias-Colmenero et al, 2020). To fit in, not break the boundaries of normative behaviours, is a common desire (Pryor et al, 2019) as the fear of negative evaluation is a significant concern (Zhang et al, 2023). As such, the secrecy components of the End of Life Choice Act (2019), while noting a rationale for these, produce a problem whereby those associated with using or delivering the service risk feel judged for doing so (Gamondi et al, 2018).

To choose to die, before what is considered to be the natural end to human life, transgresses the socially constructed normative social values of both historical and contemporary society. The notion of choosing to die 'prematurely' can be seen as deviant, not by the self-determined individual, but in relation to broader expected societal norms of wanting to live (Winnington, 2016), as death remains a discomforting and disconcerting entity for many. As such, the individual and clinician involved in, or the family member experiencing AD services, not only becomes judged for this engagement but labelled as deviant for doing so. Such labelling has the potential to burden those involved with this new means of dying through interpreting their choices as non-conformist. Often such labels are ascribed by those in positions of power (Winnington, 2016), but in this instance, it is the broader societal narrative that is holding those involved to account; despite the reality that they are not accountable given the legality of the service.

Being judged as deviant, therefore, for engaging in AD services is a multifaceted experience given the polarizing positioning of the actors. Yet, merely judgement is not a singular depiction of disapproval for all involved in service access or delivery as society attempts to monitor the use of AD. As such, this produces a fine line along which to tread whether seeking to utilize or provide the service, whereby, irrespective of the role played, judgement for doing so has the potential to lead to feeling shamed for participation, together with being stigmatized by others for doing so. Such narratives are emerging from Canada, where medical assistance in dying has been available since 2016, with families alluding to the judgement of using the AD service but also not discussing that AD has occurred in the family (Crumley et al, 2023).

Shame as a cultural phenomenon places feelings of guilt or embarrassment onto individuals dependent upon their involvement in certain social activities and can be used to change population behaviours (Tyler and Slater, 2018). It is a powerful emotion, whereby it focuses attention on those who stray from the behaviours of the majority (Simmel, 1904) as a mechanism to enforce social control and solidarity (Durkheim, 1997 [1897]). As such, the social environment is a key component of the manifestation of shame or shaming, becoming a collective mechanism of influence and social control (Bates and LaBrecque, 2020: 1). When related to the use or delivery of a legal medical service, but because it is related to the discomforting subject matter of death, this collective behaviour produces a discourse of stigmatization.

Stigmatization as a social phenomenon presents a narrative of rejection (Goffman, 1963) by social actors towards those who do not align with normative expectations. It is often displayed through judgement and punishment, ultimately defining them as deviant (Durkheim, 1982 [1895]). Further, as Goffman (1963) suggests, stigma is the idea that full social acceptance of individuals is unachievable due to their behaviours. As such, the stigmatizing behaviour of choosing death over life discredits those seeking an assisted death, while simultaneously classifying them and the service providers as other. The juxtaposed positioning of normative expectations against a new and legal mode of death produces a discourse of conflict for all involved. The individual seeking to die is constrained by social values as their choice sits in opposition to mainstream thinking.

While this paints a broad image of societal opinions on the polarizing subject of AD, it must be remembered that not all opposition and, therefore, judgement and stigmatization is emitted from the general public, but often likely within the context of close-knit family units, clinicians regarding peers and colleagues, or those with religious affiliations, for example (Yan et al, 2023). The strict guidelines halting open discussion around AD services in NZ may, in part, be considered as a safety mechanism to reduce the judgement and stigmatization of those involved in service use and provision. Yet, it is unlikely that these concepts were actually considered in the construction of the legislation.

While stigma and judgement appear to be a consequence of individuals using the AD service, together with the constraints placed upon them by the imposed secrecy, it appears that family members are similarly affected. Disclosure of an assisted death appears problematic for some family members after the event, despite the legality of the service, due to an anticipation of stigma (Gamondi et al, 2018), or being 'fearful of judgement' (Winnington and MacLeod, 2020). Thus, the reactions of others and the fear of being othered continues to feed into the cycle of obscuring the true nature of a death that has occurred (Winnington and MacLeod, 2020). As such, this practice inhibits the likelihood of constructing an inclusive and fair society regarding death and dying, but rather upholds the taboo status accorded to this life event.

Furthermore, while individuals may encounter such negative barriers and labels in pursuit of their preferred means of dying alongside family members' reluctance to share this information posthumously, the healthcare practitioners involved are positioned simultaneously as both perpetrators of death but also offering what is considered by some to be humanistic care and a 'good death' (Cain and McCleskey, 2019). Stigmatization for clinicians is multifaceted. It can emanate from engagement with family and *whānau* if invited by the individual to be part of the process but can also be at the reproach of fellow healthcare professionals.

Although any healthcare professional may be asked about AD services in NZ, and the Act gives registered professionals the option to conscientiously object to participating in the actual delivery of an assisted death (End of Life Choice Act, 2019), for the purpose of this work consideration is given primarily to medical doctors (MDs) and registered nurses (RNs). Yet, the inherent dogma surrounding AD provision provides a dichotomous positioning that these professionals must traverse, with neither option appeasing all concerned. Specifically, MDs and RNs are stigmatized by colleagues for engaging in a taboo and often considered objectionable service (Beuthin et al, 2018), but simultaneously for not wanting to provide this legal medical service through conscientious objection (Faúndes et al, 2013).

It has been suggested that for some MDs and RNs the use of conscientious objection can be used is a legal mechanism to not be involved in service delivery, even if this is not their true belief (Faúndes et al, 2013); as conscientious objection is often used as a guise by clinicians who fear 'discrimination and social stigma' (Faúndes et al, 2013: S57) by their peers. Yet, the notion of legal human killing (Szasz, 2002) as a mechanism to relieve 'unbearable suffering' (End of Life Choice Act, 2019: section 5.1.e) should theoretically be acceptable if the medical ethics of beneficence and non-maleficence are to be truly upheld.[3] The reality of these concepts in this instance, however, is not related to the conscience of the service user but that of the deliverer. As such, the controlling power of the legislation together with the socially expected norms regarding choosing death may combine to place the individual and willing clinician as deviant or other.

Although conscientious objection is a well-documented phenomenon in relation to AD services, conscientious participation (Rutherford, 2021a, 2021b) is less so. For those clinicians who actively choose to be involved in AD, this comes at a personal cost in relation to emotional impact. However, belief in and motivation for participation emanates from the need to help those in their care (Rutherford, 2021b). Thus, in doing so those engaged in conscientious participation uphold their interpretation of beneficence and non-maleficence – in other words, doing no harm: the foundation stone of medical practice (Beauchamp and Childress, 2013). While this notion of consciously considering participation is noteworthy, Rutherford (2021a, 2021b) denotes that it remains contingent on coping with the fallout, conflict and labelling that may occur.

This delineation of those abiding by social norms, and those who are other, or outsiders (Becker, 1963), inhibits inclusivity at a life point that is often stressful. The idea of social exclusion is not uncommon to those being judged or stigmatized (Berry and Greenwood, 2018; Liamputtong and Rice, 2021), yet such ascribed meanings by those external to the process considers participants as being deviant for choosing death over life (Winnington, 2016). Despite, however, the legal regulation of what has been practised as passive euthanasia for centuries, and often considered acceptable as care, it appears that active choices equate with exclusive practices occurring. As such, the use of AD legislation leaves the individual, the family and *whānau*, and the healthcare practitioners in a position of suffering, with the ascription of judgement, shame, stigma or otherness due to the dominance of normative social constraints in Western societal culture. Moreover, the End of Life Choice Act (2019) operates against the values of what is a bicultural nation, whereby a Māori worldview of inclusivity in decision-making has not been clearly considered in the construct nor implementation of the legislation, but in reality places the values of colonization above this.

Assisted dying: the institutional consequences of othering

This discussion has primarily focused on the individual players that may be involved in assisted death provision. However, the application of the Act in relation to institutional settings is noteworthy in relation to the secrecy and privacy components of the legislation. Specifically, when considering the lack of privacy afforded to individuals in hospital or residential aged care settings, true privacy regarding AD use is, therefore, neither possible nor indeed appropriate. To provide holistic and inclusive care, healthcare providers, who are bound by codes of confidentiality, need to be aware of all aspects of an individual's needs to be able to deliver suitable care (Filej and Kaucic, 2013). Yet, due to the constraints of the legislation together with the potential judgement and stigmatization for engaging with AD, individuals may not want to make their choices known to all involved. This, however, is problematic as to withhold such information from care teams at an individual's request leaves the individual unable to openly discuss their care pathway, but simultaneously stops healthcare providers from being able to support those in their care and each other.

Despite previous literature outlining potential or actual social consequences of implementing AD as a legal medical service (Gamondi et al, 2018; Winnington and MacLeod, 2020), the impact of the Act is thus further reaching than could have been anticipated. While judgement, shame and stigma are key experiences of many of those involved in the AD service, irrespective of role, the role of secrecy supersedes all of these. This is due to the fact that if the legislation were less prescriptive in situating assisted deaths as being other through the requirements of individuals initiating conversations and were less conservative as per the legislation in Western Australia, for example (VADA, 2019), open discussions could occur. Such positioning of AD as an option that can be openly discussed in an institutional setting or context, or at least an accepted legal medical service, would support the notion of AD being a contemporary mechanism of individual control and self-determination with the potential to reduce the negative social barriers that currently exist. Furthermore, the legislative requirement that only individuals can involve families and *whānau* in the process, and not clinicians with legal responsibilities for care, obscures the cultural process of *whanaungatanga* in the NZ context specifically. Moreover, the initial exclusion of *whānau* from being involved in AD conversations appears at odds with the cultural narrative of NZ, where decisions are often made collectively and are less noted for individualistic choices. As such, solid and supportive relationships are paramount if this legal service is to be successful, and success does not equate with statistical evidence of number, location or gender of assisted deaths, but relates to the experience of following this process together with a broader understanding, embracement and acceptance of a service that is unlikely to be discontinued.

Conclusion

Specifically, this AD legislation is restrictive in relation to accessibility, involvement of broader family and social connections, and media reporting. Given experiences in countries other than NZ of the fallout from AD implementation, it is disappointing to note that overseas regulations have been followed rather than revised, which is likely to lead to ongoing secrecy, judgement and stigma for those using or delivering this new legal medical service. As such, the consequences of this legislation are dichotomous, as self-centricity of individualized choice is upheld, albeit through pseudo-autonomy (Jaye et al, 2021) while the limitations of the legislation contain and constrain such autonomy; all of which remain under the power and control of medical practitioners. This, therefore, highlights the dominance of institutional drivers over the needs of all involved in AD service provision. Yet, the impact is broader than the self and the clinician, but permeates broader society, affecting many beyond the immediacy of the decision. The decision of NZ to embrace AD is a brave move in contextualizing death and dying as individualistic acts of self-determination in the contemporary era, particularly given the bicultural identity of the country. Yet, the End of Life Choice Act (2019) specifically is perhaps not an ideal piece of legislation given the constraints it places upon all of those involved in its use. Indeed, it promotes the operation of silos, and does little to encourage open and active conversations regarding AD, given the unknown and unknowable about the service unless immediately involved. While it must be acknowledged that the root of this secrecy is commendably founded in mitigating potential coercion and abusive practices, it simultaneously produces a positioning of secrecy, judgement and stigma for all involved in service use or provision, thus, following rather than learning from experiences and outcomes in other countries. The possible social consequences of implementing this legislation produces the 'potential to fracture family and community structures' (Winnington and MacLeod, 2020) which may be irreparable. Thus, this AD legislation presents a polarizing dichotomy in terms of acceptance and practice in that while the right to end life is a legal option, it is simultaneously a covert practice and, as such, continues to sequester death practices away from everyday living, with the potential to continue the divisive nature of choosing to reject societal norms.

Notes

[1] Enduring Power of Attorney is a legal document which sets out who can take care of personal or financial matters if an individual is no longer able to do so.

[2] *Whānau* is the Māori language word for the basic extended family group, which can include non-blood relatives, friends and the broader community.

[3] Beneficence refers to the fact that physicians are obliged to not only cause no harm to patients but also to ensure that interventions are beneficial to their wellbeing, whereas non-maleficence clearly refers to physicians doing no harm, including not to kill, cause pain or suffering (Varkey, 2021).

References

Achterbergh, L., Pitman, A., Birken, M., Pearce, E., Sno, H. and Johnson, S. (2020) 'The experience of loneliness among young people with depression: a qualitative meta-synthesis of the literature', *BMC Psychiatry*, 20: Article 415.

Arias-Colmenero, T., Pérez-Morente, M.Á., Ramos-Morcillo, A.J., Capilla-Díaz, C., Ruzafa-Martínez, M. and Hueso-Montoro, C. (2020) 'Experiences and attitudes of people with HIV/AIDS: a systematic review of qualitative studies', *International Journal of Environmental Research and Public Health*, 17(2): 639.

Bates, R.A. and LaBrecque, B. (2020) 'The sociology of shaming', *The Journal of Public and Professional Sociology*, 12(1): Article 3.

Beauchamp, T. and Childress, J. (2013) *Principles of Biomedical Ethics* (7th edn). Oxford: Oxford University Press.

Becker, H.S. (1963) *Outsiders: Studies in the Sociology of Deviance*. New York: The Free Press.

Beidelman, T.O. (1993) *Secrecy and Society: The Paradox of Knowing and the Knowing of Paradox*. New York: MPublishing.

Bergham, G., Came, H., Doole, C., Fay, J., McCreanor, T. and Simpson, T. (2017) *Te Tiriti ō Waitangi-based Practice in Health Promotion*. Auckland, Aotearoa/New Zealand: STIR: Stop Institutional Racism.

Berry, C. and Greenwood, K. (2018) 'Direct and indirect associations between dysfunctional attitudes, self-stigma, hopefulness and social inclusion in young people experiencing psychosis', *Schizophrenia Research*, 193: 197–203.

Beuthin, R., Bruce, A. and Scaia, M. (2018) 'Medical assistance in dying (MAiD): Canadian nurses' experiences', *Nursing Forum*, 53(4): 511–520.

Brown, J., Thorpe, L. and Goodridge, D. (2018) 'Completion of medical certificates of death after an assisted death: an environmental scan of practices', *Healthcare Policy*, 14(2): 59–67.

Cain, L.C. and McCleskey, S. (2019) 'Expanded definitions of the "good death"? Race, ethnicity, and medical aid in dying', *Sociology of Health and Illness*, 41(6): 1175–1191.

Carrigan, K. (2023) 'One-way ticket to Zürich: presentations of "suicide tourism" in European news media', *Mortality*: 1–16.

Crumley, E.T., LeBlanc, J., Henderson, B., Jackson-Tarlton, C.S. and Leck, E. (2023) 'Canadian family members' experiences with guilt, judgment and secrecy during medical assistance in dying: a qualitative descriptive study', *CMAJ Open*, 11(4): E782–E789.

Devos, T., Yogeeswaran, K., Milojev, P. and Sibley, C.G. (2020) 'Conceptions of national identity and opposition to bicultural policies in New Zealand: a comparison of majority and minority perspectives', *International Journal of Intercultural Relations*, 78: 33–42.

Durie, M. (1994) *Whaiora: Māori Health Development* (2nd edn). Auckland: Oxford University Press.

Durkheim, E. (1982 [1895]) *Rules of Sociological Method*. The Free Press.

Durkheim, E. (1997 [1897]) *Suicide*. New York: The Free Press.

End of Life Choice Act (2019) Ministry of Health, New Zealand. Available at: https://www.legislation.govt.nz/act/public/2019/0067/latest/DLM 7285905.html [accessed 20 October 2024].

Ezekiel, J.E. and Joffe, S. (2003) 'Assisted suicide and euthanasia', in Kufe, D.W., Pollock, R.E., Weichselbaum, R.R., Bast, R.C., Gansler, T.S., Holland, J.F., Frei, E., et al (eds) *Hollan-Frei Cancer Medicine* (6th edn). Hamilton, ON: BC Decker.

Faúndes, A., Duarte, G.A. and Osis, M.J. (2013) 'Conscientious objection or fear of social stigma and unawareness of ethical obligations', *International Journal of Gynaecology and Obstetrics: The Official Organ of the International Federation of Gynaecology and Obstetrics*, 123(3): S57–S59.

Filej, B. and Kaucic, B.M. (2013) 'Holistic nursing practice', *South Eastern Europe Health Sciences Journal*, 3: 1–7.

Fontalis, A., Prousali, E. and Kulkarni, K. (2018) 'Euthanasia and AD: what is the current position and what are the key arguments informing the debate?', *Journal of the Royal Society of Medicine*, 111(11): 407–413.

Fujioka, J.K., Mirza, R.M., Klinger, C.A. and McDonald, L.P. (2019) 'Medical assistance in dying implications for health systems from a scoping review of the literature', *Journal of Health Services Research and Policy*, 24(3): 207–216.

Gamondi, C., Pott, M., Preston, N. and Payne, S. (2018) 'Family caregivers' reflections on experiences of assisted suicide in Switzerland: a qualitative interview study', *Journal of Pain and Symptom Management*, 55(4): 1085–1094.

Giddens, A. (2009) *Sociology* (6th edn). Bristol: Polity Press.

Goffman, E. (1963) *Stigma: Notes on the Management of Spoiled Identity*. Hoboken, NJ: Prentice Hall.

Goodyear-Smith, F. and Ashton, T. (2019) 'New Zealand health system: universalism struggles with persisting inequities', *The Lancet*, 394(10196): 432–442.

Hart, H.L.A. (2012) *The Concept of Law* (3rd edn). Oxford: Oxford University Press.

Hendry, M., Pasterfield, D., Lewis, R., Carter, B., Hodgson, D. and Wilkinson, C. (2012) 'Why do we want the right-to-die? A systematic review of the international literature on the views of patients, carers and the public on AD', *Palliative Medicine*, 27(1): 13–26.

Hobbs, M., Ahuriri-Driscoll, A., Marek, L., Campbell, M., Tomintz, M. and Kingham, S. (2019) 'Reducing health inequity for Māori people in New Zealand', *The Lancet*, 394(10209): 1613–1614.

Jaye, C., Lomax-Sawyers, I. and Young, J. (2019) 'The people speak: social media on euthanasia/AD', *Medical Humanities*, 47: 47–55.

Jaye, C., Young, J., Lomax-Sawyers, I. and Egan, R. (2021) 'Assisted dying in New Zealand: what is known about the values underpinning citizens' positions?', *Mortality*, 26(1): 66–82.

Liamputtong, P. and Rice, Z.S. (2021) 'Stigma, discrimination, and social exclusion', in Liamputtong, P. (ed) *Handbook of Social Inclusion*. Switzerland: Springer.

Marx, G.T. and Muschert, G.W. (2009) 'Simmel on secrecy', in Rol, C. and Papilloud, C. (eds) *Soziologie als Möglichkeit*. Heidelberg, Germany: VS Verlag für Sozialwissenschaften, pp 237–248.

Masters-Awatere, B., Rarere, M., Gilbert, R., Manuel, C. and Scott, N. (2019) '*He aha te mea nui o te ao? He tāngata!* (What is the most important thing in the world? It is people!)', *Australian Journal of Primary Health*, 25: 435–442.

MCNZ (2021) *Informed Consent: Helping Patients Make Informed Decisions about Their Care*. Medical Council of New Zealand, Wellington, Aotearoa/NZ. Available at: ttps://www.mcnz.org.nz/assets/standards/55f15c65af/Statement-on-informed-consent.pdf [accessed 20 October 2024].

Mellor, P.A. (1992) 'Death in high modernity: the contemporary presence and absence of death', *The Sociological Review*, 40(1): 11–30.

Mellor, P.A. and Shilling, C. (1993) 'Modernity, self-identity and the sequestration of death', *Sociology*, 27(3): 411–431.

Miller, D.G., Dresser, R. and Kim, S.Y.H. (2018) 'Advance euthanasia directives in the spotlight', *Journal of Medical Ethics* [blog]. Available at: https://blogs.bmj.com/medical-ethics/2018/03/05/advance-euthanasia-directives-in-the-spotlight/ [accessed 20 October 2024].

Moeke-Maxwell, T., Collier, A., Wiles, J., Williams, L., Black, S. and Gott, M. (2020) 'Bereaved families' perspectives of end-of-life care: towards a bicultural Whare Tapa Whā older person's palliative care model', *Journal of Cross-Cultural Gerontology*, 35: 177–193.

Mroz, S., Dierickx, S., Deliens, L., Cohen, J. and Chambaere, K. (2021) 'AD around the world: a status quaestionis', *Annals of Palliative Medicine*, 10(3): 3540–3553.

Pryor, C., Perfors, A. and Howe, P.D.L. (2019) 'Even arbitrary norms influence moral decision-making', *Nature Human Behaviour*, 3: 57–62.

Rutherford, J. (2021a) 'Enough already about conscientious objection in voluntary AD – what about the conscientious participants?', *Journal of Medical Ethics* [blog], 9 July. Available at: https://blogs.bmj.com/medical-ethics/2021/07/09/enough-already-about-conscientious-objection-in-voluntary-assisted-dying-what-about-the-conscientious-participants/ [accessed 20 October 2024].

Rutherford, J. (2021b) 'Conscientious participants and the ethical dimensions of physician support for legalised voluntary AD', *Journal of Medical Ethics*, 47: e11.

Seale, C., Raus, K., Bruisman, S., van der Heide, A., Sterckx, S., Mortier, F., et al (2015) 'The language of sedation in end-of-life care: the ethical reasoning of care providers in three countries', *Health*, 19(4): 339–354.

Shrestha, A., Martin, C., Burton, M., Walters, S., Collins, K. and Wyld, L. (2019) 'Quality of life versus length of life considerations in cancer patients: a systematic review of the literature', *Journal of the Psychological, Social and Behavioral Dimensions of Cancer*, 28(7): 1367–1380.

Simmel, G. (1904) 'Fashion', *International Quarterly*, 10: 130–155. (Reprinted in the *American Journal of Sociology*, 62: 541–559.)

Simmel, P. and Bellman, B. (1984) *The Language of Secrecy: Symbols and Metaphors in Poro Ritual*. New Brunswick, NJ: Rutgers University Press.

Storey, J.E. (2020) 'Risk factors for elder abuse and neglect: a review of the literature', *Aggression and Violent Behavior*, 50: 1–13.

Szasz, T.S. (1970) *The Manufacture of Madness: A Comparative Study of the Inquisition and the Mental Health Movement*. Syracuse, New York: Syracuse University Press.

Szasz, T.S. (2002) *Fatal Freedom: The Ethics and Politics of Suicide*. Syracuse, New York: Syracuse University Press.

Testoni, I. and Arnau, L. (2023) 'Journey to Switzerland as a state of exception: a 'homo sacer' Italian experience', *Mortality*.

Tyler, I. and Slater, T. (2018) 'Rethinking the sociology of stigma', *The Sociological Review*, 66 (4).

Varkey, B. (2021) 'Principles of clinical ethics and their application to practice', *Medical Principles and Practice*, 30(1): 17–28.

Veenstra, G. (2011) 'Race, gender, class, and sexual orientation: intersecting axes of inequality and self-rated health in Canada', *International Journal for Equity in Health*, 10(3): 1–11.

Voluntary Assisted Dying Act (2019) Western Australia. Available at: https://www.legislation.wa.gov.au/legislation/prod/filestore.nsf/FileURL/mrdoc_42491.pdf/$FILE/Voluntary%20Assisted%20Dying%20Act%202019%20-%20%5B00-00-00%5D.pdf?OpenElement [accessed 20 October 2024].

Waitangi Tribunal (2016) *The Treaty of Waitangi/Te Tiriti ō Waitangi*. Justice. govt.nz. Available at: https://www.waitangitribunal.govt.nz/treaty-of-waitangi/meaning-of-the-treaty/ [accessed 16 October 2023].

Walter, T. (1991) 'Modern death: taboo or not taboo?', *Sociology*, 25: 293–310.

Wilson, D., Boulton, A. and Warbrick, I. (2019) 'Physical Wellbeing of Māori', in Fleming, C. and Manning, M. (eds) *Routledge Handbook of Indigenous Wellbeing*. London: Routledge, pp 71–86.

Winnington, R. (2016) *Patient Choice as Illusion: Autonomy and Choice in End-of-Life Care in the United Kingdom and New Zealand*. PhD thesis, The University of Auckland, New Zealand.

Winnington, R. and MacLeod, R. (2020) 'Social consequences of AD: a case study', *New Zealand Medical Journal*, 133(1517): 18–23.

Yan, H., Bytautas, J., Isenberg, S.R., Kaplan, A., Hashemi, N., Kornberg, M., et al (2023) 'Grief and bereavement of family and friends around medical assistance in dying: scoping review', *BMJ Supportive and Palliative Care*, 13(4): 414–428.

Zhang, Y., Li, Y. and Mai, X. (2023) 'Fear of negative evaluation modulates the processing of social evaluate feedback with different valence and contexts', *Cereb Cortex*, 33(8): 4927–4938.

4

Institutional Thoughtlessness: Prison as a Place for Dying

Renske Visser

Introduction

In preparation for writing this chapter I find myself scrolling through the website of the Prisons and Probation Ombudsman. Every death in the United Kingdom is subjected to an investigation which is subsequently published as a 'Fatal Incident Report' on this website. During 2019–2022 I conducted research on living with cancer in prison (Visser et al, 2021; Armes et al, 2024), and while death and dying was not explicitly the focus, obviously people with cancer sometimes die. As I scroll through the Prisons and Probation Ombudsman website occasionally I have a slightly perverse little peek to see if I recognize a name. Arguably this peeking is the topic for another chapter, but I open this chapter with it here as it raised a sadness for me that, for various reasons, the project was designed in such a way that I would not be able to keep in touch with participants, and evidently them being in prison altered the research dynamic. It is difficult for people in prison to call and speak with their friends and family, let alone a nosy researcher. I like to imagine that all the people I encounter are cured and living relatively happy lives. Perhaps some are released and rebuilding their lives. But every now and again I find myself scrolling to the reports to see if I recognize a name. Luckily so far this has not happened yet.

Working with prisoners was an insight into another world, shielded within this most institutionalized of settings. Globally 11.5 million people are imprisoned (Penal Reform International, 2023). This number continues to fluctuate as new people enter prisons and others are released. Disproportionally to the wider community, people in prison have a higher chance of death, with mortality rates 50 per cent higher for people in prison compared to those in the general community (Penal Reform International, 2022). Despite this, the number of deaths in prison worldwide is unknown. Thus, one of the first issues when thinking about death and dying in prison is the lack of a global definition of what constitutes a 'death in custody'. Some countries only count deaths that occur within a detention facility whereas other countries also include deaths in pre-trial detention, deaths on temporary leave and deaths occurring shortly after prison release (Penal Reform International, 2022). For example, Ireland classifies a death as a 'death in custody' up to a month post-release; Turkey only up to ten days; but Italy does not include these deaths at all in its official figures (Penal Reform International, 2022). What is more, while international standards require all deaths in prison to be investigated, this is by no means done everywhere (Penal Reform International, 2022). The data about deaths in prison is thus far from complete, and the data that *is* available deserves critical consideration. Tomczak and Mulgrew (2023) note that the current means of collecting data about prisoner deaths makes various groups invisible; for example, while prisoner death is a gendered phenomenon predominantly involving males, little is known about women dying in prison, and transgender deaths are entirely absent from official data. Moreover, race and ethnicity are not visible in international datasets on prisoner deaths, obfuscating the disproportionate number of deaths among ethnically marginalized groups (Tomczak and Mulgrew, 2023).

In identifying these data gaps, Tomczak and Mulgrew propose three tenets to adequately capture the amount of people who die in prison; first, they advocate for *counting prisoners who die* as opposed to *prisoner deaths*. Second, they advocate for the examination of characteristics of prisoners who die so that age, disability, race, ethnicity, sexuality and gender are all included and available for analysis. Lastly, they argue in favour of adopting explicitly defined, mutually exclusive categorizations as current definitions conflate different types of death.

Even with this information, deaths in custody are (or would be) reduced to numbers. At the time of writing, I can tell you that in England and Wales, '[i]n the 12 months to June 2023, there were 313 deaths in prison custody, an increase of 9% from 288 deaths in the previous 12 months. Of these, 88 deaths were self-inflicted, a 26% increase from the 70 self-inflicted deaths in the previous 12 months' (Ministry of Justice, 2023). This tells you little about the people who died and the impact their deaths have had on those around them, including fellow people in prison, prison officers, healthcare and other staff working in prisons. Likely the impact of these deaths ripples beyond the boundaries of the prison into the community. Moreover, it tells you nothing as to whether prison should be a place for death and dying at all. Liebling (2017: 28) argues that: 'Deaths in custody are, and should be, controversial. They raise issues of accountability, legitimacy, and quality of life, including safety, as well as questions about the quality of death for those who die of natural causes in prison as a result of their age or sentence.' Liebling particularly focuses on deaths by suicide and murder, two forms of violent death that occur regularly in prison. Liebling notes that these two types of death represent forms of 'death without dying' as they are often sudden. In addition to suicide and murder, she also highlights 'whole life sentences' as a form as 'dying without death' until the very end (Liebling, 2017) and is highly critical of 'a judicial system that keeps people in custody for longer than they have been alive, or that aims to keep them until they die' (Liebling, 2017: 28).

The accountability that Liebling is referring to is evident in the aforementioned death investigations. As each death in custody is investigated in the United Kingdom, Robinson (2023) has explored the extent to which the anticipation of a post-death investigation influences both understandings of acceptable end-of-life care as well as the way care was delivered to those deemed dying. Robinson notes that this anticipation shapes 'the care given to dying prisoners by encouraging staff to prioritize the issues they thought would be of interest to the investigators' (Robinson, 2023: 6). Robinson concludes that the quality of end-of-life care is defined in the context of these expected investigations. Importantly, Robinson notes that a 'striking' importance is placed on bureaucratic tasks and suggests that this shifts the focus to making a 'defensible' decision about care and action, which is not necessarily the best decision for a dying prisoner. While in principle it is good that each death receives scrutiny, in practice these investigations have consequences likely not intended by those who introduced these reports.

Overall, death and dying in prison are, like Liebling (2017) points out, highly controversial. In addition to violent deaths, societal ageing has meant that there is an increasingly older prison population in England and Wales which makes 'death of natural causes' more commonplace. In this chapter I will use the concept of *institutional thoughtlessness* (Crawley, 2005) as a lens through which to understand the ways in which death, dying and loss are dealt with in prison. While some deaths in prison occur by design as many prisons are unhealthy places (Jewkes, 2018) and through the use of, for example, capital punishment, there are a myriad of ways in which the thoughtlessness of institutions contribute to the dying experience of those in prison. Additionally, I will use the work of anthropologist Daina Stanley to illustrate how intimate research on death and dying in prison, as well as humane ways in which to enable dying, are possible.

Reflecting on my aforementioned scrolling and hope for people I have met in the course of doing research in prison, I have written this chapter to challenge readers to reflect on their thinking about prison as a place of death, dying and loss. Here, I aim to highlight the humanity of those dying in this institutional setting and to show how, as can be seen in the work of Robinson (2023) and some of the examples that follow, prisons are challenging environments with complicated bureaucratic rules and power dynamics. These rules and dynamics are not always consistent with the needs of dying prisoners. What is more, dying people in prison also challenge assumptions about whose life is deemed 'grieveable' and who is deserving of care. It is to these issues that I now turn.

Institutional thoughtlessness around death and dying in prison

Prisons are not designed with ageing and dying in mind, reflected in the experiences of older people who reside and reach their final years in prison. Previous research has argued that older people in prison are 'doing harder time' (Mann, 2012), and that they face a 'double burden' (Turner et al, 2018) as, in addition to being deprived of their liberty, they are also deprived of basic social and care needs. Crawley (2005) uses the concept of *institutional thoughtlessness* to understand the experiences of older men in prison in England and Wales, defined as 'the ways in which prison regimes (routines, rules, time-tables, etcetera) simply roll on with little reference to the needs and sensibilities of the old' (2005: 350). As a consequence, Crawley argues, the needs of older people are often not met: for example, they are not able to walk at the pace that is expected of them, and as a result some stop joining certain activities as they slow things down. As time outside cells is limited, people in prison must think carefully how to use this time (for example, take shower, go outside, make a phone call) and the limits on what can be done during this time outside of a cell can be exacerbated for older, less mobile people. Crawley suggests that this negligence and oversight of slowing down in old age is not always deliberate, but instead a consequence of the inherent thoughtlessness of institutions. In other words, institutions simply do not 'think' about the range of people inhabiting them. Prisons have been designed with young, able bodies in mind, which explains, to some extent, how older people are often forgotten.

This is not unique to England and Wales. Building on Crawley's work, Suzuki and Otani (2023) note similar issues with regards to institutional thoughtlessness in prisons in Japan. This country has experienced a rapid increase of older people in the general population, and a corresponding quick rise of older people in the prison population. The authors suggest the concept of normalization, meaning that the conditions of prison life should be made as close as possible to 'normal' life as they could be helpful in improving the prison experience. However, they go on to warn that while 'normalising prisons may lead to the enhancement of healthcare and welfare inside prisons for older adults, it should not be used as an excuse to accommodate more elders' (Suzuki and Otani, 2023: 8). In other words, while the lives of older people in prison should be as normal as possible, prison should not be normalized as a potential institution that can house older people who are not wanted, or cannot be cared for, elsewhere.

While there is a growing body of literature concerned with ageing experiences in prison, little is known about the dying experiences of those in prison (Visser, 2021). Various studies have pointed out the tension between care and custody in secure environments and how this impacts the availability of palliative care in prison settings (Turner et al, 2011; Burles et al, 2016; Lillie et al, 2018). These studies have specifically focused on the availability of palliative care in prison, showing that prisons are not designed with these forms of care in mind. Elsewhere, Burles et al (2016) question whether a so-called 'good death' is available at all to people in prison. They note that while dying well is potentially achievable in prison, there are various issues limiting this possibility, such as access to palliative care and prisons not being not suitable environments to give this type of care. Furthermore, they note that access to pain relief can be restricted since drug abuse is a wide problem in prison; as a result healthcare providers are more likely to be distrustful of the realness of people's symptoms and limit people's access to medication.

A critical barrier to supporting good deaths in prison is that prisons are simply not thought of as places for dying. If death is considered, it is predominantly in relation to violent, sudden deaths and suicides, which as forms of 'death without dying' (Liebling, 2017) by their nature do not involve things like advance care planning. As choice and preferred place of death is an important element of, for example, the United Kingdom's end-of-life care policy (Borgstrom, 2016) 'the issue of where prisoners should die [from disease or old age] raises important questions about how much choice they should have about their preferred place of care at the end of life, and whether or not they should be granted compassionate release' (Turner et al, 2011: 376). On the one hand, this raises questions as to whether people in prison could potentially die outside of prison. On the other hand, this equally raises questions for prisons if people in prison 'choose' to die in this institutional environment. To help people die well in prison, it is helpful if these institutions give some thought to how this can be arranged: 'To implement palliative strategies and services successfully, it is important to be able to identify individuals who are dying and to anticipate, and plan for, the challenges that lie ahead' (Lillie, 2018: 49).

This is no easy task. Identifying those who are dying is already a challenge for healthcare providers in the community, particularly as there is no consensus on when 'dying' begins. This challenge will be exacerbated by the prison environment as people working and volunteering in prisons are rarely trained to provide this type of care, or what to look out for. To thus improve this identification and to facilitate improved dying experiences in prison, death and dying should be on the radar not only of those providing healthcare in prison, but also to those exercising other roles, such as chaplains, prison officers and prison volunteers.

Institutional thoughtlessness with regards to death and dying is also evident in the ways in which prison staff are trained to manage their emotions in the workplace. Prison officers often do not expect to be working in close proximity to death and dying when they take up the job, yet they can witness death and dying in a myriad of ways (Turner and Peacock, 2017). Previous research has shown the complicated emotional role that prison officers play when a person in prison is dying. For example a paper by Barry (2020) aptly titled 'You can't tell anyone how you really feel', illustrated how Irish prison service staff explored the emotional labour of prison staff who have experienced a prisoner's death. Prisons are institutional settings where showing vulnerability might make one susceptible to violence or be taken as a sign of weakness, and they are notorious for being places in which everyone needs to maintain face (Jewkes, 2005). It is often expected that prison officers show no emotion, no matter what. As one prison governor in Barry's study noted:

> I can't afford an officer to get all blubbery and upset if someone is dead. I will look after them and I understand, but I need them to hold themselves together right just until I know what's going on, and then I can move them out. … You can't afford for some fella to be getting upset like that. Because is he gonna flake in the middle of something and then you're on your bloody own? (Barry, 2020: 4)

Prison staff are systematically trained that these types of emotions are not for their workplace, as not being able to manage one's emotions hinders institutional routines and protocols. Yet emotional management, debriefing and talking about death, dying and bereavement seem pertinent as a wide range of deaths – including violent deaths, suicides, including hanging, and sudden deaths due to heart attacks – can and do occur (Barry, 2020). At the same time, with an ageing prison population it is increasingly likely that gentler (or natural) deaths will inevitably be experienced among the older prison population. Older people in prison often have multiple health problems, and are likely to have more co-morbidities compared to the general population, and inevitably prison officers will be involved in their care (Peacock et al, 2018; Turner et al, 2018). This involvement in caring at the end of life tests the boundaries of the prison staff role and whether they are there for custody and security, or whether they are equally there to have a helpful function. Tension between these contrary purposes has been seen in previous studies: a senior officer who took part in a study on palliative care in UK prisons noted that the prison was 'more like a care home than a prison wing' (Turner and Peacock, 2017: 62). Ageing and dying people in prison thus challenge the prison institution, and the people working in them, in a myriad of ways.

Loss and bereavement in prison

Beyond dying, it is important to briefly note that loss and bereavement are also complex concepts and experiences in relation to prison. Vaswani (2015) has suggested that young people in Scottish prisons experience a 'catalogue of losses' including loss of liberty and loss of a potential future. Vaswani's research (2015, 2018) further shows that young Scottish men often have suffered from a disproportionate amount of bereavement and the reason they have come into contact with the criminal justice system is partly due to their own unresolved grief. Alongside a disproportionate exposure to significant bereavements, people in prison can thus often experience a so-called disenfranchised grief. Defined as 'the grief that persons experience when they incur a loss that is not or cannot be openly acknowledged, publicly mourned, or socially supported' (Doka, 1989: 4), people in prison are 'separated from kith and kin and excluded from important healing rituals, [therefore] prisoners can experience themselves as being completely alone with their grief' (Masterton, 2014: 61).

These cumulative experiences of death and loss, both inside and outside the prison walls, challenge the routine and rules of prison. Based on research in a male prison in the North of England, Wilson et al (2022) identified various ways in which institutional thoughtlessness comes to the fore in relation to grief, death and dying in prison. For example, there are various protocols and procedures that are followed when a 'close relative' is dying or dead, yet the definition set by the Ministry of Justice might hinder whether permission is granted to attend a funeral (Wilson et al, 2022). They note too that the grieving patterns experienced by people in prison might be markedly different to those residing in the community as it can be much more difficult to accept the reality of a death due to their segregation from society and the ability to say goodbye or attend a funeral service. This delay has also been observed in other research on the experience of grief among women in prison:

So I think I was still in shock. It was only a year and I don't think I have dealt with it yet. Like I have to go home and see, go to the cemetery and see for myself. I think that's what I need. I am not in denial that she is dead because I know she is dead. It's just seeing it that I think will be the moment that I will probably break down. (Woman quoted in Harner et al, 2011: 43)

The limitations placed on prisoners being able to grieve can create 'unintentional harm', 'produced due to prison protocol, for example, when verifying information, receiving bad news, attempting to visit dying relatives and attend funerals, and the limited support currently in place to process an excessive grief reaction, healthily' (Wilson et al, 2022: 166). As an institutional setting, therefore, prisons impact prisoners' experiences of loss and bereavement, compounded by it being an environment with particular rules about feelings and emotions that can make it very difficult for those grieving in prison to acknowledge and talk about their bereavement.

Dying in prison: prisoner perspectives

There is limited research about the ways in which people in prison think about and prepare for death and dying. A 2006 study with ageing prisoners concluded that some people in prison see death as an escape, while others see dying in prison as the 'ultimate defeat' whereby dying could cause stigma and humiliation to their family (Aday, 2006). This study, and a later study by Aday and Wahidin (2016), found that thinking about death, and death anxiety, were common occurrences among older women in a US prison. The researchers also note that there is often a strong distrust in medical professionals and that these women often delayed seeking medical help due to experiences of neglect and humiliation (Aday and Wahidin, 2016). Their fear of death and dying was exemplified by a 61-year-old woman in another study who commented:

> It is a bad feeling to have to sit here day after day, year after year getting older every year just to sit around here every day wondering if I will ever get to go back to my family before I leave this earth. I wouldn't want to have to leave here in a body bag. That would hurt my family so much. (Aday and Krabill, 2011: 67)

Little is known about the everyday lived reality of facing the end of life in prison. A rare insight into dying in prison has been offered through the work of Daina Stanley. In her exemplary research exploring end of life in prison, Stanley conducted fieldwork in a state prison in Maine, United States. In this prison, peer-based end-of-life care was offered and fellow prisoners were intimately involved in the dying journeys of other prisoners. In the chapter 'Touching life, death and dis/connection', Stanley (2021) focuses particularly on the sensory elements of dying in prison. The chapter describes Stanley's personal proximity to the death of prisoner Daniel. Daniel had been ill for a while and had started to refuse his antiretroviral treatment. Stanley writes:

> Shortly thereafter, amidst his declining health, Daniel was shackled and sent to a hospital located beyond the walls of the prison. Several days later, doctors indicated that life-sustaining treatment was no longer a

viable option and Daniel was transferred back to the infirmary to spend his final days in the care of fellow prisoners who were trained and state certified, through a peer-based prison hospice programme, to provide hospice and palliative care. Upon his return to the prison's infirmary, and after undergoing the humiliation of the policy-mandated strip search, Daniel was assigned a new cell, the 'terminal cell'. (Stanley, 2021: 59)

The shackles that Daniel was made to wear underscored the aforementioned tensions between whether the staff were providing secure custody or care. Even when facing the end of his life, as a person in need of care and a person residing in prison, cuffing and strip-searches were deemed necessary. Such stark and seemingly contrary practices lay bare the challenges of whether those dying in prison are 'patients', 'prisoners' or 'people' (Plugge et al, 2008). According to Stanley, despite the shackles, the presence of the peer-based hospice care returned the humanity to the care experiences of Daniel:

> Writing about the moments of Daniel's nearing death, the memories that return equally vividly are the moments of both levity and care that characterise the ways peer hospice care affirms the patient's existence. In the preceding weeks, Daniel's brother and peer caregivers had shared with me their favourite stories and memories of the gentle yet witty man whose impending death brought us together. (Stanley, 2021: 61)

Daniel spent a while in his 'terminal cell', which Stanley visited frequently. One night, while she was already leaving the prison, she was called to return to the infirmary; Daniel's death seemed imminent. When she entered the room, she decided to touch him: 'As my eyes adjusted to the greyness of the cell, I laid my hand on Daniel's arm to let him know I was present. My ears prickled at the sounds of a crackling deep within Daniel's chest. The "death rattle"' (Stanley, 2021: 62). That Stanley touched Daniel was critical, as the presence and absence of touch is particularly pertinent in prison environments with researchers actively discouraged from exchanging any form of physical touch with prisoners (Stanley, 2021). Yet in this moment, it only felt natural to Stanley to touch Daniel as he died, something she likely would have done if this was a non-prison-based hospice. Having held Daniel's hand several times during his illness, Stanley felt that this 'shared sensation of touch, of human connection, was my real entry point into Daniel's end-of-life experience, the point in which he truly invited me into his life' (2021: 64).

As Daniel's dying was not as quick as anticipated, Stanley returned home for a few hours. When she returned two peer caregivers, Agelu and C.R., were holding vigil around his bed and Stanley joined them. She recounted his death as follows:

> I sat in silence at the foot of the bed beside C.R., who was also experiencing a hospice death for the first time. I listened intently to Daniel's breathing, each breath fewer and further between. ... I sense a natural intimacy as Agelu tenderly stroked Daniel's head with large hands that experienced nearly a decade of death as a peer caregiver. An electric calm, an impenetrable tranquillity came over the cell. With ears that I had learned to open in new ways, I caught Agelu's whispered words: 'Enjoy the journey'. As the moon glistened through the small window, Daniel's chest rose in a large breath. Froze. And then fell for the last time. (Stanley, 2021: 62)

Peer caregiver C.R. was extremely moved by witnessing Daniel's death and started to cry. While it had felt appropriate to touch Daniel's arm earlier, Stanley fought the impulse to comfort C.R., as she felt this 'remained beyond the bounds of acceptability in prison' (Stanley, 2021: 63). Prior to Daniel's death, a different energy had been present in the room, and his death marked a return to the prison's usual routine and rules. As an officer entered the room, it was time to leave Daniel's body as the prison investigator had to see him (Stanley, 2021).

Stanley's research offers a rare glimpse into the world of naturally dying behind the closed walls of a prison. On the one hand, it highlights the continued tensions between care and custody and the way dying and death challenge routines and rules. On the other hand, both the peer caregiving as well as Stanley's presence show how death opens up space for humanity to return to prison, for discretion to be applied to the implementation of rules and protocols, if only temporarily. Furthermore, it shows how the dying and death of people in prison have an impact on those working in prison and others residing in prison.

Conclusion

In this chapter I have introduced some ideas around the reality of death and dying in prison. I am mindful that different dynamics and power relationships are at play during violent deaths, suicides and other types of death such as deaths in detention centres, which this chapter has not examined. Instead, here I have focused on death in older age and deaths due to untreatable diseases, such as terminal cancer, and I have found the notion of institutional thoughtlessness particularly helpful in starting to unpack the complexity of these types of death and dying in this particular setting. Prison as an institution shapes the way people think and feel about death and dying in this environment. Death and dying also play a role in people's general wellbeing as people in prison often experience more co-morbidities and have a lower life expectancy compared to people in the general population (Visser et al, 2019; Visser, 2021). The growing prison population and the ageing of said populations will mean that increasingly people will die in prison. Those who run these institutions thus have a responsibility to ensure that dying can be well managed.

It is very difficult to conduct empirical research about this topic both due to the emotional labour involved as well as the power dynamics at play. Getting access to prisons is not easy and consists of continuous negotiations between the researcher and the institution. Due to the pandemic I, and all other researchers in the UK, were ordered to halt face-to-face studies in prison from March 2020 onwards. I am not sure if research has started again. I hope research on death and dying will increasingly be allowed behind bars; Stanley (2021) has shown how ethnographic research on end of life in prison can reveal the humanity present during the dying of people in prison, which I believe are stories that need to be told more often. Studies can put death in prison on the radar, but equally highlight why prisons might be reluctant to open their doors to researchers, as they can scrutinize their ways of working and highlight failings. However, stories that reveal the real lived experience of people in prison are important as they show what actually happens versus what is told in sensational media headlines, how prison could potentially happen to all of us, and how we are all just people in the end. Like Stanley, I met the people I interviewed for the cancer study in prison for research purposes. I was not interested in why they were in prison or what their so-called 'index offence' was. What I wanted to know is how they were diagnosed with cancer and how they experienced their illness. There was a relief and gratitude from prisoners, I felt, that I spent time with them, just wanting to hear their story without judgement. For some there was a notion of not deserving care; they felt they had wasted their lives and that the National Health Services spending money and resources on their care was wasteful too. While some had received a terminal prognosis, others were curable, and I strongly hope they continued to receive the stellar care that the National Health Service can provide. Nevertheless, I do worry, with a 'cancer emergency' predicted due to COVID-19 and delays in access to treatment (Gregory, 2022), what this will mean for those in need of care behind locked doors, and whether some will have been or will become just another statistic, another preventable death in prison.

References
Aday, R.H. (2006) '"Aging prisoners" concerns toward dying in prison', *Omega: Journal of Death and Dying*, 52(3): 199–216.

Aday, R. and Krabbill, J. (2011) *Women Aging in Prison: A Neglected Population in The Correctional System*. Lynne Rienner Publishers Inc.: Boulder.

Aday, R. and Wahidin, A. (2016) 'Older prisoners' experiences of death, dying and grief behind bars', *Howard Journal of Crime and Justice*, 55(3): 312–327.

Armes, J., Visser, R., Lüchtenborg, M., et al (2024) 'Cancer in prison: barriers and enablers to diagnosis and treatment', *eClinicalMedicine*, 72: 102540.

Barry, C. (2020) '"You can't tell anyone how you really feel": exploring emotion management and performance among prison staff who have experienced the death of a prisoner', *International Journal of Law, Crime and Justice*, 61: 1–11.

Borgstrom, E. (2016) 'National end-of-life care policy in the English context: the problem and solution to death and dying', in Foster, L. and Woodthorpe, K. (eds) *Death and Social Policy in Challenging Times*. Basingstoke: Palgrave Macmillan, pp 35–53.

Burles, M.C., Peternelj-Taylor, C.A. and Holtslander, L. (2016) 'A "good death" for all? Examining issues for palliative care in correctional settings', *Mortality*, 21(2): 93–111.

Crawley, E. (2005) 'Institutional thoughtlessness in prisons and its impacts on the day-to-day prison lives of elderly men', *Journal of Contemporary Criminal Justice*, 21(4): 350–363.

Doka, K.J. (1989) 'Disenfranchised grief', in Doka, K.J. (ed) *Disenfranchised Grief: Recognizing Hidden Sorrow*. Lexington, MA: Lexington Books, pp 3–11.

Gregory, A. (2022) Treatment delays leave UK facing cancer emergency, doctors warn, *The Guardian*. Available at: https://www.theguardian.com/society/2022/dec/14/treatment-delays-leave-uk-facing-cancer-emergency-doctors-warn [accessed 14 January 2024].

Harner, H.M., Hentz, P.M. and Evangelista, M.C. (2011) 'Grief interrupted: the experience of loss among incarcerated women', *Qualitative Health Research*, 21(4): 454–464.

Jewkes, Y. (2005) 'Loss, liminality and the life sentence: managing identity through a disrupted lifecourse', in Liebling, A. and Maruna, S. (eds) *The Effects of Imprisonment*. London: Routledge, pp 366–388.

Jewkes, Y. (2018) 'Just design: healthy prisons and the architecture of hope', *Australian and New Zealand Journal of Criminology*, 51(3): 319–338.

Liebling, A. (2017) 'The meaning of ending life in prison', *Journal of Correctional Health Care*, 23(1): 20–31.

Lillie, K. (2018) 'Loss at the end of life: palliative care in prisons', in Read, S., Santatzoglou, S. and Wrigley, A. (eds) *Loss, Dying and Bereavement in the Criminal Justice System*. London: Routledge, pp 43–53.

Lillie, K., Corcoran, M., Hunt, K., Wrigley, A. and Read, S. (2018) 'Encountering offenders in community palliative care settings: challenges for care provision', *International Journal of Palliative Nursing*, 24(8): 368–375.

Mann, N. (2012) *Doing Harder Time? The Experience of an Ageing Male Prison Population in England and Wales*. London: Ashgate.

Masterton, J. (2014) 'A confined encounter: the lived experience of bereavement in prison', *Bereavement Care*, 33(2): 56–62.

Ministry of Justice (2023) 'Safety in Custody Statistics, England and Wales: Deaths in Prison Custody to June 2023 Assaults and Self-harm to March 2023'. *Crown Copyright*. Available at: https://assets.publishing.serv ice.gov.uk/media/64c253b0f921860014866613/safety-in-custody-q1-2023.pdf [accessed 14 January 2024].

Peacock, M., Turner, M. and Varey, S. (2018) '"We call it jail craft": the erosion of the protective discourses drawn on by prison officers dealing with ageing and dying prisoners in the neoliberal, carceral system', *Sociology*, 52(6): 1152–1168.

Penal Reform International (2022) *Deaths in Prison: Examining Causes, Responses, and Prevention of Deaths in Prison Worldwide*. London: Penal Reform International.

Penal Reform International (2023) *Global Prison Trends 2023*. London: Penal Reform International.

Plugge, E., Douglas, N. and Fitzpatrick, R. (2008) 'Patients, prisoners, or people? Women prisoners' experiences of primary care in prison: a qualitative study', *British Journal of General Practice*, 58(554): 630–636.

Robinson, C. (2023) 'The anticipation of an investigation: the effects of expecting investigations after a death from natural causes in prison custody', *Criminology & Criminal Justice*, 23(1): 3–19. https://doi.org/10.1177/17488958211028721

Stanley, D. (2021) 'Touching life, death, and dis/connection in a state prison infirmary', in Herrity, K., Schmidt, B. and Warr, J. (eds) *Sensory Penalties: Exploring the Senses in Spaces of Punishment and Social Control*. Leeds: Emerald Group Publishing Ltd, pp 53–68.

Suzuki, M. and Otani, A. (2023) 'Ageing, institutional thoughtlessness, and normalisation in Japan's prisons', *International Journal of Comparative and Applied Criminal Justice*, 48(4): 363–374. https://doi.org/10.1080/01924 036.2023.2188236

Tomczak, P. and Mulgrew, R. (2023) 'Making prisoner deaths visible: towards a new epistemological approach', *Incarceration*, 4. https://doi.org/10.1177/26326663231160344

Turner, M. and Peacock, M. (2017) 'Palliative care in UK prisons: practical and emotional challenges for staff and fellow prisoners', *Journal of Correctional Health Care*, 23(1): 56–65.

Turner, M., Payne, S. and Barbarachild, Z. (2011) 'Care or custody? An evaluation of palliative care in prisons in North West England', *Palliative Medicine*, 25(4): 370–377.

Turner, M., Peacock, M., Payne, S., Fletcher, A. and Froggatt, K. (2018) 'Ageing and dying in the contemporary neoliberal prison system: exploring the "double burden" for older prisoners', *Social Science and Medicine*, 212: 161–167.

Vaswani, N. (2015) 'A catalogue of losses: implications for the care and reintegration of young men in custody', *Prison Service Journal*, 220: 26–35.

Vaswani, N. (2018) 'Beyond loss of liberty: how loss, bereavement and grief can affect young men's prison journeys', in Read, S., Sanatatzoglou, S. and Wrigley, A. (eds) *Loss, Dying and Bereavement in the Criminal Justice System.* London: Routledge, pp 177–188.

Visser, R.C. (2021) 'Dying in the margins: a literature review on end of life in English prisons', *Religions*, 12(6): 413.

Visser, R.C., MacInnes, D., Parrott, J. and Houben, F. (2019) 'Growing older in secure mental health care: the user experience', *Journal of Mental Health*, 30(1): 51–57.

Visser, R., Barber, A.E., X, A., et al (2021) 'Collaboration with people with lived experience of prison: reflections on researching cancer care in custodial settings', *Res Involv Engagem*, 7: 48. https://doi.org/10.1186/s40900-021-00284-z

Wilson, M., Johnston, H. and Walker, L. (2022) '"It was like an animal in pain": institutional thoughtlessness and experiences of bereavement in prison', *Criminology and Criminal Justice*, 22(1): 150–170.

5

Out of the Ashes in New York City: Body Storage Bottleneck in COVID-19's First Wave

Sally Raudon

Introduction

Mere weeks into the COVID-19 pandemic in New York City (NYC), the bottleneck of the dead demanded improvisation. On 6 April 2020, NYC Council Health Committee chair Mark Levine tweeted that due to the climbing daily COVID-19 death toll, the Office of the Chief Medical Examiner's morgue freezers in Manhattan and Brooklyn would soon be full because 'traditional burial system has largely frozen up'. Despite crematoria receiving dispensation from the city to operate at all hours, cemeteries and crematoria simply could not keep up.

Phil Tassi of Ferncliff Cemetery in Westchester, just north of NYC, told me that they usually cremated about 12 bodies a day. By early April 2020, Ferncliff was cremating about 40 bodies before 11am. 'We're running 16 hours a day and we hit capacity ... we can't keep up with the number of bodies coming in', he said, adding that cremators are fragile and expensive to repair, as two of NYC's crematoria had retorts[1] break down, likely from overuse. Cremation slots became so difficult to book that funeral directors started taking bodies to nearby states like New Jersey for cremation.

New Yorkers are all too familiar with congestion and traffic jams when the volume of transport overwhelms the city's roads and vehicles snarl up along bottlenecked arterial routes. But in April 2020, the city faced a far grimmer gridlock. When New York become COVID-19's early global epicentre, its death rate rapidly reached six times its average, and jammed up the city's deathcare systems. Every step in NYC's entire chain of death infrastructure – the Office of the Chief Medical Examiner, hospital morgues, funeral homes, cemeteries and crematoria – strained under the extraordinary burden. The city was strangely muted and eerily still: lockdowns meant people were confined to their apartments, forbidden from gathering, and unable even to claim their dead from the morgue. Many New Yorkers had to adapt their ideas about funerals. Thousands of deceased New Yorkers started to be stored in refrigerated trucks that had been transformed into temporary morgues, sometimes for months, while their families tried to figure out how to conduct a funeral in these exceptional circumstances. The sudden visibility of the dead during New York's first wave, and the care they demanded, substantially shaped the dislocated, distressed sense of collective experience of that time. And New Yorkers began, for the first time, putting aside their strong historical preference for burial to choose cremation (NFDA, 2021a).

As readers of this collection likely already know, cremation transforms the corpse into fragments so that it no longer resembles a body. Mechanized fire burns away bodily remains to leave only bones, then all fragments are swept up and pulverized, and the 'ashes' or 'cremains' (the US hybridized term for cremated remains) are returned to family in an urn. It has long been stigmatized in American society (Walter, 1993), with Anglo-American cultures often associating it with secularism and industrialization, an association that has sat uneasily with many. In contrast, in Australasia, where people prefer cremation, people have described it to me as clean, modern, quick and more efficient, compared with burial. But in NYC funeral directors often reminded me that cremation would destroy the body, or make it difficult for mourners to visit it, as well as being problematic for Catholics and forbidden for Jews and Muslims. Even professionals who supported cremation would tell me, 'It's an economical option for families', reflecting the reality that cremation is often significantly less expensive than burial in the United States, but they would fall short of endorsing it in its own right. And even though there have been gradual increases in cremation across the United States, pre-COVID-19 suspicion of it as 'industrial incineration' had remained stubbornly persistent (Dawdy, 2021: 94) with a perception that it can be 'numbingly transactional' (Dawdy, 2021: 159).

This chapter analyses New Yorkers' shift to cremation during COVID-19, examining how the city's deathcare infrastructure had historically marginalized cremation, and analysing cremation's local meanings within this shifting context. NYC's limited physical provision for cremation, and the legal and bureaucratic limits to it, provided structural accommodations that prioritized burial over cremation in ways which had, many locals argued, simply reflected local preferences. As I will show, COVID-19 clarified, in turn, how existing institutional infrastructure had shaped those preferences and possibilities. Taking the concept of the logjam as both a lived reality and an analytic tool helps illuminate what this institutional infrastructure limited – and what it facilitated – especially when overloaded with the dead. Crucially, to think infrastructurally (Chu, 2014; Appel et al, 2018) about the problem of excess mortality means examining the often taken-for-granted activities of collecting, caring for, moving, placing and settling the dead into spaces dedicated to them. This kind of daily logistics often go unnoticed until one is personally affected by 'infrastructural inversion' when 'the normally invisible quality of working infrastructure becomes visible when it breaks' (Bowker and Star, 1999: 35).

The chapter comes from a 15-month fieldwork period during 2019–2020 in NYC. During that time, I was focused on Hart Island, NYC's massed grave, and in doing so learned about NYC deathcare from many perspectives. I met bereaved relatives, activists, artists, community organizers, funeral directors, policy makers and officials, politicians, former inmates, city councillors, cemetery managers and staff, lawyers, religious leaders, urban planners, historians, journalists, and others. Some spoke openly and others wanted anonymity. I complemented these ethnographic interviews with participant observation across NYC's five boroughs, attending meetings and events, council committee hearings, onsite visits and funerals, before the city closed due to COVID-19. I also analysed documents including statutes and policy texts, legal files, death certificates, activist campaign materials, and contemporary and archival media coverage found in archives, libraries, universities and museums. In 2020, as the pandemic arrived, I conducted ethnographic interviews during NYC's lockdowns in COVID-19's first and second waves, and before vaccines arrived. I spoke with fewer bereaved families during this time and this chapter thus draws predominantly on interviews with funeral professionals and experts. This material captures a moment of time, when the trajectory of the pandemic and its societal impact remained uncertain, and at a time where there was still much ambivalence towards cremation. In these interviews we discussed deathcare practices that were unfolding during local and global crisis, and how New Yorkers were beginning to choose cremation over burial. Such a choice may seem a self-evident practicality in a city as crowded as NYC and during a disaster, yet it represented a significant transformation and, as interviewees told me, it was not without practical challenges, most notably being that NYC has only four crematoria (Green-Wood, Brooklyn; Pinelawn, Queens; Fresh Pond, Queens; and Woodlawn, Bronx).

The bereaved's legal right to the deceased

New York State legally protects the next of kin's right to a relative's dead body. The Right of Sepulchre, used throughout the United States but first claimed in New York State (Ruggles, 1856; Marsh, 2015), refers to the next of kin's right to possess and control human remains and to choose how and where they are disposed. Here the law understands the body as a form of property, the possession of which should not be delayed – because without this, next of kin may feel agonizing sorrow and suffering. The next of kin's right to control the deceased's remains accords with how values such as individual autonomy and agency are regarded in matters of death and dying in the United States (see Kaufman, 2006), as well as recognizing the relationship between deceased and bereaved. This law recognizes the corpse as both object and person; as property, but also somewhat human and therefore sharing some of the rights of living bodies.

The problem of understanding human remains as property, and how this shapes how people choose to dispose of a body, rests on how property manifests a set of relations (Strathern, 2005). Within Anglo-American legal traditions, the body is understood as the inalienable foundation of legal individualism (Pottage, 1998), in which a person is embodied in and by their body, equating a person with their individual body. As Strathern described, while 'a corpse may be treated as a whole body, no one would think of regarding it as a whole person' (2007: 210), and yet corpses 'cannot be property although there is a duty to effect a decent burial and a corresponding right to possession for that purpose' (2007: 212). The Right of Sepulchre effectively secures this. Correspondingly, New York State law implies that the dead have rights that the living must protect, including the right to a decent burial, or alternative. To place this historic right to the body in a contemporary practical perspective – because after cremation, nothing that resembles a body will remain – I begin with a brief cultural context of cremation and its gradual adoption in the United States.

How cremation's meanings vary

Cremation's meanings are particular to the culture in which it is practised. For instance, it has long been almost ubiquitous in Buddhist traditions, and is being readopted in postcolonial Asian states, embedded within beliefs about facilitating reincarnation by promptly destroying the corpse. In contrast, when modern European cremation was reinvented in the late 19th century, it was seen as a novel practice for atheists, intellectuals and dissenters (Prothero, 2001) and initially understood as counter to Christian values and especially lingering convictions that the corpse should be as intact as possible to ease resurrection (Meier, 2020). In some countries, such as Great Britain, as well as in some settler societies such as Australia and New Zealand (see Schafer, 2012), it has become the default (although not universal) choice, where it is perceived as a quick, hygienic and practical way to avoid the distress of a body rotting in the earth. In Great Britain, cremation has become so normalized over time that it has been described as 'the British way of death'

(Jupp, 2006), now accounting for around 78 per cent of the dead (The Cremation Society, 2022).

Despite its popularity elsewhere, for many Americans cremation has retained a sense of being an innovation that is something of a compromise: slightly risky, perhaps expedient, and somehow conveying less dignity and respect for the deceased person than burial. It is also usually significantly less expensive than burial in the United States and has, over time, become associated with need, which funeral directors told me created a slight stigma around it.

It is not universally negatively viewed, however, with historian Stephen Prothero predicting that cremation might suit the austerity of lingering US Puritanism, and that cremation was 'a preparation for memorialization' (2001: 196). In this way, Prothero imagined that the stigma of cremation could be transformed into something deeply meaningful, potentially heralding 'a new era in American ritual life' (2001: 199) as it could be well suited to a culture that valorizes choice and personalization, as ashes offer rich potential for memorialization. Already dematerialized, they can be easily moved, divided, transformed into objects and stored in various places.

Cremation's slow adoption across the United States

Despite growing US cultural diversity, its funeral rituals have been judged remarkably homogeneous (Metcalf and Huntington, 1991; Troyer, 2020), with burial understood as a profoundly and enduringly American act (Walter, 1993; Prothero, 2001). NYC funeral directors told me that burial was so standard a practice in the United States that even immigrants from strong cremation traditions often opted for burial as a way of demonstrating their US citizenship. This is an unusual assimilation, because often mortuary traditions are among the most enduring of immigrants' cultural practices, persisting after others have been adapted (Walter, 1993). One reason for such strong associations between burial and belonging is that early associations with the Civil War helped crystallize the notion that US soil was fertilized by the bodies of its citizens (Faust, 2008). Even earlier, Thomas Jefferson wrote of the Republic's ongoing need for sustenance from the bodies of its sons, patriotic and otherwise: 'the tree of liberty must be refreshed from time to time with the blood of patriots and tyrants. it is it's natural manure' ([sic], Jefferson, 1787).

In the 1920s, approximately 1 per cent of the dead were cremated across the United States (Prothero, 2001). Forty years later, in 1963, with the instruction Piam et Constantem, Pope Paul VI approved cremation as long as the ashes were interred in consecrated land (Holy See Press Office, 2016). In the same year Jessica Mitford (1963), in her best-selling exposé of the US funeral industry, championed cremation as a simple, dignified and affordable option. Despite this, by 1981 only 10 per cent of people in the United States chose cremation and by 1999 this stood at 25 per cent. By 2020, however, 56 per cent of US deceased people were cremated, more than doubling the rate over two decades (NFDA, 2021a). The growth in cremation's national popularity had been slow to start, but the recent accelerating trend was clear.

New York City's history of cremation

For most of its history, the most popular kind of NYC funeral has involved burial, so much so that burial could be understood as a literal claim on the city's most iconic resource – real estate. Cremation was considered at best a compromise, though rates had gradually increased over the 20th century, albeit at a slower rate than national trends. The New York Cremation Society was formed in April 1874 (Prothero, 2001) and despite an initial flurry of interest cremation remained unpopular. In 1879 *The New York Times* announced 'The end of cremation', dismissing it as a fad and stating accurately that 'cremation has not come into fashion' (NYT, 1879). In 1881, as there was not enough local interest to justify its existence, the New York Cremation Society was quietly transformed into the US Cremation Company (Prothero, 2001).

By the mid-1880s, cremationists had taken up germ theory (Prothero, 2001) and in a stance that would resonate during COVID-19, the US Cremation Society president and naval chaplain, Reverend John Beugless, delivered a paper to the American Public Health Association entitled 'Cremation as a safeguard against epidemics' (Beugless, 1884). He argued that cremation was 'the only never-failing germicide' that could be relied on to avoid 'epidemics of contagion' (Beugless, 1884). Evocatively, he called for 'a crematory at every quarantine station and in connection with every public hospital and in every Potter's Field' (Beugless, 1884: 57). Such a proclamation was a potent foreshadowing of the local nexus that would develop for cremation as a practical technology well-suited for dealing expediently with bodies, including those of the poor, unfortunate, immigrants, and the diseased and potentially contagious, who were perceived to pose higher risks to the living.

While Reverend Beugless was not successful in changing national practices, in 1889 NYC opened the country's first publicly operated crematory on Swinburne Island, the tiny artificial island off Staten Island's South Beach. Effectively replacing the island's potter's field, Swinburne had been strategically built to quarantine and hospitalize unwell immigrants before they reached Manhattan, and officials started cremating immigrants who had died of infectious diseases, especially cholera (Prothero, 2001).

Over one hundred years later and just before the onset of the pandemic, by 2019 in New York State approximately 47 per cent of the dead were buried and just over 47 per cent were cremated (NFDA, 2021b). The remaining

5.5 per cent were donated to science, sent out of state, or otherwise unknown. It took the pressure of the pandemic to increase cremation rates, and even then, relatively slowly. In part this slow uptake can be attributed to the persistent widespread and oft-repeated view that cremation was the inferior, or somehow lesser, option. The NY State Association of Cemeteries (NYSAC) website details that cremation's extreme heat reduces the deceased's remains to bone fragments, clarifying that '[i]t is an irreversible process' (New York State Association of Cemeteries, nd). They also strongly opposed the idea of scattering: 'If a person's remains are scattered, there is no permanent place for future generations to come and pay their respects to the deceased' (New York State Association of Cemeteries, nd). This remonstration not only indicates the funeral industry's financial interest in selling goods and services that make use of cremains – such as an urn, plaque engraving, columbarium niche, perhaps memorial jewellery or other options – but also emphasizes the US social norm of memorialization of connecting the body with the land and dedicating a defined location permanently to remembering and honouring each deceased person – as a grave does (see Laqueur, 2015).

Such a view was echoed by funeral home executive Elisa Krcilek, who similarly framed cremation as problematic for memorialization. She said in a press interview that the funeral industry had 'to do a better job informing people that there's a time to say goodbye and a place to say hello. The moment you scatter someone, you're done. People need a memorial, to be remembered' (Heller, 2022). When talking with me, interlocutors frequently articulated cremation as the problem when they meant the lack of memorialization that often accompanied cremation. However, as the Cremation Authority of North America estimated that only 20 to 40 per cent of cremains are interred, the data supported this conflation (Heller, 2022).

When I asked people outside the funeral industry about their views on cremation before COVID-19, a common reaction was mild disgust, such as a wrinkled nose and a statement like, 'My family doesn't cremate, I don't know, we prefer burial. It's just what we do.' The usual exception was Asian New Yorkers. However, when people whose families did cremate discussed it, they often rationalized cremation by the options it enabled, in statements like, 'Our family is spread out over several states now, so the last couple of people who died got cremated. We can bring them home more easily. But scattering? No. We got an urn, interred the cremains.'

Saliently, these pre-pandemic anecdotes show the drive to return the deceased home for disposition as an assertion of community belonging (Woodthorpe, 2010). When I mentioned the popularity of scattering ashes in other cultures, New Yorkers were often bemused and assumed that this was motivated by cost, as cremation is generally perceived to be the cheaper option to burial in the United States. Indeed, this is for the large part true: in 2020 the average price for a US funeral including viewing and burial was

US$7,848, against the average direct cremation (cremation only, without viewing or funeral) costing $2,550. A cremation with a viewing and funeral cost an average of $6,970, only slightly less expensive than a traditional burial (NFDA, 2021b). When I explained that in other countries the costs of burial and cremation were often similar, people were puzzled, often asking why someone who could afford burial would choose cremation.

One possible reason is that cremation has various temporal implications. Hertz described cremation as 'neither a final act, nor sufficient in itself; it calls for a later and complementary rite' (1960: 42; cf Prothero, 2001: 196). Cremation's new popularity in the Euro-American world in the 20th century prompted new secondary rituals of re-enchantment (Prendergast et al, 2006), such as scattering, earth burial or columbarium placement. As 'the mobile material residue of the corpse' (Prendergast et al, 2006: 881), ashes remain material yet flexible, meaning they can travel, be divided and, crucially, be held for further action later. Conversely, a lack of ritual urgency means ashes can also sit indefinitely in a closet or funeral home storeroom. Such inertia around ashes is not limited to closets: across Australasia, up to a third of ashes are not returned to the bereaved (Clayden et al, 2014), suggesting that, contrary to Hertz, mourners find cremation itself a sufficient ending, or possibly choose to postpone indefinitely the final disposal for which they have not yet found an accessible and satisfactory ritual. This ability to postpone certainly bore out during my pandemic fieldwork, when funeral directors suggested that cremation became more popular during COVID-19 *because* families found it more flexible, as they could postpone the funeral and decisions about what to ultimately do with the ashes until the lockdowns, travel bans and funeral restrictions were finally over.

Certainly, ashes offer extraordinary potential for creative expression and reuse. After cremation people might use some of the deceased's ashes to create jewels, reefs, tattoos, explode them as fireworks, shoot them from cannons, or send them into orbit. Most of these are new to the 20th and 21st centuries, and relatively unusual choices. More commonly, families might bury the ashes at a cemetery, store them at a vault or a shelf at home, or scatter them in significant places or anonymously in nature. New Yorkers who plan to scatter remains, despite the advice from NYSAC mentioned earlier, are strongly advised to gain permission from the landowner before doing so. However, in most cultures, even where authorization is officially expected, some degree of collusion and surreption is both intrinsic and routine to rituals of ash scattering (Engelke, 2019). This is especially common when it involves a small amount of ashes being placed in a public spot of great private emotional significance, such as a favourite sports ground or holiday spot. Informal ash-scattering rituals often involve a smaller ceremony of close family and friends in places of personal meaning more associated with life than with death (Prendergast et al, 2006). Indeed, British mourners have reported that the ritual act of scattering and the associations of scattering locations with good memories were more important than the consequent absence of memorialization (Prendergast et al, 2006; Rumble et al, 2014).

Such practices represent an important counterpoint to Laqueur's (2015) necronominalism (the urge to individually name and place the dead), as the bereaved can choose not to inter individually and not to publicly memorialize, yet still find the ritual deeply significant. Moreover, anonymous scattering can affirm the bonds between the closest family and friends, by privately claiming the scattering place for the deceased. These findings on scattering support the concern that there will be fewer physical memorials as the trend for cremation continues, but also suggest that this may distress other community members (and funeral directors) more than the bereaved themselves.

How New Yorkers understood cremation

So what shaped New Yorkers' preference for burial pre-pandemic? Many of my interlocutors believed that, given the size and political and cultural influence of the Irish and Italian Catholic and European Jewish populations, those communities' attitudes towards or abhorrence of cremation had shaped New Yorkers' lack of interest in the method. The influence of migrant practices is perhaps unsurprising given that NYC has always been 'America's quintessential immigrant city' (Foner, 2007: 1001). The city reported that, in 2019, immigrants accounted for some 37 per cent of NYC's population and 45 per cent of its workforce (NYC Mayor's Office, 2019). Within NYC's population those categorized as White comprise largely of first-, second- and third-generation Irish and Italian Catholics, and Jews, reflecting consecutive, massive immigration waves, especially of Italian and Eastern European Jewish immigrants in the early 20th century (Foner, 2000). Following migration flows in recent decades from Central America, NYC's Catholic churches and neighbourhoods have often been 'Mexicanized', 'Dominicanized' and 'Haitian-Creolized' (Foner, 2007) and these traditionally minded Catholic immigrants may have had a similar reluctance to embrace cremation.

However, since the 1960s, immigration flows have also risen from East Asian cultures such as the Philippines, where inherited Buddhist traditions support a preference for cremation, even among other faiths. For example, the Catholic Basilica of Regina Pacis, the Pope's church in Brooklyn, affords a striking example of changing attitudes towards cremation. The original 1905 church was known as the 'Mother Church of Italian immigrants' at a time when the Vatican had forbidden cremation. Today, Regina Pacis offers Mass in English, Spanish and Mandarin, for the Latin American and East Asian immigrants who make up the parish – and the Vatican permits cremation.

In response to its parishioners' preferences, Regina Pacis had converted a chapel into a sizeable columbarium, offering niches for families to deposit cremains. Parishioners seemed proud of their columbarium, describing a sacred, beautiful, convenient place for their dead available because the church responded to community needs and, especially given NYC's high burial costs, made good use of its resources to serve its people. Of course, papal recommendations aside, ash has long had a religious resonance in Christian traditions in the celebration of Ash Wednesday, and the committal in the Book of Common Prayer reminds mourners of life's transience in the phrase 'ashes to ashes'. The parish of Regina Pacis has thus solved the stigma of cremation to its own satisfaction through a significant change in practice that sustained the social value of memorialization.

Religious acceptance was not the only popular explanation, however, and cremation would be especially unsuitable, people told me, for those who needed the city to pay for their funeral. Views were almost entirely against cremation for the poor or unclaimed: surely cremating people who needed a public funeral would be unseemly, would frustrate families who might later seek disinterment, and risk offending against the deceased's faith? Ultimately, if the deceased died unlawfully, cremation might destroy criminal evidence and prevent justice being served, I was told. When I discussed this with Professor Tanya Marsh, a property and funeral law expert and licensed funeral director, who teaches the only course in the United States on funeral and cemetery law, she commented, 'In most other states, if there's a body at the coroner and it goes unclaimed for some time, they're just going to cremate it.' These views and the practices they underpin illustrate common local perceptions of cremation as something expedient, uncaring, disrespectful and, ultimately, risky.

Officials sometimes mused to me that families opting for public burial (that is, paid for by the city) might even prefer cremation because it would offer more options for memorialization. Currently, and perhaps curiously given the popular beliefs about cremation being the less expensive option, New York State law permits only burial for those needing a public funeral. Given the turn towards cremation during the pandemic, perhaps this will become an option for consenting families in the future.

How New York infrastructure and institutions shape ritual

While people often rationalized the local preference for burial with cultural heritage narratives in their conversations with me, it is important to note that New York's unusual cemetery legal environment has also prioritized burial. Most New York funeral professionals I met believed cemeteries were economically constrained by this legal framework, and that the organizational inflexibility of New York State's death infrastructure – legal, bureaucratic and physical resources – made it harder to respond to COVID-19.

In the United States, laws regarding death, funerals, cemeteries and so on are managed by each state individually. New York State cemeteries are institutionally distinctive in three main ways. First, all public cemeteries must be owned by a non-profit organization, which is highly unusual in the United States. If the cemetery fails economically, its ownership returns to the local municipality. Many funeral professionals believed that this non-profit requirement limited New York cemeteries' ability to earn enough through sales to have adequate surplus funds to innovate and adapt, an assumption that arguably reflects the common American confidence in private enterprise. Second, New York State requires crematoria to be located at and owned by cemeteries, rather than independently operated. Industry professionals I met described this as significantly restricting cremation capacity across the city, which became important during COVID-19. Third, New York State itself approves cemetery pricing and cemeteries cannot set their own rates. Many interlocutors believed that this kept prices artificially low, although there was also evidence that many people already found funeral costs prohibitive.

I discussed these institutionally distinctive issues with David Fleming Jr, who has been a lobbyist for the trade association, NYSAC, for 25 years. NYSAC has 520 cemetery and crematory members. In his role, David has helped write most funeral laws that New York State has introduced over the last 25 years. He is also a local politician, a supervisor for Long Island's Nassau County, and holds governance or advisory roles for many cemeteries. David summarized these issues simply: 'Prices are lower in New York than the market would have them.' When I raised them with legal scholar Tanya Marsh, she agreed, 'All of those things together mean that cemeteries in New York are very economically challenged.'

Notwithstanding economic problems, New Yorkers, under the Right of Sepulchre, expected to be able to choose how to dispose of their dead, employing funeral directors to exercise that right. COVID-19 exacerbated capacity and commercial constraints and, during its first wave, NYC funeral directors had to improvise as they struggled to keep up with the volume of the dead.

How funeral directors perceived cremation, for the bereaved and for themselves

Early in COVID-19, NYC funeral directors cranked up air conditioning to approximate morgue conditions for storing bodies, revised tasks and processes to limit infection in workplaces, scrambled to fill rosters as demand surged but staff became ill or needed to isolate, and dealt with shortages in equipment like body bags, coffins and protective clothing. They spent hours trying to book burial and cremation at bottlenecked cemeteries, and streamlined funerals to comply with changing legal orders on public gatherings. Ironically, in a period of excess death and while dealing with these constraints, the funeral industry also faced potentially serious revenue losses, as the lack of rituals reduced the goods and services that they could sell.

As well as operating under enormous pressure in challenging conditions, the gap between what funeral directors wanted to provide for bereaved families, and what was possible, burdened them emotionally too. Often ethically motivated to provide services to the grieving, many funeral directors believe funeral rituals to be psychologically beneficial for those grieving (Mathijssen, 2023). As one funeral director explained to me, a funeral serves a profound need for the bereaved, so minimizing or avoiding the funeral could cause serious emotional suffering in the future. Increased demand for cremation and minimal funerals worried them for other reasons too: how could funeral businesses remain economically viable when faced with significantly falling demand for their services, and a proliferation of 'cheaper' options?

Even before COVID-19, when families were opting for cremation, many funeral directors found that they did not want goods and services that they might have wanted with a burial. They often preferred only minimal body preparation as opposed to having the deceased embalmed; they were also less likely to want a viewing event over several days at the funeral parlour; and they often purchased only a basic urn, which the family might keep at home or maybe place in a columbarium niche. Families typically did not choose a large, heavy wood or metal coffin, and would not need to have a grave opened and burial vault prepared, or to purchase a headstone and other burial goods. Lost sales like these represented an alarming trend for the industry.

Yet, this is not always so. When families choose cremation elsewhere it does not automatically follow that they will purchase fewer services from funeral directors. Certainly this is not necessarily so in Great Britain, for instance.[2] Recall that Hertz (1960) assumed cremation demanded a second ceremony, Prothero (2001) reckoning that cremation suited American appetites for memorialization celebrating agency and individualism, and Laqueur's (2015) diagnosis of modernity's necronominalism. But funeral directors' concerns about making a living or going out of business as cremation rates rose reflect how cremation is understood in the United States: as a cut-price option, both economically and with a perceived lower ceremonial value.

Pre-pandemic, NYC funeral directors told me that New Yorkers' long-standing preference for burial was yielding gradually to cremation. A reduced interest in full funeral services had been underway, many funeral directors reported, since the 2001 World Trade Center attacks. Then, few intact corpses were recovered and often small fragments were the only physical remains recovered of the deceased. Many funeral directors associated the declining importance of viewing the body and the corpse's presence at the funeral with this historical event. The rationale was that because so many people knew of families who had had to conduct funerals without bodies, in deeply traumatic circumstances, it had prompted greater social acceptance for funerals to focus less on the deceased's body.

Funeral lawyer, Tanya Marsh, believed the bottleneck of NYC's death toll during the pandemic's first wave resulted from the combination of the sharp increase in deaths over a limited area, and the inflexibility of its cemetery and crematory institutional infrastructure. 'New York has one of the most rigid [deathcare] systems in the United States', she said, adding:

> It did not have any room to give ... it would not have gone down that way in other states because they just had to go to the state for everything, to get anything out of them. ... In other states, you would have just been sending bodies to out-of-state crematories or out-of-city crematories and be done with it, you wouldn't have had this whole backlog, it was because there are a ridiculously low number of crematory retorts in New York City for the demand and the population.

She described a self-defeating circle when it came to root causes: state regulators limited crematoria to cemeteries, and limited bodies from being sent out of the city or state to crematoria with capacity, cemetery ownership was limited to non-profit organizations; prices were restricted by the state; and economic constraints made it hard for operators to upgrade their retorts. Consequently, the crematoria were old, fragile, costly to repair and could not be run at capacity as they needed time to cool between cremations; and so, even under normal circumstances (let alone emergency conditions) there was inadequate crematoria capacity. Tanya was also unsurprised that others I had spoken with had not made these points. 'It's a heavily regulated industry, they cannot criticize their regulators very easily', she told me.

From David Fleming's perspective, the problems of managing the excess mortality had been logistical rather than total physical capacity being reached across the city. Between the place of death and the point of cremation or burial, bodies needed to be authorized for transfer, transported and stored, and it was the weaknesses in these systems that caused the lag during the pandemic, he felt. Moreover, more people died in deprived neighbourhoods in Queens and the Bronx (Horton, 2020; NYC Council Data Team, nd), so demand for death care was concentrated in these areas. Ideally, this demand would have been better distributed across the state's network of funeral directors, cemeteries and crematories, but there was no feasible institutionalized process for this to happen. David described how there had obviously been an extraordinary volume of work required within cemeteries, 'these poor people who were worked around the clock', but the real bottleneck was storing bodies before cremation. Logistically, this had been a counterintuitive moment for the move to cremation, as it would have been practically easier and faster to dig more graves. As David explained:

> Pinelawn for instance, I think they were doing y'know four hundred and some burials a month, they put in shifts, they were able to do it … it's obviously a lot easier to bury people than it is to cremate them as far as time commitment, you can do 14 holes to get them done, but doing 14 bodies in the same retorts not going to happen in one day … it still takes three hours to cremate a body. … The capacity to properly store the remains until they could be cremated was the biggest problem … it was seven days a week on the phone with State Mortuary Task Force … really just trying to get the storage we needed, dealing with the City of New York, dealing with the State … [people in] government who will go unnamed just said 'Yeah we're providing refrigeration' and I said well go to the store and get three pounds of raw chicken and stick it in your refrigerator and then come back and talk to me in a month and a half and tell me how that's going. It does not prevent decomposition.

Post-pandemic David saw increasing cremation capacity as a clear priority for NYC: more crematoria at more cemeteries, and urgent maintenance and upgrading of those already in use: 'That has to be done. And it has to be done at cemeteries, that's New York law, but that's really about [economic] sustainability, providing a revenue stream for the cemeteries.'

There were other administrative problems besides capacity, however. When the pandemic began, a cremation had to be purchased in person by the funeral customer, and the forms authorizing it had to be signed in person ('wet signed'). If there were errors in the form, a new one would have to be prepared and wet signed. This became unworkable during COVID-19: did a funeral director really need to go back across town to get a signature to reauthorize a cremation for the deceased husband from the wife who was herself infectious and ill? Legislators drafted and passed laws so that cremation paperwork could be completed electronically. David worked through the pandemic to amend law so that people could authorize and purchase a cremation online.

David understood these changes as inevitable given the public need for more efficient funeral organization during the pandemic, and even for efficient, unmemorialized funerals, as part of a larger (and to him, troubling) trend. He added, 'We do view this [cremation] as the cheap alternative' to burial. He reiterated a popular industry view, commenting: 'Scattering is a real problem for a lot of reasons but particularly for cemeteries and revenue and what a cemetery is, which is really memorialization [for families, historians and genealogists]. It's incredibly irritating if someone gets cremated and there's no monument.' For David, cremation was a commercial reality that the industry needed to grapple with, especially regarding how to make it more financially viable. However, he saw ash scattering and its lack of physical memorialization as creating difficulties for the bereaved, other members of the community, future generations and researchers.

Conclusion

In ordinary conditions, we take the mobility of the dead for granted: we assume that someone will get them to the right place at the right time. But during NYC's first wave of COVID-19, the dead's transportation and disposition became increasingly constricted and unpredictable. For some, the difference between what the bereaved imagined a funeral should be and what was possible represented further suffering. Funeral directors told me the overcrowded morgues created errors like mistaken identities of the deceased that could cause great anguish.

People adjust and remake ritual, amid changing understandings of what a given practice means. In some ways, then, improvisation is perpetual in ritual. Practice theory argues that improvisation is not only about knowing the rules but knowing how to apply them appropriately, as in the regulated improvisation of Bourdieu's (1977) concept of habitus. In NYC in COVID-19's first wave, as people constantly tinkered with individual death rituals, these constant adaptions also sustained a gradually honed core practice, or appropriate new social rules and norms for funerals (namely, cremation), for the wider social group.

Compared with everyday tinkering, COVID-19 required improvisation at a distorted, desperate pitch and intensity, however. Creative arrangements mostly happened when people tried to evade the bottleneck, rather than within the bottleneck itself (see Melly, 2017). In these emergency conditions, tensions emerged between caring for the dead in general and the dead in particular (Engelke, 2021), as municipal authorities, deathcare professionals and the bereaved grappled with the breakdowns and ruptures in devising and doing bodily, material and spiritual care. Against decisions such as shipping a relative's body to a neighbouring state for burial, waiting over a month for a burial slot, attending a burial by cell phone video, or storing a relative's body in a morgue truck for months, ordering a cremation no longer seemed like a weighty decision.

For almost 60 years, disposal practices in NYC have followed a fairly predictable trajectory, responding over time to changes in immigration patterns, religious practice, and economic constraints and opportunities, just as Regina Pacis has adapted to its changing parishioners. Even the cultural rupture of the World Trade Center attacks in 2001 had not significantly interrupted this pattern. Yet in 2020, New Yorkers who had historically strongly preferred burial began for the first time to embrace cremation, as burial slots became hard to access and funerals were forbidden or stringently restricted. Such phenomena challenged expected rhythms of mourning and complicated people's temporal experiences of caring for the dead, including the competing responsibilities of care that shift between bureaucrats, deathcare professionals, mourners and others.

Although burials would have been easier to scale than fragile cremators, in the crisis of the bottleneck cremation shed some of the stigma with which New Yorkers, like many Americans, had long regarded it: as something distastefully cheap and, for some religious groups, doctrinally dubious. Instead, cremation meant people could pause rituals until circumstances were safer, and it gave them time to make memorialization choices, if they wanted. Through this turmoil, New Yorkers demonstrated imagination and flexibility in reworking death rituals, including sequence and speed, as rituals, gathering and formal memorialization were delayed indefinitely.

When New Yorkers shifted to cremation as a majority choice for the first time during COVID-19, it illustrated how ritual forms can alter, yet their intended meanings and significance may remain relatively stable even, or especially, in crisis. The change recalls Prothero's (2001) prediction that Americans could come to see cremation as suitable because of its memorialization potential, austere utility and the cultural appeal of dematerialization. This potential was, perhaps unexpectedly, borne from the disruption created by the bottleneck, itself a product of institutionalized laws, practices and norms. The relationship in NYC between COVID-19 and cremation thus reiterates the resilience of ritual: when a practice is abruptly dismantled, it will also be remade with what is to hand in the moment.

Notes

[1] The individual chamber with an industrial furnace for cremating the body, also known as a cremator.

[2] The rapid increase in direct cremation, when there is no funeral, is a separate issue.

References

Appel, H., Anand, N. and Akhil, G. (eds) (2018) *The Promise of Infrastructure*. Durham, NC: Duke University Press.

Beugless, J. (1884) 'Cremation as a safeguard against epidemics', *Public Health Papers and Reports*, 10: 140–144.

Bourdieu, P. (1977) *Outline of a Theory of Practice*. Cambridge: Cambridge University Press.

Bowker, G.C. and Star, S.L. (1999) *Sorting Things Out: Classification and its Consequences*. Cambridge, MA: MIT Press.

Chu, J. (2014) 'When infrastructures attack: the workings of disrepair in China', *American Ethnologist*, 41(2): 351–367.

The Cremation Society (2022) *Progress of Cremation in the British Islands from 1885 to 2021*. The Cremation Society. Available at: https://www.cremation.org.uk/progress-of-cremation-united-kingdom [accessed 12 September 2022].

Dawdy, S.L. (2021) *American Afterlives: Reinventing Death in the Twenty-First Century*. Princeton: Princeton University Press.

Engelke, M. (2019) 'The anthropology of death revisited', *Annual Review of Anthropology*, 48(1): 29–44.

Engelke, M. (2021) 'Some moods and modes of enchantment in the human sciences: on the troublesome dead', *Religion*, 51(4): 551–565.

Faust, D.G. (2008) *This Republic of Suffering: Death and the American Civil War*. New York: Alfred A. Knopf.

Foner, N. (2000) *From Ellis Island to JFK: New York's Two Great Waves of Immigration*. New Haven: Yale University Press.

Foner, N. (2007) 'How exceptional is New York? Migration and multiculturalism in the empire city', *Ethnic and Racial Studies*, 30(6): 999–1023.

Clayden, A., Green, T., Hockey, J. and Powell, M. (2015) *Natural Burial: Landscape, Practice and Experience*. London: Routledge.

Heller, K. (2022) 'The stunning rise of cremation reveals America's changing idea of death', *Washington Post*, 19 April. Available at: https://www.washingtonpost.com/lifestyle/2022/04/18/cremation-death-funeral/ [accessed 11 September 2022].

Hertz, R. (1960) *Death and the Right Hand*. Translated by R. Needham and C. Needham. Aberdeen: Cohen and West.

Holy See Press Office (2016) *Instruction Ad resurgendum cum Christo Regarding the Burial of the Deceased and the Conservation of the Ashes in the Case of Cremation, The Vatican: Summary of Bulletin*. Available at: https://press.vatican.va/content/salastampa/en/bollettino/pubblico/2016/10/25/161025c.html [accessed 11 September 2022].

Horton, R. (2020) 'Offline: COVID-19 is not a pandemic', *The Lancet*, 396(10255): 874.

Jefferson, T. (1787) 'Thomas Jefferson to William Smith – Paris'. Available at: https://www.loc.gov/exhibits/jefferson/105.html [accessed 12 September 2022].

Jupp, P.C. (2006) *From Dust to Ashes: Cremation and the British Way of Death*. Basingstoke: Palgrave Macmillan.

Kaufman, S.R. (2006) *And a Time to Die: How American Hospitals Shape the End of Life*. Chicago: Chicago University Press.

Laqueur, T.W. (2015) *The Work of the Dead: A Cultural History of Mortal Remains*. Princeton: Princeton University Press.

Marsh, T. (2015) 'The law of human remains', *Lawyers and Judges Publishing Company*, Wake Forest University Legal Studies Paper No. 2646184. https://papers.ssrn.com/sol3/papers.cfm?abstract_id=2646184

Mathijssen, B. (2023) 'The human corpse as aesthetic-therapeutic', *Mortality*, 28(1): 37–53.

Meier, A. (2020) 'How cremation lost its stigma', *JSTOR Daily*. Available at: https://daily.jstor.org/how-cremation-lost-its-stigma/ [accessed 13 September 2022].

Melly, C. (2017) *Bottleneck: Moving, Building, and Belonging in an African City*. Chicago: Chicago University Press.

Metcalf, P. and Huntington, R. (1991) *Celebrations of Death: The Anthropology of Mortuary Ritual*. Cambridge: Cambridge University Press.

Mitford, J. (1963) *The American Way of Death*. New York: Simon & Schuster.

New York State Association of Cemeteries (nd) 'FAQs: New York State Association of Cemeteries'. Available at: http://nysac.com/faqs/ [accessed 11 September 2022].

NFDA (2021a) *2021 NFDA Cremation and Burial Report*. Available at: https://dailymontanan.com/wp-content/uploads/2021/09/2021-nfda-cremation-and-burial-report.pdf [accessed 7 September 2022].

NFDA (2021b) *2021 National Funeral Directors Association General Price List Study Shows Funeral Costs not Rising as Fast as Rate of Inflation*. Available at: https://nfda.org/news/media-center/nfda-news-releases/id/6182/2021-nfda-general-price-list-study-shows-funeral-costs-not-rising-as-fast-as-rate-of-inflation [accessed 12 September 2022].

NYC Council Data Team (nd) *COVID19 Demographics*. Available at: https://council.nyc.gov/data/covid19-demographics/ [accessed 17 August 2022].

NYC Mayor's Office (2019) *State of Our Immigrant City: MOIA Annual Report for Calendar Tear 2019*. New York City Mayor's Office of Immigrant Affairs. Available at: https://www1.nyc.gov/assets/immigrants/downloads/pdf/MOIA-Annual-Report-for-2019.pdf [accessed 20 October 2024].

NYT (1879) 'The end of cremation', *The New York Times*, 17 October, p 4.

Pottage, A. (1998) 'The inscription of life in law: genes, patents, and bio-politics', *Modern Law Review*, 61(5): 740–765.

Prendergast, D., Hockey, J. and Kellaher, L. (2006) 'Blowing in the wind? identity, materiality, and the destinations of human ashes', *The Journal of the Royal Anthropological Institute*, 12(4): 881–898.

Prothero, S.R. (2001) *Purified by Fire: A History of Cremation in America*. Berkeley: University of California Press.

Ruggles, S. (1856) *An Examination of the Law of Burial: In a Report to the Supreme Court of New York*. New York: D. Fanshaw.

Rumble, H., Troyer, J. Walter, T. and Woodthorpe, K. (2014) 'Disposal or dispersal? environmentalism and final treatment of the British dead', *Mortality*, 19(3): 243–260.

Schafer, C. (2012) 'Corpses, conflict and insignificance? A critical analysis of post-mortem practices', *Mortality*, 17(4): 305–321.

Strathern, M. (2005) *Kinship, Law and the Unexpected: Relatives are Always a Surprise*. Cambridge: Cambridge University Press.

Strathern, M. (2007) 'Losing (out on) intellectual resources', in Pottage, A. and Mundy, M. (eds) *Anthropology, and the Constitution of the Social: Making Persons and Things*. Cambridge: Cambridge University Press, pp 201–233.

Troyer, J. (2020) *Technologies of the Human Corpse*. Cambridge, MA: MIT Press.

Walter, T. (1993) 'Dust not ashes: the American preference for burial', *Landscape*, 32(1): 42–48.

Woodthorpe, K. (2010) 'Buried bodies in an East London cemetery', in Maddrell, A. and Sidaway, J. (eds) *Deathscapes: Spaces for Death, Dying, Mourning and Remembrance*. Farnham, Ashgate: Routledge, pp 57–74.

6

Governing the Dead's Territory

Hajar Ghorbani

Introduction

Arriving in Tehran's *Behesht-e Zahra* cemetery to conduct ethnographic fieldwork was a unique experience because the cemetery's employees referred to it as 'an institution', a term I had never associated with a burial ground. Like many Iranians, I had assumed it was simply a place for burying the deceased. However, during my preliminary interviews, it became evident that this cemetery is more than just a cemetery. Tehran's *Behesht-e Zahra* cemetery is one of Tehran's 22 districts, designated as a *Shar-dari* (شهرداری), *Shahr* (شهر) meaning city, and *Dari* (داری) referring to the charge of the city. Linguistically, *Shar-dari* can be considered the administrative organization of a city, which, in terms of etymology, is equivalent to the English word 'municipality'.[1] This term is derived from the Latin root 'Municipum', which represents 'a social agreement among "municipals", duty holders, or the residents of the town' that has come together for common goals (Saeedi Rezvani, 2000: 17). As a municipality the cemetery is managed by a *Shar-dar* (شهردار), a mayor, who oversees the cemetery which includes theshrine of Khomeini,[2] the founder of the Islamic Republic of Iran. The cemetery is the only place where the paperwork for burial can be completed, thereby compounding the site's control over the dead and their disposal in Tehran (although another site can be used for burial once the paperwork is complete).

In previous publications, the cemetery has been studied as a case to explore the impact of modernization and bureaucratization of labour. These processes have significantly transformed cemeteries and reshaped understandings of death in contemporary Iran (Rahmani and Ghorbani, 2017; Bayatrizi and Ghorbani, 2019). Additionally, work on and within the cemetery has shed light on how inscriptions and symbols on graves can serve as valuable means for discovering the sociopolitical dynamics of modern Iranian society (Shams, 2020). While these studies have provided a more general overview of the impact of modernization on the cemetery's appearance, to date nobody has offered a more in-depth analysis of the site as a necropolitical space. It is this that forms the core of this chapter.

I am not the first to make this point, as political systems have always held distinct perspectives on the treatment of dead bodies and where they are buried, actively seeking to control and appropriate them as a means to legitimize their authority. This intricate relationship has been a relatively overlooked subject within scholarly discourse in Western social science, with dead bodies essentially silent as the living impose their meaning (Verdery, 1999). This silence is despite the fact that the dead can be used symbolically and politically to claim new territories and establish messages of sovereign power. What is more, beyond the dead, their graves and monuments, especially those dedicated to martyrs and heroes, can be potent tools employed by states to convey national identity (Rizvi, 2003; Elling, 2009; Pippidi, 1995; Ghorbani, 2017). As spaces designated for the commemoration of the deceased, cemeteries thus inherently carry a symbolic weight that extends beyond individual mourning to encompass collective memory and societal identity. Governments play a crucial role in their regulation, manipulation, maintenance and preservation, reflecting their involvement in shaping the narratives of the past and present. Issues such as urban planning, land-use policies and heritage conservation intertwine with their governance, illustrating the broader impact of state intervention on the commemorative landscape.

Existing literature surrounding this topic has considered how governments navigate the delicate balance between respecting cultural traditions, ensuring public access, and addressing the evolving needs of diverse communities within the context of cemetery governance (see Larkin, 2012; Fontein, 2014; Myrttinen, 2014; Trans, 2014). Building on these, this chapter explores the complex interplay between the cemetery landscape and the nation-state, examining the sociocultural factors that have contributed to this cemetery's transformation into an institution and its subsequent recognition as one of Tehran's urban districts, governed by a mayor. In addition, I seek to examine how the Iranian government has expertly employed the mechanisms of institutionalization, modernization and more importantly centralization to transform a conventional cemetery into a complete municipality.

To make this argument I draw on a six-year ethnographic project conducted at the cemetery, where I actively participated in numerous official institution meetings; observed both official and unofficial rituals, ceremonies and events; took photographs of the spaces and their material culture; and conducted interviews with practitioners responsible for site management. Additionally, I used an archival studies method to analyse historical records and primary source materials, providing insights and contextual background for my fieldwork while facilitating comparative analysis. This desk-based method complemented my ethnographic research, offering valuable historical perspectives for a more comprehensive understanding of the subject under study. In the process of data analysis, I applied Lefebvre's concept of the 'social production of space' (1991), in which space is viewed as a social construct that attempts to conceal the conflicts inherent in its production (Low, 2009). Lefebvre identified three modes of space: the first space, which he referred to as 'the perceived', encompasses materials like urban planning, human design and spatial organization. 'The conceived' space he identified comprises any visual signs and imagined space[3] produced and controlled by those in power. Lastly, 'the lived' space represents the space experienced by citizens that holds personal significance for them (Hanssen, 2005). Through my research, I found that these spatial modes served as a valuable framework for understanding how the state has designed this institution of death, shaping its space and purpose as a way to exert control over its wider population.

The institutionalization and centralization of death in Iran

In the evolution of Iranian society, there has been a significant transition in the management of death rituals. In pre-industrial Iran, echoing Aries' (1975) oft-cited term, death was considered 'tame', occurring at home where relatives gathered to perform mortuary rituals and bury the deceased in nearby cemeteries or the yards of holy shrines, which were constructed by and within communities. Burial was thus highly localized, with the yard of a mosque, a holy shrine or a local cemetery considered appropriate places for interment (Bayatrizi and Ghorbani, 2019). In contrast, contemporary Iran portrays death as a 'wild' phenomenon, with dying shifting from homes to hospitals, and public services assuming the mantle of responsibility for death rites and their consolidation in centrally located cemeteries (Rahmani and Ghorbani, 2017). These centrally located sites have evolved beyond being a mere place of burial for the deceased, and instead have emerged as a key public organization with functions extending beyond the realm of death and serving as a pivotal institution politically. This political dimension plays a significant role in shaping and influencing the dynamics of these cemetery spaces, further underscoring their importance in the broader societal landscape.

The development of modern urbanized and centralized institutions in Tehran began during the Qajar and later in the Pahlavi dynasty (1878–1979) with the introduction of nationalistic policies in the form of the nation-state aimed at gradually erasing cultural diversity (Abrahamian, 2008; Scot Aghaie and Marashi, 2014; Amanat, 2017). Reza Shah's governance in particular (1925–1941) represents a significant chapter in Iranian history, characterized by a concerted effort to modernize and centralize state institutions while promoting a unified sense of national identity. The most pivotal transformations during this time took place in Iranian state institutions, social structures and cultural forms during these two dynasties. Reza Shah's policy of authoritarian modernization aimed at centralizing government power in the capital city, ignoring ethnic influences and creating a modern Iranian 'citizen', was based on his state's definition of a nation-state. Through this he encouraged educational reforms, language policies and cultural initiatives that ignored local voices in favour of fostering a new sense of national unity and a modern identity (Atabaki, 2014). These efforts, governed by strict bureaucratic frameworks, laid the foundation for the contemporary Iranian nation-state, and set the stage for subsequent political developments in the country, and policies quickly expanded after the 1979 Iranian Revolution,[4] also known as the Islamic Revolution, in the form of 'religious nationalism'.[5] This is where religion is not regarded as separate to nationalism nor merely an ethnic signifier or cultural by-product, but rather a core component of national identity. Via this religion is positioned as central to a nationalist discourse, involving ideals, symbols, identity, culture and social values. Since the late 1970s and building on this religious nationalist discourse, the capital city of Tehran has become the central point for the consolidation and expansion of Iran's modern centralized institutions (Scot Aghaie and Marashi, 2014) governed by a strict bureaucratic structure. These institutions reflect the current regime's emphasis on effective control and management.

Within Tehran's evolving sociopolitical landscape, cemeteries have become more than places to bury the dead. Tehran's *Behesht-e Zahra* cemetery has transformed into a city-cemetery, underpinned by a combination of political discourse and ideology and operating as an institution with rules that aim to control over the territory of the dead and suppress political protests by the living. Yet how does an urban necropolis possess or generate such authority? One key method is arguably the alignment of death rituals and memorialization with political narratives and processes. In doing so, death rituals and mourning rites have become required to follow predetermined bureaucratic processes and guidelines, such as the singular approved method for *Ghusl* (cleaning, washing and purifying a corpse in Islamic rituals and practices), and the running of funeral prayers and performance of mourning rites. The playing of live music[6] during mourning is prohibited while reciting the Quran or religious lyrics is permitted, and grave design is subject to strict controls, with restrictions on the publication or carving of women's portraits on headstones and limitations on specific gravestone sizes and shapes.

Such regulation and policing of death rituals and memorialization deliberately leads to a standardized and monolithic space that (deliberately) homogenizes funerary practices and memorials, rendering cultural and religious diversity invisible. The transformation of the cemetery is, however, not merely symbolic of a broader Iranian societal transition from traditional to modern approaches to managing death rituals. Now intricately woven into the administrative institutional fabric of Tehran, the cemetery has instead transcended its role as a place for the dead and bereaved, instead becoming a pivotal connection between the sacred and political ideology. Now a microcosm of the capital city, *Behesht-e Zahra* not only reflects the evolving nature of death rituals in modern Iran but also presents as a necropolis closely monitored by the state. In this new regime, death is no longer a family or community phenomenon; it is a meticulously regulated and standardized process, used to reflect and (re)present the broader narrative of the Islamic Republic.

Navigating ideological arenas

As already noted, the evolution of *Behesht-e Zahra* cemetery into a municipal institution with a mayor can be traced back to the 1979 revolution. During this period, the concept of religious nationalism emerged as a powerful ideological force, connecting Islam, martyrdom and the Iranian nation-state. When Ruhollah Khomeini arrived in Iran in 1979, he chose Tehran's *Behesht-e Zahra* cemetery, rather than the parliament, as the location to make his public speeches and establish the new Iranian state. In his first speech at the cemetery the dead, not the living, were his audience. Martyrdom, as a sacred death, played a crucial role in shaping the policy of the new Iranian

Figure 6.1: The martyrs' site, Tehran's *Behesht-e Zahra* cemetery

Source: Hajar Ghorbani (2015)

state, and with many martyrs buried on site, the cemetery was a critical choice for Khomeini (Figure 6.1). This significance deepened during the Iran–Iraq war in the 1980s, when over 30,000 Iranian soldiers died. They included youths and teenagers, who were buried in the cemetery and transformed the site into a sacred ground as a space that symbolized religious national unity and the defence of Shiite Islam over other ethnic identities. The cemetery subsequently became synonymous with expressions like 'Islamic-Shiite identity' in political discourse, reflecting the growing dominance of religious nationalism.

In 1988 the identity of Tehran's *Behesht-e Zahra* cemetery as a political institution gained another layer of complexity with the massacre of political prisoners and the burial of over 300 prisoners in the site.[7] With their interment came increased concerns within the government that this space could potentially become a site of protest. Consequently, strategic decisions were made to protect and control the cemetery from dissidence, leading to its transformation from a mere burial ground to a municipal institution managed by a mayor (Nasiri and Faghfouri Azar, 2024). This high degree of regulation was further reflected in the cemetery's design, with monuments and memorials serving to control oppositional voices and erase anything that did not conform to the government's agenda. Monuments, for example, including the location of Khomeini's speech, have over time been transformed into holy tombs for assassinated Iranian politicians. Additionally, as places like *Golzar-e Shohada*,[8] where martyrs of the revolution and the Iran–Iraq war are buried, were becoming increasingly decorated with martyrs' personal belongings, their photos and army clothes (Figure 6.2), the mayor decided to remove and replace the original graves and the mementoes left with unified gravestones representing the symbols and ideologies of the Islamic Republic of Iran.

Another explanation for *Behesht-e Zahra*'s transformation into a municipal institution is the city's increasing population. As a result of technological advancements, urbanization and industrial growth, Tehran has experienced significant demographic changes, with 12 million citizens now living in the city. With this population growth, mortality rates have also increased, necessitating the establishment of a system for managing the influx of bodies and conducting funeral rituals efficiently. As a consequence, from an Iranian perspective, the cemetery has evolved from a traditional burial ground into a bureaucratic organization. The administrative system implemented within the cemetery now serves a practical purpose in coping with the challenges posed by the growing population and the associated demands for burial services, and oversees the organization of various activities that were once handled by families and communities, namely grave preparation, burial arrangements, maintenance of burial records and the management of funeral ceremonies (Rahmani and Ghorbani, 2017). Overseen by the mayor, it is

Figure 6.2: The martyrs' material cultures, Tehran's *Behesht-e Zahra* cemetery

Source: Hajar Ghorbani (2015)

regarded as a municipality because of its synergy with the Persian definition of a municipality as:

> [B]eing defined as institutions responsible for urban affairs, such as constructing streets and squares, public gardens and parks, providing sources of light and water, maintaining hygiene and health, overseeing physical education and public welfare, taking action against floods and fires, regulating the activities of merchants and shopkeepers, supervising food and daily necessities of the people, monitoring public places such as cafes, restaurants, and cinemas, and examining urban planning projects. The Ministry of Interior appoints the mayor to manage this institution. (Mo'in, 2017: 4562)

In no definition of municipalities is the realm of death the main focus. However, Tehran's *Behesht-e Zahra* cemetery is unique, operating as one of the 22 municipalities of Tehran, established with the purpose of managing the realm of the dead and their burial. This management is embodied by the presence of a mayor, who directly interacts with key political institutions in Iran, including the legislative branch of the Islamic Republic of Iran, the judiciary system of the Islamic Republic of Iran, the presidential institution and the office of the Supreme Leader. Operating as a municipality, the site transcends its original function as a burial ground and it has become a place for amalgamation of religious and nation-state identity in the Iranian post-revolution era.

Conclusion

Tehran's *Behesht-e Zahra* cemetery serves as a testament to the intricate interplay of history, politics and ideology in post-revolutionary Iran. Originally conceived as a traditional burial ground, the cemetery has undergone a profound transformation into a municipal institution intricately entwined with the upper level of Iranian political structures. In this web of political, social and bureaucratic contexts and purpose, Tehran's cemetery becomes a micro-political landscape, reflecting the complexities of the post-revolutionary era in Iran. To understand this metamorphosis, in this chapter I have explored the historical context and the evolution of the cemetery. At the core of this transformation has been the establishment of religious nationalism after the Iranian Revolution in 1979, which led to the creation of the cemetery as a municipal institution, complete with a mayor closely aligned with key political institutions. Such a transition marked a strategic move by the state to assert control over a space laden with political and ideological significance, and a potential site of protest. Over time, the government's objective has become clear; to shape Tehran's *Behesht-e Zahra* into a microcity where cultural and ethnic diversity is supplanted by a unified ideological narrative. This intentional effort transforms *Behesht-e Zahra* into a governed municipal institution, firmly under the sovereignty of political structures. As a 'perceived space' (Lefebvre, 1991), the government deliberately shapes the cemetery – and its inhabitants – through urban planning and spatial organization, the suppression of diverse design and memorials, and through a high degree of bureaucratic regulation. This management and tight control over the aesthetics of the cemetery landscape are the manifestation, and re(presentation) of power and control wielded by those in authority, intended to both suppress objectors and reinforce religion nationalism. Simultaneously, the 'conceived space' materializes through the promotion of symbols of this religious nationalism. It is this historical and political life of the cemetery, as a plurality of simultaneous spaces with clear governance structures and a close alignment to the nation-state, that renders *Behesht-e Zahra* a municipality in its own right.

Notes

[1] In Iran, the place and importance of the municipality are determined by the laws and legal systems. The Tehran Municipality: After the announcement of the Constitutional Revolution in 1325 AH (1907 AD), the Municipal Law was passed by the National Consultative Assembly. According to the Municipality Law, in any location where the population reaches at least five thousand people, a municipality must be established. The municipality is a public, non-governmental organization (as part of metropolitan management) that is founded based on the principle of administrative decentralization to manage local affairs such as urban development, city sanitation, and the welfare of residents.

In all the definitions, the municipality is where community affairs should be managed, and the lives of the living are organized. Tehran's *Behesht-e Zahra* cemetery as a municipality was also established with the aim of managing and supporting the presence of the living in death rituals. The key point is that none of the definitions of a municipality considered the territory of death as a primary focus of the institution (the cemetery) aims. Yet today we see that the most important task of *Behesht-e Zahra*, as a municipal organization, is the governance of the dead, not the living.

[2] The shrine of Ruhollah Khomeini not only becomes part of the *Behesht-e Zahra* organization, but it also stands as an independent entity, managed by Khomeini's descendants. However, the institutional duties of the Khomeini shrine are ultimately carried out by the mayor of *Behesht-e Zahra*.

[3] In Lefebvre's theory, the concept of 'imagined space' refers to the mental or conceptual space that individuals or groups create in their minds. It is not a physical or concrete space but rather a representation or idea of space. This concept is closely related to the idea of 'social space', where space is not just a physical entity but also a product of social practices, perceptions and imagination.

[4] In less than seven months between August 1978 and February 1979, Iran underwent a profound revolution that toppled the Pahlavi regime, dismantled the monarchy, and established the Islamic Republic under Ayatollah Khomeini's leadership. The revolution, supported by diverse groups including Islamic activists, urban poor and elements of the middle class, exhibited a complex ideological amalgamation of Islamic principles, anti-Pahlavi sentiment, and influences from both leftist and third-world postcolonial discourse. Initially expressing aspirations for democracy and human rights, the revolution's evolution proved more encompassing and geopolitically significant than its predecessors, while deviating from its initial democratic promises and demonstrating a lineage from the earlier National Movement (Amanat, 2017).

[5] Examples of religious nationalism include Islamist movements in the Middle East, religious Jewish nationalism, certain forms of Hindu nationalism, evangelical Christian nationalism in the United States, and some Islamist movements in Turkey and the Arab world. Minoo Moallem (2003) introduces the concept of 'religious nationalism' and argues that Islamic national identity was constructed during the Islamic Revolution by defining it against the West and emphasizes that aspects of nationalism survived within revolutionary ideologies (Scot Aghaie and Marashi, 2014).

[6] The post-Islamic Revolution era in Iran was marked by a strict prohibition on music, ran by official views that consider it potentially corrupting and contradictory to religious principles. Despite these bans, music kept on in Iranian society, but mainly in private spheres. Over time, there were gradual shifts in the government's stance towards music, resulting in some relaxation of restrictions and a growing recognition of its cultural significance. However, it is crucial to acknowledge that music still lacks a defined place within Islamic thought and rituals in post-revolution Iran. Due to the sanctity attributed to Islamic rites, the performance of music is viewed as breaking the sacred principles

defended by the Islamic Republic and its ideology. The only forms of music found acceptable within the government's ideology are those that involve recitations of the Quran and religious texts expressing grief and sadness for the death of the Prophet Mohammad and the martyrdom of Shia imams.

[7] In 1988, the Iranian government, under Supreme Leader Ruhollah Khomeini's Fatwa, executed approximately 30,000 political prisoners. These executions were carried out by 'Death Commissions' formed across Iran. In Tehran's *Behesht-e Zahra* cemetery, remains of individuals executed between June 1981 and March 1982 are found in five distinct sections known as 'sections of executed dissidents', including sections 41, 85, 87, 91 and 92. These sections house dissidents from various periods, with section 85 containing a mass grave of over 300 individuals. Despite the cemetery providing an online database for locating burial places, over 86 per cent of dissidents' records have been removed, indicating deliberate efforts by the Iranian government to conceal facts about the massacre and avoid accountability.

[8] *Golzar-e Shohada* (گلزار شهدا): in the discourse of the Islamic Republic, vocabulary that resonates with the values and ideology of the Islamic Revolution is utilized to sanctify individuals and events. These words typically include spiritual and metaphorical attributes and names that are considered symbols of another worldliness and paradise. By selecting these terms, the Islamic Republic tries to strengthen its connection to revolutionary values and ideals, aiming to align individuals and events with the revolutionary perspective and interpret them within the framework of these values. The Martyrs' Graveyard (*Golzar-e Shohada*) is no exception to this practice. The burial place of martyrs, referred to as the 'Martyrs' Garden', with the graves of martyrs likened to flowers, uses these metaphorical images of beauty and life to associate the martyrs' graveyards with a sacred place filled with spiritual beauties.

References

Abrahamian, E. (2008) *A History of Modern Iran*. New York: Cambridge University Press.

Amanat, A. (2017) *Iran: A Modern History*. New Haven: Yale University Press.

Aries, P. (1975) *Western Attitudes toward Death: From the Middle Age to the Present*. Baltimore: Johns Hopkins University Press.

Atabaki, T. (2014) 'Contesting marginality: ethnicity and the construction of new histories in the Islamic Republic of Iran', in Scot Aghaie, K. and Marashi, A. (eds) *Rethinking Iranian Nationalism and Modernity*. Austin: University of Texas Press, pp 219–232.

Bayatrizi, Z. and Ghorbani, H. (2019) 'The bureaucratic professionalization of funeral rites in Tehran's *Behesht-e Zahra* cemetery', in Selin, H. and Rakoff, R.M. (eds) *Death Across Cultures: Death and Dying in Non-Western Cultures*. New York: Springer International Publishing, pp 103–118.

Elling, R.C. (2009) 'Bring in the dead: martyr burials and election politics in Iran', *MR Online*. Available at: https://mronline.org/2009/03/21/bring-in-the-dead-martyr-burials-and-election-politics-in-iran/ [accessed 13 March 2024].

Fontein, J. (2014) 'Remaking the dead, uncertainty and the torque of human materials in northern Zimbabwe', in Steputtat, F. (ed) *Governing the Dead*. Manchester: Manchester University Press, pp 114–142.

Ghorbani, H. (2017) *From Death to Martyrdom: Cultural Analyze of Visual Elements in Martyrdom in the Behesht-e-Zahra Cemetery of Tehran*. Master's dissertation, Tehran University of Art.

Hanssen, J.P. (2005) *Fin de Siècle Beirut: The Making of an Ottoman Provincial Capital*. Oxford: Oxford University Press.

Larkin, C. (2012) *Memory and Conflict in Lebanon: Remembering and Forgetting the Past*. London: Routledge.

Lefebvre, H. (1991) *The Production of Space*. Oxford: Basil Blackwell.

Low, S.M. (2009) 'Towards an anthropological theory of space and place', *Semiotica*, 175: 21–37.

Moallem, M. (2003) 'Cultural nationalism and Islamic fundamentalism: the case of Iran', in Kaiwar, V. and Mazumdar, S. (ed) *Antinomies of Modernity: Essays on Race, Orient, Nation*. Durham, NC: Duke University Press.

Mo'in, M. (2017) *The Mo'in Encyclopedic Dictionary*. Tehran: AmirKabir Publication.

Myrttinen, H. (2014) 'Claiming the dead, defining the nation: contested narratives of the independence struggle in post conflict Timor-Leste', in Steputtat, F. (ed) *Governing the Dead*. Manchester: Manchester University Press, pp 95–114.

Nasiri, S. and Faghfouri Azar, L. (2024) 'Investigating the 1981 massacre in Iran: on the law-constituting force of violence', *Journal of Genocide Research*, 26(2): 164–187.

Pippidi, A. (1995) *Graves as Landmarks of National Identity*. Budapest: Budapest Collegium.

Rahmani, J. and Ghorbani, H. (2017) 'Burial as a bureaucratic phenomenon death rituals in Tehran's *Behesht-e-Zahra* cemetery', *Quarterly of Social Studies and Research in Iran*, 6(3): 409–430.

Rizvi, K. (2003) 'Religious icon and national symbol: the tomb of Ayatollah Khomeini in Iran', *Muqarnas Online*, 20(1): 209–224.

Saeedi Rezvani, N. (2000) 'Planning: future in the mirror of today', *Municipalities Monthly*, 6: 13–64.

Scot Aghaie, K. and Marashi, A. (2014) *Rethinking Iranian Nationalism and Modernity*. Austin: University of Texas Press.

Shams, F. (2020) 'Dialogues with the dead: necropolitics of Zahra's paradise', *Iranian Studies*, 53(5–6): 893–909.

Trans, L.O. (2014) 'Travelling corpses: negotiating sovereign claims in Oaxacan post-mortem repatriation', in Steputtat, F. (ed) *Governing the Dead*. Manchester and New York: Manchester University Press, pp 75–94.

Verdery, K. (1999) *The Political Lives of Dead Bodies: Reburial and Postsocialist Change*. New York: Columbia University Press.

7

'The Bluecoat Boys to Walk and Sing an Anthem before the Corpse': The Children of Christ's Hospital in London Funerals of the 18th Century

Dan O'Brien

Introduction

On a June afternoon in 1732 a funeral procession made its way through the city of London between Bassinghall Street and the church of St Lawrence in Cateaton Street (now Gresham Street). It was a relatively short journey, taking only one street corner to reach its destination, but this did not prevent a solemn spectacle performed in honour of its subject, Edwin Rawsterne (*Daily Courant*, 1732: 2). Preceding the coffin on that June afternoon was a party of mourners dressed in blue, whose presence would have been recognized by any who saw the funeral on its short journey to the church. The mourners clad in blue were schoolchildren from Christ's Hospital, an institution located close to the site of the funeral and of which Rawsterne had been a governor before his death.

The Christ's Hospital schoolchildren had participated in the funerals of benefactors since the 16th century, and the practice can be traced through a ledger begun in 1622 which recorded the time of the funeral and the identity of the deceased (London Metropolitan Archives, 1622–1754). Each record in the ledger also indicates the amount of money which was given to the school on behalf of the deceased. This chapter analyses this ledger to understand what roles the schoolchildren performed at the funerals, and how their participation was shaped by the relationship between the institution and its benefactors. By examining the funerary duties of the schoolchildren, this chapter expands upon literature which has mostly focused on the traditions of the school and the experiences of schoolchildren. Broad histories of the school pay particular attention to the events surrounding the school's foundation in the 16th century, a development which distinguished the school from later charity schools (Manzione, 1995). Many of the school's histories were written with people close to the institution and arguably invested some of their lived experience of the school into their writing (Christ's Hospital, 1953). For example, G.A.T. Allan was a boy at the school and later served the school in various administrative roles as an adult (Morpurgo, 1984). Biographies of pupils illustrate the traditions of the school and the experiences of famous pupils such as Thomas Coleridge, Leigh Hunt and Charles Lamb (Johnson, 1896; Treadwell, 1998). Other writing has identified the contribution which notable public figures made to the life of the school, such as architect Christopher Wren, and these demonstrate the significance of the school (Foxall, 2008). It is arguable that within this literature there is little opportunity to discuss in the detail the funerary duties of the schoolchildren, even though these represent an important part of the school's interaction with its city and the negotiation of its relationship with the citizens.

This chapter will focus on the early 18th century, a period during which the practice of the Christ's Hospital schoolchildren attending funerals was in decline. In 1624 the schoolchildren had attended 83 funerals, a total which was larger than the 69 that they attended in the five decades between 1700 and 1750. The last recorded attendance by the schoolchildren was the funeral of James St Amand in 1754 (London Metropolitan Archives, 1622–1754). E.H. Pearce, a historian of the school, notes that practice 'came to an unlamented end' in the 1750s, but does not contribute significantly to our understanding of the children's funerary duties in what is a very broad history of the institution (Pearce, 1901). While the present chapter does not interpret the children's participation in 18th-century funerals quite so severely, it does recognize that they were mourners who attended on request rather than for reasons of personal grief. In order to understand the nature of their presence at these funerals, we must first consider the institution which sent them.

The institutional context

Christ's Hospital was founded in 1552 with the intention of providing relief and education to poor and orphaned children. It was not a hospital in the medical sense, but a school in which the children of the deserving local poor were educated and provided with an opportunity for advancement. Enrolment at the Hospital was determined by the individual's need, with candidates assessed on the severity of their poverty and lack of pre-existing support (Morpurgo, 1984). From the late 17th century, special rules also dictated that the children must be residents of London and also related to inhabitants of the city. Christ's Hospital was by no means the only charitable school in the city, and other successful institutions founded during this period included John Cass's school (which would later become the modern Aldgate School). The City's livery companies also funded schools of their own in the City, and this custom would continue into the 19th century which saw the foundation of schools that continue to educate to this day.

For the sake of clarity, the chapter focuses on the City of London, the traditional square mile that was divided into an ever-fluctuating number of wards, each electing a senior official known as an alderman. The City was governed by the Corporation of London which was formed of the Lord Mayor, a council of the City's aldermen and the Court of Common Council. Common Council was an elected body comprised of local freemen, who were members of the livery companies. The livery companies covered a wide variety of the different trades practised within the City, and had been an integral part of business and civic life since the medieval period, with membership of a company enabling an individual to work and trade within their chosen field. The livery companies were also an important part of civic life as they held functions, supported charitable causes and endorsed churches within the City of London. Liverymen were the subjects of many of the funerals attended by the schoolchildren.

Christ's Hospital had a very close relationship with the Corporation, which had existed since its origin with Henry VIII's grant of Greyfriars monastery to the City of London. The City influenced the administration of the school through the election of its governors, many of whom were heavily engaged in the politics of the City. The Lord Mayor, the symbolic leader of the City, had a prominent role in many of the school's ceremonial functions, and appeared alongside the schoolchildren at events where the City of London welcomed visiting monarchs (Morpurgo, 1984). Both the Lord Mayor and the livery companies possessed the right to refer children to the school and the Mayor sat on the school council as vice president (Maxwell, 1819; Wilson, 1821).

As a charitable school, Christ's Hospital depended upon financial contributions from the City, which came in a variety of different forms. Subscriptions from the City's parishes and livery companies provided a regular income to the school, which was supplemented by special privileges granted by the civic authorities. For example, the right to register carts within the City provided the school with an income which might be received directly or could be leased to another party for a fee (Morpurgo, 1984). In addition to its regular forms of income, the school could rely upon monies donated in the wills of affluent City residents, many of whom were members of the livery companies or the City authorities (Morpurgo, 1984). The burden of funding the school was therefore an important context for the schoolchildren's participation in funeral processions, as each occasion brought additional money to the school.

How the children participated

The participation of the schoolchildren followed certain patterns, although there appears to be no direct link between the amount of money given by the deceased person and the number of children who took part in the funeral. The children's attendance was not explicitly purchased by the deceased nor directed by a rate system. While the sums of money gifted to the school varied from 50 pounds to 1,000 pounds, the school typically decided to send one of two group sizes: 100 or 200 children (London Metropolitan Archives, 1622–1754). In the period analysed by this chapter, 29 funerals featured 100 children and 21 funerals featured 200 children (London Metropolitan Archives, 1622–1754). At three funerals in the period a smaller group of 50 children participated although there is no clear cause for these numbers in the identity of the deceased or the money given to the school, to explain the smaller group. The schoolchildren who attended were frequently identified as 'boys' although they are also described more generally as 'children' (London Metropolitan Archives, 1622–1754). Girls from the school were specifically recorded as attending funerals of women and in this duty they participated alongside boys. At the funeral of Dame Martha Clayton a group of 60 girls were joined by 20 boys for the procession of her body before its funerary journey. The gender-imbalanced groups seen at the Clayton funeral can also be observed in the funeral of Mrs Mary Bearcroft, where a large group of 90 boys were accompanied by 60 girls (London Metropolitan Archives, 1622–1754). There is no explanation from the school regarding these uneven groups, but it is clear that the cohort of schoolchildren would have been considerable in number compared to a private funeral party consisting of just friends and family. The children would therefore have added to the scale of the funeral procession, while their presence would also have been valuable public exposure for the school.

Ostentation

The schoolchildren of Christ's Hospital participated in many large funerary processions, where they were part of an expensive display which testified to the status and significance of the deceased. The children marched alongside pall-draped hearses, mourning coaches and in the company of mourners bestowed with funerary gifts. All of these items represented expenditure by the executors of the deceased, payments intended to secure a 'respectable' funeral from the undertakers or allied trades. Money could buy a visual spectacle that ensured that the deceased would not go to their grave unrecognized or unacknowledged by the people of their neighbourhood and peers within civic life. The crowds who watched these funerals were clearly impressed with the spectacle but there were critical voices who condemned funerary display as 'pomp'. Critics asserted that popular decorative elements had no practical value and constituted a vain display at wasteful cost. Bernard de Mandeville drew a comparison between an undertaker and a dancing master, suggesting that the funeral was little more than a performed routine with no genuine emotion (Mandeville, 1723). Criticism was frequently targeted at the decorative items which adorned the hearse and the gifts given to mourners who joined the funeral. John Trapp (1748) questioned whether there was a purpose for decorative, heraldic elements which spectators did not understand, even if they found them visually appealing. The writer, John Gay, encouraged people to consider how funeral display served the family members' desire to appear successful through items which did not assist the dead person in any way, even though they might be popular (Gay, 1716).

Contemporaries were divided on whether the presence of schoolchildren constituted pomp, and so could be considered unnecessary. Alderman Sir Peter Vandeput had 100 Christ's Hospital children in his funeral procession, having expressed a desire for a modest funeral in his will. Vandeput left directions that there would be no mourning rings and no funeral sermon read. His will further stipulated that the funeral was to be a private occasion in which his body should be accompanied by 'nearest relations and particular friends'. Vandeput's vision of modesty featured compromises and he was willing to give mourning tokens, although not rings, to this cohort of family and friends (TNA, 1708). These instructions might seem quite contradictory to the alderman's desire for modesty through restraint, because the children added to the scale of the funeral and they were not in attendance to mourn personally. Though statements were made by contemporaries about shared sorrow and respect, the children were not his family or friends. It can be argued that two factors legitimized the children's participation in a 'modest' funeral or at least provided a justification. First, the children were a reminder of the deceased's charity, a personal quality which could be more easily championed than social status, wealth or military achievement. Second, the children were not professionals and did not receive payment for their participation as mutes, banner carriers and undertakers' attendants did. Such paid roles were described by the critics of funerary pomp as 'a masquerade' because their presence was motivated by business rather than respect or sorrow (Mandeville, 1723: 402).

There were still arguments that schoolchildren were part of funerary pomp and therefore an unnecessary presence in the rite. In 1736, the will of affluent Newington gentleman Samuel Wright gave detailed instructions for his funeral which included schoolchildren in a list of 'pompous' elements that were to be avoided by his executors. Wright stipulated: 'I desire my funeral may be performed in a grave, decent manner, not in a pompous manner, would have no blue coat boys nor parish boys at my funeral, nor any escutcheons, guidons or the like' (TNA, 1736). This brief statement equates the schoolchildren, the 'blue coat boys' as being of a similarly decorative and ostentatious nature as the frequently criticized escutcheons or banners. We can be certain that Wright was not criticizing the schoolchildren or their schools, because his will also gave a sum of 1,000 pounds to Christ's Hospital, around £117,792 today; a total which was comparable to some of the notable individuals discussed elsewhere in this chapter such as Richard Hoare or Peter Vandeput. Similarly to these men, Wright possessed a considerable wealth when he died and dispensed his money widely to support charitable causes. Wright gave money to support the poor, and also to advance the Christian faith through the funding of clergymen or missionaries. He behaved comparably by dispensing sums of money to institutions in the City of London which housed the vulnerable such as hospitals, prisons and workhouses. In the context of these similarities, it is challenging to consider why Wright's funerary choices differed so significantly. Wright's decision could be interpreted as a condemnation of the use of recipients of charity as emblems of one's identity in the funeral procession. This is because Wright's equation of schoolchildren with decorative devices suggests that he believed the children were performing the same purpose as escutcheons and guidons; devices which traditionally told spectators who a person was or what they stood for.

The differing choices of Wright and Vandeput demonstrate how the participation of schoolchildren was influenced by the intentions and the attitudes of the deceased (or their bereaved relatives). There was therefore no fixed understanding of the schoolchildren's funeral roles, and in this respect it is quite similar to many other funerary services which people could choose to criticize or endorse depending on their own values.

The funerary roles of the schoolchildren

The schoolchildren of Christ's Hospital were expected to be present during the processional stage of the funeral when the body was transported through the city streets. The presence had two distinct forms: lining the route along which the funeral travelled or marching in the funeral procession. Examples from the early 18th century indicate that marching was the most common form of participation, with children joining the close friends and family of the deceased. Lining the funeral route was less common and this is perhaps because it was a more limited form of participation with the children restricted to part of the route or dispersed along its length. Both forms of participation in the procession ensured that the schoolchildren would be seen by spectators and spontaneous bystanders who encountered the funerals passing through the city. We will now consider how children participated in route-lining and marching during the early decades of the 18th century.

Lining the funeral route

The 1719 funeral of former Lord Mayor and banker Sir Richard Hoare was a grandiose occasion, in which his coffin was carried along Fleet Street from his house to the church of St Dunstan-in-the-West. Fleet Street was a busy throughfare, and the funeral was consequently staged in the evening, a choice which would lessen disruption to the procession. Christ's Hospital was an integral part of this procession, with 280 schoolchildren committed to the funeral to lead the coffin and also line the route which the funeral party travelled from the household to the church (*Weekly Journal or Saturday's Post*, 1719). It is possible that the children provided illumination with torches because this was an established custom for nocturnal burials of fellow pupils in the school cloisters (Trollope, 1834). The short distance travelled by the coffin arguably made lining the route a more feasible choice than at those funerals which made journeys through several streets, and at times of the day which would have complicated the act of placing children along a public street. As route-liners, the schoolchildren were in a prominent position throughout the funeral and could be easily seen by the large crowd which gathered to witness the funeral. The visibility of the schoolchildren was a reminder of the important role which Hoare had played in their lives as President of Christ's Hospital prior to his death. For both the school and Hoare's family it was mutually beneficial to recognize this association so prominently in the composition of the funeral procession. Hoare's status demonstrated that the school was important to the City's elites and the civic community of which they were members; the coffin of the deceased was carried by his fellow aldermen. It was also a reminder to other members of the elite that they could support the school as Hoare had done. For Hoare's family, the presence of the schoolchildren was beneficial because it demonstrated that they were philanthropical people who were actively engaged in the betterment of disadvantaged members of their city. Displays of charity in Hoare's funeral also included the distribution of food to local poor people (TNA, 1719). The distribution of food was a more overt form of charity than that which was represented by the children, but carried the risk of disorder if the invited poor did not behave in manner that fulfilled the mourners' expectations of solemnity and sobriety. At a notable occasion in Hampshire, an affluent funeral was reportedly stormed by local poor people who had grown tired of waiting for their charity to be presented (*Daily Post*, 1729). By comparison, the neatly organized schoolchildren could be expected to be a more predictable presence at the funeral, particularly as their attendance was carefully planned.

Marching in the procession

Marching in the funeral procession was the most common role for the Christ's Hospital schoolchildren, and it brought them to many different streets and churches in the City. Marching was a suitable activity because it demonstrated the children's discipline and reminded the audience of the role played by the school in the children's lives.

The journeys made by the schoolchildren varied in length, depending on the distance of the procession to the church. It was common for funerals to start from the location where the body had lain in state, which was either the household of the deceased or a livery company hall. The livery halls were situated throughout the City of London and were grand buildings which offered large spaces for company administration and gatherings, including funerals. They were primarily used by the members of their own livery company, but some halls were used for the funerals of people who were not company members. The Upholders Hall was particularly unique as it served as a lying-in-state location for individuals who were the customers of its liverymen (Houston, 2006). By the early 18th century Upholders had established a reputation for performing the funerals of the affluent, so it is therefore unsurprising that their hall was a frequent starting point for the schoolchildren's funerary participation.

The distance travelled through the City was typically short, as the proximity of parish or guild churches meant that the procession was limited to a few streets. There were some exceptions, often where the deceased was going out into the countryside for burial at a distant family vault, and on these occasions there were pragmatic limitations on the children's participation. In 1711, the body of Heneage Featherstone was taken from his house at Tower Hill out to the stones end in Whitechapel from whence it was carried to Stanford Le Hope in Essex (London Metropolitan Archives, 1622–1754; ERO, D/P 404/1/1, 1680–1812). It was typical for their march to finish at the end of the paved roadway, known widely as the 'stones end'. There were several 'stones end' locations which represented a clear boundary between city and countryside (Darlington, 1955). This was therefore a good point for the funeral to transform from a performative to a more functional state for its remaining journey along the country roads; with this transition, the children no longer had a purpose. The culmination of the journey at the stones end was determined before the funeral began and was clearly indicated in the instructions for the funeral, reflecting the extent to which the children's participation was planned and structured.

The use of the stones end at Blackman Street in Southwark demonstrates how these boundaries functioned in both directions, as a point where the schoolchildren could begin or end their funerary participation. Blackman Street was over London Bridge and on the other side of the Thames, beyond the limits of the City of London but close enough to ensure that most of the children's participation would be on the streets of the City that supported them. In 1711, the combined party of boys and girls marched with the coffin of Dame Martha Clayton from her house in Old Jewry to the stones end in Blackman Street where the coffin travelled on to her burial at Bleckingley in Surrey (London Metropolitan Archives, 1622–1754). Three years earlier, this same point in Southwark had been the start of a procession for the coffin of Sir Peter Vandeput, as it travelled from his home in rural Richmond to St Margaret Pattens at Rood Lane in the City (London Metropolitan Archives, 1622–1754). Like those being carried out of the city for burial, Vandeput was brought to St Margaret Pattens to be buried in a vault with his parents (TNA, 1708). Two hundred Christ's Hospital children waited at the stones end in Blackman Street to escort the coffin on its journey across London Bridge to the destination of his funeral.

Many of those who were transported into the countryside for their burial were former presidents of Christ's Hospital, and the school appears to have been willing to recognize their contribution by committing the children to funerals which occurred outside of the limits of the City of London. At Sir Francis Childs' funeral in 1740, a party of 200 schoolchildren finished their participation at the stones end having started at Lincoln's Inn Fields just to the west of the City of London (London Metropolitan Archives, 1622–1754). As in the funeral of Sir Richard Hoare, Childs' status as a former president of Christ's Hospital led to a more involved participation than usual; both funerals began and ended near the limits of the City of London. The schoolchildren did not attend the provincial funerals or burials of the people who were transported out of the city. This is significant because it supports the interpretation of the children's participation as a display for the people of the city who might be institution's sponsors or neighbours. Sarah Lloyd has argued that viewing charity recipients was an important part of charities' fundraising and promotional activities. While Lloyd's focus is on convivial activities and anniversaries, the funeral procession has clear parallels with the street processions before banquets and church services; recipients and benefactors were brought together to process in a location that was relevant to the institution's charitable activities (Lloyd, 2002).

Demonstrating discipline

The funeral procession was an opportunity for the school to present itself as an influential institution that was making a significant contribution to life in the city. This influence was demonstrated through the institution's control over the circumstances of the schoolchildren who had been raised from poverty into disciplined and orderly citizens who could participate in the City's future. Visibly showing its work on/with the children, and therefore its contribution to the City, through funeral involvement was beneficial for Christ's Hospital given it required charity to function and therefore needed to justify itself to sponsors, and appeal to prospective sponsors.

Discipline was demonstrated through the clothing worn by the schoolchildren throughout their funerary appearances. Discussing a 16th-century funeral at which the schoolchildren appeared, Litten (1997) suggests that the school may have provided black gowns for the children to wear over their usual uniform, rather than accepting multiple clothing gifts from benefactors. The Christ's Hospital funeral book makes no reference to gowns and this may be because the frequency of funerals attended by the school had declined significantly since the 16th and 17th centuries, reducing the need to keep gowns. When Thomas Aynscombe requested the presence of the children at his funeral in 1740, he made no reference to the provision of gowns for the mourners stating only that he desired them to attend (TNA, 1740). Uniformity, rather than colour, was sometimes seen as a respectable quality such as in the funeral of a city trumpeter whose body was accompanied by musicians in scarlet gowns which 'made a very decent appearance' (*Lloyd's Evening Post*, 1761). Gowns were still gifted to other charity recipients in this period (*Read's Weekly Journal or British Gazetteer*, 1736) and if they were used by the school, they were likely worn over the distinctive blue outfits which had become a recognizable emblem of the school and charity education more widely.

The children were frequently described with the term 'bluecoat' or 'blewcoat', referring to the long blue coat which they wore in addition to a coloured cap and yellow garters (R.B., 1730; Blanch, 1877). The term 'bluecoat' had been used to describe a variety of schools from the 17th century onward but in contemporary accounts of funerals we see that it was one of the defining elements of Christ's Hospital participation (Stephenson, 2021). The *Daily Courant* described that the funeral of Edwin Rawsterne included 'the bluecoat boys of Christs Hospital' (*Daily Courant*, 1732: 2) and later an account of the Hoare funeral described 'bluecoat boys' lining the route (*Weekly Journal or Saturday's Post*, 1719: 4). The uniforms primarily ensured that the children appeared to be neat and orderly, demonstrating that they had been elevated above contemporary ideas about the disorderly and tattered poor (Simonton, 2000). In a sermon at Christ Church in 1752, John Chapman drew parallels between the physical uncleanliness and the tattered appearance of the poor and a moral weakness which led to suffering and criminality. 'Rags and want', Chapman argued, were the most visible and superficial of the poor's problems, which would end in 'barbarism and inveterate vice' if charitable intervention did not occur (1752: 16–17). However the significance of the uniforms went beyond an act of giving, because the uniforms identified the children as members of the school rather than individuals. As a consequence, they could be seen as members of a historic community of fellow Christ's Hospital bluecoats, who had all worn the same uniform and participated in the same activities. Uniformity was important, as the schoolchildren were requested and deployed as a group, representing the school which the deceased had supported through their monetary gifts.

The uniform was an emblem of the school, recognizable in the local community where inhabitants may have seen students moving around or attending other functions at churches or civic buildings (Morpurgo, 1984). The uniform was the most tangible of the ways in which the school had influenced the children's lives as their education and spiritual instruction were less easy to represent in the funeral procession (Rose, 1991; Lloyd, 2003; Payne, 2006). In this context, the school uniform was more than sufficient in supporting the reputational claims of the funeral and ensuring that spectators could recognize proof of the deceased's good works in their own community.

Location in the funeral procession

Accounts of the funerary roles of the schoolchildren give a good sense of their position within the procession, and their consequent importance to the mourning party. The children were commonly positioned before the coffin or hearse, thus occupying a location of historic significance. In the heraldic funeral rite of the preceding centuries, the body was preceded by important devices which represented the status and rank of the deceased. The ceremonial armour of knights was carried before their coffin with additional attendants bearing different flags (Cunnington, 1972). The coat of arms were also borne in this busy, symbolic space where the identity of the deceased was condensed into a brief display summarizing who they were and what made them important. This rite was traditionally restricted to the social elite, but has relevance for the funerals discussed here. Those discussed earlier in this chapter were eligible for such funerals, although many such as Hoare chose to refuse such display. The authority of the heralds still lingered in the early 18th century, even if their legal challenges could not stop the entrepreneurialism of early undertakers (Gittings, 1984; Fritz, 1994). Many of those entrepreneurial businessmen would adopt elements of these rites into their own funerals for people of status, ignoring the conventions which the heralds had once upheld.

When viewed in the context of these funerary traditions, the position of the schoolchildren before the hearse may be understood as an attempt to recognize philanthropy as one of the defining qualities of the deceased. Spectators could observe the children as evidence for the generosity of the deceased, and as proof that they had contributed to the future of their city as well as its present. The children's appearance and behaviour was made possible, at least in part, by the actions of the deceased and the institution which they had funded. Before seeing the coffin, the spectators were presented with evidence for the person within, framing their understanding of the individual. This was beneficial to any attempt by the individual or their family to secure a posthumous reputation through funerary display.

For the institution, the procession was an opportunity to demonstrate their positive influence on the children's lives and present these orderly marchers as proof of their institutional success. The funerals in which the children marched were complicated and meticulously planned occasions requiring discipline from all who participated. The schoolchildren's ability to perform their duties in this environment was proof of how the school had positively transformed what might be perceived as the 'unruly' poor into model members of urban society.

The schoolchildren were not alone in the funeral procession, they preceded friends and family, for whom the funeral was a private occasion. Convention dictated that the mourning party would walk just after the coffin, with invited friends following afterwards. Within this structure, the procession was divided between the private grief of the mourners and the civic grief of the school. Interpreting the funeral as a form of civic display, albeit one with clear personal aims, we can understand the children as part of a celebration of the civic achievements of the deceased and the institution which they had sponsored.

Times of day

The timing of the funeral is an important detail because it informs our understanding of the wider purpose of funerary display. It is notable that the presence of the children did not influence the timing of the funeral, and the variety of different times listed in the Christ's Hospital funeral book indicates that the children attended as they were required to. The funeral of Thomas Bateson provides a stark indication of how the school was influenced by the demands of others. Bateson was a retired mariner from Stepney, who was being processed from Upholsterer's Hall to the town's end for his burial in Middlesex in late April 1701 (TNA, 1701). The Christ's Hospital schoolchildren were directed to accompany his coffin from the hall in Leadenhall Street to the town's end from six o'clock in the morning. During the early 18th century the schoolchildren were recorded as attending eight funerals in the morning, of which all but one was for a body being taken out of the city for rural burial. It is arguable that the children attending the early funeral of Thomas Bateson were not significantly visible as they processed through the city: here the schoolchildren were attending at a time that was clearly suitable to the funeral party, and their practical desire to embark on a long overland journey. All of these funerals occurred between six and eight o'clock in the morning, too early to command a large audience of spectators.

The majority of funerals occurred during the daytime, when the processions might be expected to pass through the busy streets where they could be easily witnessed by casual and intentional spectators. During the early 18th century the schoolchildren were recorded as participating in a total of 23 afternoon funerals, predominantly occurring between two o'clock and five o'clock.

Schoolchildren alone in the funeral

It is notable that the schoolchildren were the only charity recipients to participate in the funerals studied by this chapter. This was not a reflection of the limited charity dispensed by affluent men and women of early 18th-century London, indeed large sums of money were frequently given to other prominent City institutions such as St Bartholomew's Hospital, Bridewell Prison and also St Thomas' Hospital. Francis Forbes and Thomas Carpenter both gave 100 pounds to each institution in addition to their donations to Christ's Hospital (TNA, 1727a, 1731). John Crowley donated to both the Bridewell and St Bartholomew's with each receiving 100 pounds, a total which is worth around £11,610 today (TNA, 1727b). These institutions were similar to Christ's Hospital because they housed the City's vulnerable and depended upon financial support from the people of the City including the affluent elites who comprised the aldermanry (Anon, 1901). In addition to financial support, many of those elites also served as governors of more than one institution, thereby playing an active role in the organization of the institution and becoming part of its community. Governorship was a prestigious position and one which demonstrated the civic spirit of the individual who gave their time to support the institutions and people of the City. It was therefore, a highly attractive position and something that was worthy of commemoration in the funeral. There was clearly a social aspect to participation in governorship, occasioned by the overlapping relationships of London's commercial elite: the governors knew one another outside of their civic responsibilities and friendships were part of their charitable activity too (Rogers, 1985).

Sir Francis Forbes occupied gubernatorial positions at all of the institutions, albeit offering significantly more money to Christ's Hospital in his will: 800 pounds to the schoolchildren and 100 to each of the other institutions (*Daily Post*, 1727; TNA, 1727a). The same imbalance in bequests can be observed in the wills of other benefactors, although the trend is probably a consequence of this chapter's particular focus on individuals who were closely aligned to Christ's Hospital.

Some benefactors distributed their money equally to the different institutions although this parity was not represented in the composition of the funeral procession. Thomas Pinder, who had served as a governor of the hospital, directed that 'Christ Church, St Bartholomew's and Bridewell' were to receive 100 pounds each upon his death in 1741 (TNA, 1741). In his funeral, 60 children led the coffin from St John's Square to the point of its embarkation for Lincoln Hill in Hertfordshire. However there were no representatives of St Bartholomew's or the Bridewell present in Pinder's procession. Pinder's selection of school, hospital and debtors prison was a common combination, although there were some who also gave to the hospitals of St Thomas' and Bethlem; both of which were closely affiliated with the City. Where equal sums of money were given to the respective institutions there was no participation by other institutions.

There is a practical reason why the school was the only institution represented in the funeral procession. The schoolchildren represent a more viable group of participants than the patients of the hospitals or the inmates of the debtors' prison. By comparison with these other groups, the children were able to parade on the streets without being compromised by infirmity or posing a risk of abscondment. The staff of the institutions might be more viable candidates but accounts of the funerals indicate that they did not attend on behalf of their institutions either. The schoolchildren of Christ's Hospital were therefore a unique presence, something which would have drawn attention to them.

In addition to these practical considerations, the schoolchildren symbolically represented the deceased's contribution to the future. Individually their circumstances would be improved by the school which the deceased had funded, and consequently they might be rescued from a future of poverty and depravity. This contribution to the future can be understood more widely because the children would be members of the future City, and thus potential contributors to the civic community of which the deceased had also been a member. In this interpretation, the sight of a positive and flourishing school community was an encouraging message about the deceased's role in improving the future of their own City.

Conclusion

When the children of Christ's Hospital participated in the funerals of early 18th-century London they served the intentions of both their institution and its benefactors. For the institution, the children were a visual reminder of the school's influence on the lives of the poor and a prescribed reading of its success in creating future members of the City guided by discipline and morality. For the benefactors, the children were evidence of philanthropic activity which had occurred in life and at death. The institution had been supported by their money, often guided by their governance and in the funeral this relationship was communicated to the friends and neighbours of the deceased. Through the participation of the children both the institution and its benefactors could recognize their positive contribution to the city.

References

Anon (1901) 'Nova Et Vetera. St. Bartholomew's and Christ's Hospitals', *British Medical Journal*, 2(2135): 1607–1608.

Blanch, W.H. (1877) *The Blue-coat Boys. Or, School Life in Christ's Hospital. With a Short History of the Foundation.* London: E.W. Allen.

Chapman, J. (1752) *The Ends and Uses of Charity Schools. A Sermon Preached in the Parish-church of Christ-Church, London, on Thursday April the 30th, 1752: Being the Time of the Yearly Meeting of the Children Educated in the Charity-schools, in and about the Cities of London and Westminster.* London: Christ-Church.

Christ's Hospital (1953) *Christ's Hospital. Four Hundred Years Old.* London: Christ's Hospital.

Cunnington, P. (1972) *Costume for Births, Marriages and Death.* London: A. and C. Black.

Daily Courant (1732) 26 June.

Daily Post (1727) 6 October.

Daily Post (1729) 11 October.

Darlington, I. (1955) 'Borough High Street, Blackman Street and Newington Causeway', in *Survey of London*, volume 25, St George's Fields (The Parishes of St. George the Martyr Southwark and St. Mary Newington). London: London County Council. Available at: http://www.british-hist ory.ac.uk/survey-london/vol25/pp1-8 [accessed 2 January 2024].

Foxall, T. (2008) 'Schooled by Wren, or a school by Wren? The conception and design of Christ's Hospital Writing School, London', *Architectural History*, 51: 87–110.

Fritz, P.S. (1994) 'The undertaking trade in England: its origins and early development, 1660–1830', *Eighteenth-Century Studies*, 28(2): 241–253.

Gay, J. (1716) *Trivia: Or, the Art of Walking the Streets of London. By Mr. Gay.* Bernard Lintot: London.

Gittings, C. (1984) *Death, Burial and the Individual in Early Modern England.* London: Croom Helm.

Houston, J.F. (2006) *Featherbedds and Flock Bedds: The Early History of the Worshipful Company of Upholders of the City of London.* London: Three Tents Press.

Johnson, R.B. (ed) (1896) *Christ's Hospital. Recollections of Lamb, Coleridge, and Leigh Hunt.* London: G. Allen.

Litten, J. (1997) *The English Way of Death: The Common Funeral since 1450*. London: Reaktion Books.

Lloyd, S. (2002) 'Pleasing spectacles and elegant dinners: conviviality, benevolence and charity anniversaries in eighteenth-century London', *Journal of British Studies*, 41: 23–57.

Lloyd, S. (2003) '"Agents in their own concerns"? Charity and the economy of makeshifts in eighteenth-century Britain', in King, S. and Tomkins, A. (eds) *The Poor in England 1700–1850: An Economy of Makeshifts*. Manchester: Manchester University Press, pp 100–137.

Lloyd's Evening Post (1761) 5–7 August.

London Metropolitan Archives (1622–1754) *Record of attendance at funerals by pupils of the school as mourners, giving the name, status and occupation of each individual to be buried, and details of arrangements for the funeral service, number of pupils requested to attend and amount of money given or promised*, CLC/210/F/035/MS22566 (1622–1754).

Mandeville, B. (1723) *The Fable of the Bees: or, Private Vices, Publick Benefits. The second edition, enlarged with many additions. As also an essay on charity and charity-schools. And a search into the nature of society*. J. Tonson: London.

Manzione, C.K. (1995) *Christ's Hospital of London, 1552–1598: A Passing Deed of Pity*. East Brunswick: Susquehanna University Press.

Maxwell, J.I. (1819) *A Key to Christ's Hospital, containing an account of the ... foundation by Edward the Sixth; and the subsequent additional institutions. With extracts from Mr. Alderman Waithman's Pamphlet, shewing the abuses with respect to the cases of Warren, Proby, etc. To which is added a list of Governors, etc.* Richardson: London.

Morpurgo, J.E. (ed) (1984) *Christ's Hospital. By G.A.T Allan. Revised by J.E. Morpurgo*. London: Town and Country Books.

Payne, D. (2006) 'London's charity school children: the "scum of the parish"?', *Journal for Eighteenth Century Studies*, 29(3): 383–397.

Pearce, E.H. (1901) *Annals of Christ's Hospital*. London: Methuen and Co.

R.B. (1730) *A New View, and Observations on the Ancient and Present State of London and Westminster*. A. Bettesworth, and C. Hitch: London.

Read's Weekly Journal or British Gazetteer (1736) 13 November.

Rogers, N. (1985) 'Clubs and politics in eighteenth-century London: "The Centenary Club of Cheapside"', *The London Journal*, 11(1): 51–58.

Rose, C. (1991) 'Evangelical philanthropy and Anglican revival: the charity schools of Augustan London, 1698–1740', *The London Journal*, 16(1): 35–65.

Simonton, D. (2000) 'Schooling the poor: gender and class in eighteenth-century England', *British Journal for Eighteenth Century Studies*, 23: 183–202.

Stanford-Le-Hope, St Margaret of Antioch: Register of baptisms, marriages and burials, Essex Records Office, D/P 404/1/1 (1680–1812).

Stephenson, K. (2021) *A Cultural History of School Uniform*. Exeter: University of Exeter Press.

TNA (The National Archives) (1701) *Will of Thomas Bateson*, PROB 11: Piece 460: Dyer, Quire Numbers 46–88.

TNA (The National Archives) (1708) *Will of Peter Vandeput*, PROB 11: Piece 501: Barrett, Quire Numbers 89–133.

TNA (The National Archives) (1719) *Will of Sir Richard Hoare*, PROB 11: Piece 567: Browning, Quire Numbers 1–48.

TNA (The National Archives) (1727a) *Will of Sir Francis Forbes*, PROB 11: Piece 618: Farrant, Quire Numbers 251–313.

TNA (The National Archives) (1727b) *Will of John Crowley*, PROB 11: Piece 619: Brook, Quire Numbers 1–47.

TNA (The National Archives) (1731) *Will of Thomas Carpenter*, PROB 11: Piece 644: Isham, Quire Numbers 98–143.

TNA (The National Archives) (1736) *Will of Samuel Wright*, PROB 11: Piece 678: Derby, Quire Numbers 144–191.

TNA (The National Archives) (1740) *Will of Thomas Aynscombe*, PROB 11: Piece 705: Browne, Quire Numbers 251–297.

TNA (The National Archives) (1741) *Will of Thomas Pinder*, PROB 11: Piece 716: Trenley, Quire Numbers 49–91.

Trapp, J. (1748) *Thoughts upon the four last things: death; judgment; heaven; and hell. A poem. In four parts. By Joseph Trapp, D.D. The second edition.* W. Russel: London.

Treadwell, J. (1998) 'Impersonation and autobiography in Lamb's Christ's Hospital essays', *Studies in Romanticism*, 37(4): 499–521.

Trollope, W. (1834) *A History of the Royal Foundation of Christ's Hospital, with an Account of the Plan of Education, the Internal Economy of the Institution, and Memoirs of Eminent Blues.* London: W. Pickering.

Weekly Journal or Saturday's Post (1719) 17 January.

Wilson, J.I. (1821) *A Brief History of Christ's Hospital. From its foundation by King Edward the Sixth to the present time. With a List of the Governors.* Effingham Wilson: London.

8

Inside-Out and Outside-In: Learned Institutions and Garden Cemeteries in 19th-Century Britain

Lindsay Udall

Introduction

Across Britain in the early 19th century, garden cemeteries emerged alongside the precursors to civic museums – learned societies – as places intended for education, reflection and to document societal progress. While the cemetery's resemblance to a museum has previously been noted (see Meyer and Woodthorpe, 2008) the manner in which these unlikely cousins came to be, and their exact relation to one another, has largely been overlooked. Building upon the work of Rugg (1992) and Scott (2005) in identifying civic 'networks of influence' upon the 19th-century garden cemetery's development, this chapter draws on my previous work (Udall, 2019) and the idea of institutional networks of influence (Mee, 2023), to show that cemeteries and learned societies (called learned institutions from hereon to accommodate their evolution from learned societies to scientific, literary and philosophical institutions, then in some cases to civic museums) were intricately intertwined within various British provincial cities at that time. In so doing, it problematizes the typical emphasis on John Claudius Loudon (1783–1843) as an influential figure in British cemetery development (see Rugg, 1997), due in large part to the 1970s impact of Nicholas Penny (1974) and James Stevens Curl (1975, 1980, 1983, 2000, 2019). It is the position of this chapter that the extent of Loudon's individual contribution to the British garden cemetery's development has been overstated by academics and Cemetery Friends' groups alike. In contrast, this chapter situates Loudon and his work within a much wider network of Georgian and early Victorian British civic society.

After establishing the significance of networks of influence in the origins of the 19th-century garden cemetery, the chapter argues that the cemetery and learned institutions were (and still are) examples of what Foucault and Miskowiec (1986) term 'heterotopias'; that is, they are both spaces that possess the ability to be multiple things at once, both real or reimagined. Indeed, Foucault and Miskowiec go so far as to describe the cemetery as an '*atypical* heterotopia' (Ní Éigeartaigh, 2021: 160, emphasis added) because of its ability to incorporate and simultaneously suspend within it 'other' spaces, such as an educative or recreational space, alongside a space for body burial and mourning. Theorizing further, Foucault and Miskowiec highlight how certain types of heterotopic space – such as the cemetery and a learned institution – are the mirror of each other. Building on this, the argument in this chapter is that, at the time of their creation, cemeteries and learned institutions were *inversions* of one another.

But what does this inversion mean? It means that from the outset these spaces, according to Foucault and Miskowiec (1986), were transitory. Recognizable to one another, they (re)presented city geographies, peoples and 'slices' of time, acting as what Saumarez-Smith (1998) calls 'memory banks'. In other words, the learned institution (and subsequent civic museum) was (and still is) akin to a mausoleum or an 'internal cemetery' as the final resting place of objects (that belong to the dead). Simultaneously the cemetery was intended to be the 'outdoor museum', full of ideas, artefacts and antiquarian style architecture and sculpture. Together and over time, both spaces contain a unique type of power over both the living and the dead, (re)creating typology, innovation and an attempt at social order.

The role of learned institutions and networks of influence

Born towards the end of the 18th century, John Claudius Loudon is often heralded by cemetery historians as the creator of the Victorian British garden cemetery landscape. Yet while Loudon was certainly of an antiquarian persuasion (Simo, 1988), others in London, and more widely in the provinces, were also researching and documenting population data, and generating statistics and medical topographies. This acquisition of knowledge, and its collection and curation, enabled these individuals across the country to justify and build burial sites within their new cityscapes – and to make their case they were disseminating this newfound knowledge through learned institutions. Notable individuals involved in this mission included Thomas Asline Ward of Sheffield, James Cleland of Glasgow, Charles Bowles Fripp of Bristol and John Clayton of Newcastle, all of whom were involved in the creation of new cemeteries for their respective cities. Around the same time Joseph Livesey of Hull (writing in 1831) and J.A. Picton of Liverpool (published by Loudon) were also both authoring on the potential to develop and restyle burial grounds (Udall, 2019). Together, these individuals and their associated networks functioned as early 'scaffolds for institutions' and they featured heavily in social and cultural institutions' 'production at that time' (Klancher, 2022: 135).

The individuals who comprised these networks typically came from the influential middle-class elites of new urban cities and although they rarely feature in historical scholarship, their concurrent presence and involvement in both learned institutions and cemeteries of Georgian and Victorian Britain is without doubt. Becoming founders, directors, presidents, secretaries, treasurers and/or curators of both spaces, as evidenced by their listings in institutions' records and contemporary city guides (Rugg, 1992), the networks in which these influential individuals were involved also featured in other important historical sources, which at the time reflected the perceived importance and value of different people, spaces and places, and functioned as an extension of learned institutions (Udall, 2019). Notable publications included the *Penny Magazine*, *Blackwell's* and the *Architectural and Gardeners Magazine* (the latter edited by Loudon, with his wife and sisters acting as contributors and amanuenses) (Brake and Demoor, 2009: 380). An 1838 edition of the *Penny Magazine* lists the development of cemeteries immediately below that of learned institutions within cities, indicating how these two emergent institutions were thought of by contemporaries as being related.

In exploring the networks of influence that built the learned institution (and subsequently the museum) and the garden cemetery, the first individual examined in this chapter is Charles Bowles Fripp (1805–1849), a prominent figure in Bristol society during the early to mid-19th century. A soap manufacturer, as well as Financial Secretary of the Bristol Institution until 1848, Bowles Fripp was the first Director of the Bristol General Cemetery Company from 1836 to 1848. He was also a respected statistician, who wrote extensively on the populations of Bristol and New York City. This interest extended to populations and remaining burial space in the city of Bristol, to justify the need for the new cemetery at Arnos Vale (Udall, 2019). During the early to mid-1830s, with Bowles Fripp's help, networks of influence in Bristol set about establishing a need for a cemetery through the in-depth assessment of available burial space. Statistical analysis was used to assess the capacity of existing churchyards and private burial grounds within the city and, as often happened at that time, agents were employed to gather this data. In the case of Bristol, Savery Clark was commissioned to do this in 1835 (Udall, 2019). Having established there was a perceived need, Bowles Fripp was instrumental in founding Arnos Vale Cemetery in 1837 (opening in 1839). His antiquarian interests are evident in his original vision for the cemetery's neoclassical appearance (Udall, 2019) and he employed architect Charles Underwood (1791–1883) to materialize his vision at the new cemetery site. Underwood would later go on to design the neoclassical interior of the Royal West of England Academy (opened in 1844). Such was the success of the design, Underwood's maquette of the Nonconformist chapel at Arnos Vale was displayed at a Royal West of England Academy exhibition, in a reversal of roles whereby the cemetery became an exhibit in the gallery of a learned institution – the outside being brought back inside the museum as an artefact.

Bowles Fripp was critical to establishing a garden cemetery in Bristol, with his advocation for the analysis of burial as an essential need for the city's growing population. His work in Bristol, however, was distinctive for its thoroughness, since the depth and detail of analysis of burial capacity for other cities varied considerably (Rugg, 1992). It was also the case that his analysis benefited from being in a port city where there tended to be more extensive population analyses carried out, which then contributed to local and national public health reports, including the Chadwick Report (1842). Another port city, Glasgow, had similar such statistics available and it is unsurprising, therefore, that Bowles Fripp's mentor James Cleland (1770–1840), Superintendent of Public Works in Glasgow from 1814, also wrote extensively about population growth and mortality statistics in relation to his own port city. Exemplifying the networked nature of emergent learned institutions, Bowles Fripp provided a foreword to one of the volumes produced by the Glasgow Statistical Society, and also read Cleland's paper on the population of Glasgow to a scientific conference held at the Bristol Institution in 1836 (Scott, 2005). Cleland shared Bowles Fripp's antiquarian interests, specializing in genealogy and heraldry, and it was these intersecting interests – of statistics, with heritage and culture – that would influence the development of cemeteries. This is exemplified at the Glasgow Necropolis cemetery in a dramatic arcadian style across a gorge intended to (re)create a historically themed landscape.

Within this English southwest network of influence, Bowles Fripp would likely have known the genealogist, collector of memorial inscriptions and archaeologist Joseph Hunter (1783–1861), given that Hunter was an honorary member of the Bristol Institution in 1833. Hunter moved to Bath from Sheffield in 1809, and in 1824 he established the Bath Literary and Scientific Institution. From his time in Sheffield, Hunter was a lifelong friend and correspondent of Thomas Asline Ward (1781–1871), with whom he shared a deep interest in antiquarianism. Asline Ward was a significant figure within the city of Sheffield as the long-time editor of the *Sheffield Telegraph*, and he even stood for Parliament in 1831. During the 1820s he was secretary of the Sheffield Institution and he became the first chair of the local Board of Health after the cholera outbreak of 1832. Asline Ward was aware of the connection between burial spaces and public sanitation and, like Bowles Fripp in Bristol and Cleland in Glasgow, was also aware of the importance of statistical data analysis in proving this. In 1843 Asline Ward commissioned local doctor George Calvert Holland to conduct a survey of the city to better understand Sheffield's public health, and to justify the recent opening of a cemetery. In 1836 Sheffield General Cemetery was created, of which Asline Ward was a co-founder.

Evidently, with these three connections and cities alone (Bristol, Glasgow and Sheffield), the power and influence of individuals and networks was becoming obvious, bolstered by the 19th century's growing interest in debating matters of life (and death) (Ruston, 2021). This purposeful energy was reflected in an eclectic range of lectures presented by learned institutions during this period, with topics ranging from nature and anatomy (such as Dr Richard Smith's lectures to the Bristol Institution, which were illustrated with examples from his collection, and in 1824, the very first public unwrapping of an Egyptian mummy [Udall, 2019]) to anthropology, architecture, medical topography, statistical analysis and mechanical engineering. These events provided a central meeting point for surgeons and architects, together with town clerks and businessmen, enabling individuals to exchange knowledge and to commission, create and analyse new surveys to generate evidence for their local area. This new knowledge was profoundly shaped by a shared interest in antiquarianism, whereby past thought and aesthetics were considered better than anything contemporary. Indeed, drawing on the past was regarded as just as innovative and at times even superior in aiding the development of new initiatives at the time (Lowenthal, 1985).

It was through these networks of influence and their consolidation in learned institutions that academic disciplines began to become more defined. This was another watershed moment for cemetery development as it was through the lens of these emerging academic disciplines that public health began to be assessed. A growing emphasis on civic hygiene established the need to bury the dead away from the everyday life and most, importantly, the water sources of the living. Concerned that the moving of burial spaces to the outskirts of cities (to be at a distance from the living) would be detrimental to business, early cemetery owners determined that to attract custom these new sites needed to be aesthetically pleasing, and thus the garden aesthetic of the cemetery was born.

This taxonomical mentality thus influenced the design of these new garden cemetery spaces, with a 'typology' of interments, memorials and biographies carefully planned to be placed and experienced as a journey through the beautiful, landscaped grounds of the cemetery. The idea of a journey through a landscape resonated strongly with the idea of journeying through a learned institution's collection. Thus, the idea of the cemetery as a collection emerged in line with – and a product of – a wider desire in the 19th century to 'collect the world' (Kelly, 2020). 'Collecting the world' in these new outside cemetery spaces now extended to 'collecting' the dead and became infused with well-networked individuals' interests in genealogy and heraldry, which had by this time filtered down from the upper to the civic middle classes (Litten, 1991). In 1837 this expanding interest led to a new formal system of recording births, deaths and marriages. Data gathering on the population became an increasing area of activity and was followed four years later by the first nationwide census in 1841.

These new, intensive processes of collecting and documenting information on the living (and the dead) required institutional-style management methods, rules and regulations – seen in the newly established cemeteries in Bristol, Glasgow and Sheffield, as well as in Liverpool, Manchester, Leeds and Newcastle. Rules, regulations and cemetery records needed implementing and policing – in other words, curating – and as a result, the emergent garden cemeteries were given their equivalent of museum curators in the form of superintendents and gardeners to manage the landscape (Marchant de Beaumont, 1828). Managing these spaces overall were the cemetery company directors, who were often found sitting on the boards of learned institutions and were instrumental in the decision-making for both spaces. Indeed, this was the case for Bowles Fripp (Bristol), Asline Ward (Sheffield) and Cleland (Glasgow).

The inside-out (and outside-in) of cemeteries and learned institutions

The Georgian and early Victorian provincial learned institution and garden cemetery thus shared founding principles and features. Their common roots were within contemporary civic 'networks of influence' and associated key figures. As noted earlier in this chapter, their founders intended both to be 'heterotypic' spaces – worlds that mirrored each other – bringing the lives of the living (and dead) into the learned institution and taking the inside of the museum out to new burial spaces to explore and expand previously segmented understandings of time and memory, presence and absence (Lord, 2006; Meyer and Woodthorpe, 2008; Johnson, 2012). Both were conceived as spaces to educate, reflect and progress.

While these comparable founding principles were admirable, in operational reality the collections of the dead within cemeteries often proved far less suitable for curation than the objects from their lives which inhabited the learned institutions. Within these spaces objects were relatively easy to curate; Henning refers to the museums of the 19th century as being full of 'glass coffins', housing the belongings of the dead (2006: 5). In contrast, the cemetery held the remains of deceased *people* (such as Samual Stutchbury, the Bristol Institution's first museum curator, who is buried in Arnos Vale Cemetery) and the ability to categorize deceased people via their lives and professions to create a coherent educative narrative through which to journey was less feasible. As it progressed, the garden cemetery thus became less methodical in its organization owing to the influence of personal choice and costs in burial location and memorial, practicalities relating to the act of burial itself, and the impact of, for example, epidemics or times of war.

Despite the varying degree of control in both sites, similar to how Foucault and Miskowiec saw museums and libraries (in the 19th century, learned institutions were both) as 'accumulating time indefinitely' (Prescott, 2008), the same may also be said of the new garden cemetery at this time. Like the learned institution, this novel burial space was designed to recreate the living landscape, becoming the 'other city' (Foucault and Miskowiec, 1986) with potential for learning journeys through its myriad of pathways, terraces, islands and areas of burials and memorials, and attempted to be broadly organized according to status, education and class. Moreover, the garden cemetery aesthetic and its content, such as monument display and memorialization, was deliberately intended to be performative. As part of an exhibit-like approach a strictly neoclassical/Greek Revival architectural aesthetic prevailed (Kselman, 1993; Tarlow, 2000; Mytum, 2004), with perhaps the most dramatic expression of this at Liverpool with its unashamedly Acropolis-like oratory chapel which overlooked the quarried-out site in the manner of an open-air museum park. In the 1980s, the Oratory became a museum containing funerary plaques and monuments – a contemporary example of the cemetery becoming the outside-in, and the museum becoming the inside-out of the cemetery. Garden cemeteries from this era can thus be interpreted as outdoor experiments as to what could be achieved with an external version of a learned society – recreating an antiquarian scene on a monumental scale. Operating as a supersizing of the dioramas, models and maquettes that were shown in learned institutions they provoked the question of how far this new approach to knowledge collection and curation could be taken in recreating life-size antiquarian scenes.

Moreover, this worked both ways. In a significant example the cemetery became a travelling and movable exhibit which could be brought inside a museum or gallery space. For instance, during the 1820s, architectural dioramas such as Bristol-based M. Choffin's model of Père Lachaise Cemetery toured the British provinces and were hosted by learned societies and gallery spaces (Dungavell, 2015). From the 1851 Great Exhibition, on a national level (Laqueur, 1993), to smaller local events such as that at the Bristol Royal West of England Academy in the same year (Udall, 2019), these portable, miniaturized landscapes educated the public and civic elites alike, showcasing, for example, a more aesthetically pleasing way to bury and memorialize. Approximately five years before it was published by Loudon (Udall, 2019) these miniaturized landscapes likely inspired Bristol nurseryman P. Masey Junior to create his template garden cemetery design, which would go on to influence the British garden cemetery aesthetic ideal (Penny, 1974; Curl, 1983). Masey's template was not intended to be used wholesale, with its elements to be selected and adapted to suit each setting (*Gardener's Magazine*, 1836), as exemplified at Arnos Vale in his home city of Bristol. Importantly however, the Masey template created a highly organized open-air cemetery-cum-museum where the 'exhibits' (that is, the memorials) were categorized by profession or organizational affiliation. This attempt at organization and management was seen in early iterations of Bristol's Arnos Vale Cemetery's rules and regulations, which stipulated the placement of burials and appearance of monuments in specific locations. Ironically this stipulation hindered plot sales during the cemetery's early years, when most of the demand for interments proved to be from the unprofessioned and unaffiliated, children (due to generally high infant mortality rates), asylum patients and the working-class victims of cholera and typhoid epidemics.

The challenge for cemetery directors and staff at Liverpool and elsewhere was to reconcile the clash between this 'beautifying' aesthetic (Kselman, 1993; Tarlow, 2000; Mytum, 2004), and educative ideal, derived from the learned institution on the one hand, and the practicalities of running a cemetery on the other. In particular, what were regarded as aesthetically disruptive objects and activities in the cemetery – such as crematoria ovens (later), staff movements and the transport of coffins – had to be kept out of public sight. Innovative solutions were found to do so, including an underground tunnel between the two lodges at Arnos Vale, for example, along with a concealed underground crematorium. Such efforts to obscure these components of the cemetery were intended to keep the aesthetically pleasing 'front stage' exhibit-esque landscape of the cemetery separate and distinct from the 'backstage' of its function to dispose of bodies. This backstage required a lot of toing and froing of staff, alongside the movement of equipment such as funeral biers for transporting coffins to chapels and in and out of hearses, and risked the sight of a cremation furnace or catafalque machinery – things that disrupted the 'theatre' of the funeral (Udall, 2019).

Another ideal which experienced disruption when the inside-museum was taken outside to the cemetery was that of a civic institution as an apolitical, agnostic space. Wilson (1998) discusses how 'for the urban male middle classes, cultural societies, in particular … played an important role in helping to forge a sense of class solidarity amongst urban elites, otherwise sharply divided by their religious and political convictions' (Wilson, 1998: 55–80). Local press coverage promoted newly established cemeteries as being egalitarian and intended for all – for example, with their inclusion of consecrated and unconsecrated sections. However, the practical reality was more complicated, with – for example – Arnos Vale effectively excluding working-class visitors by initially charging for admittance on Sundays, a measure which attracted complaints in the *Bristol Mercury* (Udall, 2019). Across the country elsewhere, many newly established cemetery companies had strict rules about which monuments could be erected within their sites, and there was also much guidance about personal conduct in the cemetery – what one could not do, such as walking a pram through or playing ball games. The extent to which these rules were enforceable was debatable. Thus, in practice, the translation of the egalitarian principle from the controlled indoor spaces of the learned institution to the outdoor cemetery space could be difficult.

Conclusion

This chapter has shown how the Georgian and Victorian garden cemeteries that emerged across Britain during the 18th and 19th centuries were intended to extend the scientific and educational functions of learned institutions. In parallel with public lectures provided for the working classes (via the hosting of them in new learned institutions), a walk through these sites was intended to educate the visitor on the emerging disciplines of architecture, history, natural history, geology and botany. In sites such as Arnos Vale in Bristol visitors could journey through the ascending classical orders (Udall, 2019), from Doric-style gate lodges and an Iconic-columned Nonconformist chapel to a Corinthian-capped Italianate Anglican chapel. Indeed, the cemetery was deliberately designed to evoke the comparable learned institution of the same time, with curved amphitheatrical terraces recalling the 19th-century surgeon's lecture hall.

In establishing the origins of cemeteries in this era, historians to date have emphasized the individual role and impact of Loudon in the creation of the British garden cemetery aesthetic. However, this chapter has shown that Loudon was only one person within a 'network of influence' of multiple actors across Britain at this time. Key influential figures and the learned institutions to which they were affiliated functioned as a network for individuals to meet, share and develop their antiquarian and scientific values and interests. Borne of an interest in collecting and documenting life (and death) it was in this sharing that an ideal of the garden cemetery emerged, of these new burial sites (and later, cremation) as the 'inside-out' of the learned institution, writ upon the suburban landscape in monumental scale. In so doing, a type of experimental archaeology could be achieved in seeing whether architectural templates and illustrations from ancient architecture found in learned institutions' records could be replicated architecturally.

Fittingly, many of these individuals, including Bowles Fripp at Arnos Vale in 1849, are now buried in the cemeteries they helped to create. During their lifetimes, however, operational pressures and priorities meant that the process of institutional reproduction from the learned institution to the garden cemetery, the inside to the outside, was not always straightforward in practice. While learned institutions could be managed in an ordered way and their purpose was clear (an intention to educate) this was not the case for the novel and emergent cemetery, which was serving multiple functions. Moreover, learned institutions curators had a high degree of control over what was entering their sites and how objects were interpreted and presented, and there was less ability to exercise this degree of control in a cemetery.

Nonetheless, the commonality between learned institutions and cemeteries is that they were there to both inform and reform: accessible in providing an education to all, functioning as heterotopic spaces merging multiple functions and times together. Garden cemeteries were intended to provide an outdoor version of these emergent intellectual institutions, accumulating a comparable collection and social history to be perused by visitors. Given these similarities (and differences) in terms of their origin the garden cemetery may best be described as an unusual cousin, rather than a sibling, of the 19th-century learned institution.

References

Brake, L. and Demoor, M. (2009) *Dictionary of Nineteenth-Century Journalism in Great Britain*. London: Academia Press.

Chadwick, E. (1842) *Report to Her Majesty's Principal Secretary of State for the Home Department from the Poor Law Commissioners, on an inquiry the Sanitary Conditions of the Labouring Population of Great Britain*. London: W. Clowes and Sons.

Curl, J.S. (1975) 'The architecture and planning of the nineteenth-century cemetery', *Garden History*, 3(3): 13–41.

Curl, J.S. (1980) *Death and Architecture*. Stroud: Sutton Publishing.

Curl, J.S. (1983, Autumn) 'John Claudius Loudon and the garden cemetery movement', *Garden History*, 11(2): 133–156.

Curl, J.S. (2000) *The Victorian Celebration of Death*. Stroud: Sutton Publishing.

Curl, J.S. (2019) *On the Laying Out, Planting and Management of Cemeteries and on the Improvement of Churchyards*. Holywood, County Down, Northern Ireland: Nerfl Press.

'Design for a cemetery to be formed at Bristol by Mr P.Masey Jun', *Gardener's Magazine, Vol 2* (1836), pp 341–347.

Dungavell, I. (2015) 'On the model of Père Lachaise', paper presented at The Cemetery Research Group Colloquium, University of York.

Foucault, M. and Miskowiec, J. (1986) 'Of other spaces', *Diacritics*, 1(16): 22–27.

Henning, M. (2006) *Museums, Media and Cultural Theory*. Maidenhead: Open University Press.

Johnson, P. (2012) 'The cemetery: a highly heterotopian place'. Available at: www.berfrois.com [accessed 12 January 2024].

Kelly, J.M. (2020) 'The reception of Greek architecture in eighteenth century Britain', in Miles, M. (ed) *A Companion to Greek Architecture*. Hoboken, NJ: Wiley Blackwell, pp 509–525.

Klancher, J. (2022) 'Lecturing networks and cultural institutions 1740–1830', in Mee, J. and Sangster, M. (eds) *Institutions of Literature 1700–1900: The Development of Literary and Cultural Production*. Cambridge: Cambridge University Press, pp 135–156.

Kselman, T.A. (1993) *Death and the Afterlife in Modern France*. Princeton: Princeton University Press.

Laqueur, T. (1993) 'Cemeteries, religion and the culture of capitalism', in Garnett, J. and Matthew, C. (eds) *Revival & Religion Since 1700: Essays for John Walsh*. London: Hambledon Press, pp 183–200.

Litten, J. (1991) *The English Way of Death: The Common Funeral Since 1450*. London: Robert Hale Publishing.

Lord, B. (2006) 'Foucault's museum: difference, representation, and genealogy', *Museum and Society*, March: 1–14.

Lowenthal, D. (1985) *The Past is a Foreign Country*. Cambridge: Cambridge University Press.

Marchant de Beaumont, F.-M. (1828) *Transactions of the Massachusetts Horticultural Society 1833*. Printed by J.T. Buckingham in Boston, USA.

Mee, J. (2023) *Networks of Improvement: Literature Bodies and Machines in the Industrial Revolution*. Chicago: Chicago University Press.

Meyer, M. and Woodthorpe, K. (2008) 'The material presence of absence: a dialogue between museums and cemeteries', *Sociological Research Online*, 13(5): 127–135.

Mytum, H. (2004) *Mortuary Monuments and Burial Grounds of the Historic Period*. London: Kluwer Academic/Plenum Publishers.

Ní Éigeartaigh, A. (2021) *The Graveyard in Literature: Liminality and Social Critique*. Cambridge: Cambridge Scholars Publishing.

Penny, N.B. (1974) 'The commercial garden necropolis of the early nineteenth century and its critics', *Garden History*, 2(3): 61–76.

Prescott, A. (2008) 'The textuality of the archive', in Craven, L. (ed) *What Are Archives? Cultural and Theoretical Perspectives: A Reader*. Aldershot: Ashgate, pp 32–50.

Rugg, J. (1992) *The Rise of Cemetery Companies in Britain 1820–1853*. Doctoral thesis, University of Stirling.

Rugg, J. (1997) 'The origins and progress of cemetery establishment in Britain', in Jupp, P. and Howarth, G. (eds) *The Changing Face of Death: Historical Accounts of Death and Disposal*. London: St Martin's Press, pp 105–119.

Ruston, S. (2021) *The Science of Life and Death in Frankenstein*. Oxford: Bodleian Library Publishing.

Saumarez-Smith, C. (1998) 'Museum as memory bank', *Prospect Magazine*. Monthly Arts & Culture Magazine produced in London. Viewable online [accessed 10 October 2023].

Scott, R. (2005) *The Cemetery and the City: The Origins of the Glasgow Necropolis 1825–1857*. Doctoral thesis, University of Glasgow.

Simo, M. (1988) *Loudon and the Landscape: From Country Seat to Metropolis 1783–1843*. New Haven, CT: Yale University Press.

Tarlow, S. (2000) 'Landscapes of memory: the nineteenth-century garden cemetery', *European Journal of Archaeology*, 3(2): 217–239.

Udall, L. (2019) *The Life of a Cemetery: Arnos Vale, South Bristol*. Doctoral thesis, University of Bristol.

Wilson, A. (1998) 'The cultural identity of Liverpool 1790–1850: the early learned societies', *Transactions of the Historic Society of Lancashire and Cheshire*, 147: 55–80.

9

'They Attached No Blame to the Staff in Charge': The Role of Dublin Workhouse Administration in Preventing and Contributing to Institutional Mortality, 1872–1913

Shelby Zimmerman

Introduction

In the early morning on 22 January 1913, Ellen Walsh, a 55-year-old workhouse inmate with epilepsy, got out of her bed in the South Dublin Union (SDU) workhouse's lunatic department and fell on the hot-water pipes.[1] Anne Connolly, an untrained inmate night attendant, assisted Walsh back into bed. In the morning, a ward attendant dressed Walsh and noticed extensive burns on her body. Despite receiving medical attention, Walsh died from shocks following her burns on 2 February in the lunatic department (*Evening Herald*, 1913b: 6; National Archives of Ireland, 1913c: 136). During the coroner's inquest into the cause of her death, one of her sons interjected that his mother's death 'occurred in such a manner showed that the institution was mismanaged' (*Evening Herald*, 1913b). Dublin City Coroner, Dr Louis A. Byrne, declared that the jurors 'attached no blame to the staff in charge' (National Archives of Ireland, 1913c: 172). The coroner's jury issued a telling verdict into Walsh's death by absolving the workhouse's medical officers and nursing staff of liability with regard to the death. In late 19th and early 20th-century Ireland, coroner's inquests rarely held administrators and staff accountable for institutional deaths (Clark, 2010; Breathnach, 2022). Although workhouse administrators and officials avoided legal responsibility, in practice their decisions indirectly influenced the institution's mortality rate.

Using the SDU as a case study, this chapter will examine the ways that workhouse administrators and officials contributed to mortality in periods of normal operation, and how these ways contrasted with their attitudes towards infectious disease. The historiography of Irish workhouses centres on the role of the institution during the Famine from 1845 to 1852. As the Irish workhouses were in their infancy during the Famine, the unprecedented high mortality rates and increased demand for admission put pressure on the nascent institution. This research contributes to our understanding of the post-Famine Irish workhouse by approaching the functioning of the workhouse during periods of normal operation, and by examining institutional deaths from causes other than infectious disease. Analysis of the post-Famine Irish workhouse during years without epidemics provides insight into the standard daily functioning of the workhouse and the administrators' priorities. This research focuses on 1913 since it was a standard year epidemiologically, despite the occurrence of significant labour disputes in Dublin in the latter half of the year. Public health reports recorded a decrease in Dublin City's death rate in 1913 with no significant disease outbreaks (Cameron, 1914). 1913 has also been chosen as a year from which a particular abundance of archival material has survived.

Although 99.3 per cent of deaths in the workhouse in 1913 were attributed to disease or old age, the SDU's Boards of Guardians and officials played a crucial role in shaping the institution's mortality rate (National Archives Ireland, 1913a). The Guardians' priorities and considerations shaped their influence on institutional mortality as their financially frugal measures benefited the ratepayers who funded the Poor Law Union. These perspectives influenced the daily administration of the workhouse, responses to infectious disease, and ultimately the inmates' lives.

The workhouse

In 1838, Parliament enacted the Irish Poor Relief Act to establish a national system of poor relief funded by local taxes (Gray, 2009). Based on the English New Poor Law of 1834, the workhouse functioned as the predominant institution for relief with conditions intentionally austere in order to serve as a deterrent for those seeking relief. Unlike its English counterpart, the Irish workhouse did not limit admission to those residing within the Poor Law Union's jurisdiction. Upon admission, inmates were either classified as 'able-bodied' or 'aged and infirm' while children were classified based upon their age. These classifications were reflective of the primary purpose of the workhouse as an institution for the administration of poor relief, in which classes referred to work capacity rather than health (Crowther, 1981; Driver,

1993; Gray, 2009; Crossman, 2013b). By the early 20th century, Ireland was divided into 163 Poor Law Unions. Dublin City encompassed two Poor Law Unions, the North and South Dublin Unions, with a workhouse on each side of the River Liffey. The SDU was one of the largest workhouses in the country with an average occupancy of 3,846 inmates in 1913 (National Archives Ireland, 1913c). The workhouse was a sprawling institution with distinct buildings for the various classifications that were divided along gender and religious lines. The workhouse had individual buildings for the infirmary, hospital and other medical spaces. The Guardians referred to the individual buildings as 'hospitals' and referenced individual units in the hospitals as 'wards'. They also used the term 'department' interchangeably to refer to the hospitals. The Guardians differentiated the medical facilities from the main workhouse, which indicated different activities, experiences and expectations for inhabitants of the medical departments as opposed to other workhouse buildings.

By the end of the 19th century, the workhouse was the predominant and most accessible medical institution for the Irish poor, with the sick and aged comprising the majority of the workhouse population. Crossman notes that on average, the sick and infirm comprised between one-half and two-thirds of the Irish workhouse population after 1870 (Crossman, 2013a). Legislative change in the latter half of the 19th century shaped the role of the Poor Law as a medical provider. Acts such as the Medical Charities (Ireland) Act of 1851 and the Poor Law Amendment Act of 1862 established a state-run medical network funded by the Poor Rates and removed destitution as criteria for medical admission (Mooney, 1887; Cassell, 1997; Geary, 2004; Lucey, 2015).

The changing status of the workhouse coincided with the professionalization of medicine and a greater understanding of epidemiology. Hospitals sought to establish themselves as curative institutions in the late 19th century, resulting in restrictive admission policies. Voluntary hospitals sequestered dying patients from the rest of the institution as death was perceived as failure on the part of the hospital and the attending medical practitioner (Clark, 2016). The notion of segregating the dying coincided with the medical profession classifying patients as suffering from either acute or chronic conditions. Hospital administration used chronic disease as a euphemism for 'incurable' and thus it functioned as a mechanism to deny admission to these types of patients to ensure beds were available for curable cases (Weisz, 2014). As a result, three institutions for the dying were founded in Dublin in the late 19th and early 20th centuries to provide a comfortable place where the terminally ill sick poor could die as an alternative to Dublin's crowded and unsanitary workhouses (O'Brien and Clark, 2005; Clark, 2016). However, the limited number of beds in these hospices and high demand resulted in prioritizing admission for moribund patients (Dublin Hospitals Commission,

1887; *Thom's Official Directory*, 1914). As a result, the workhouse was coerced into serving as an institution for chronic patients and the dying.

Despite the workhouse's status as a medical institution in post-Famine Ireland, the stigma of pauperism and the Famine lingered in public consciousness.[2] Workhouse hospital patients were still mandated to wear the uniform and comply with workhouse policies (Crossman, 2013a). Hospital patients were also registered in the same admission records as inmates in receipt of poor relief, thus indicating that although the sick comprised a separate category for inmate classification, they did not constitute a separate entity. Gilleard observes that as the workhouse's demographics changed in post-Famine Ireland, resulting in a higher percentage of aged and infirm inmates, the institution's reputation changed to a 'pitiable place for old men to go to before they died, rather than as the badge of shame that it had once been for illegitimate children, fallen women and unemployed workers' (Gilleard, 2017: 65). The stigma associated with workhouse admission and the institution's reputation was reflected in instances of individuals refusing to enter the workhouse. The reluctance to seek workhouse admission resulted in individuals dying without receiving medical attention. For instance, on 14 March 1886, 36-year-old Laurence Matthews died while being conveyed to the SDU workhouse. According to Matthews' sister, he had suffered from lung disease for the past year and refused to enter the workhouse for treatment. Matthews was brought to the workhouse when he was too weak to resist. At the coroner's inquest, his sister asserted that he 'would not allow himself to be brought into the workhouse, and said he would never die there' (*Weekly Irish Times*, 1886: 5). Considering that the Famine had ended in 1852, public consciousness remembered the horrors of the workhouses. For instance, in the 1930s Kathleen Burns recorded her grandfather's recollection of the Dunmanway Workhouse in County Cork burying the bodies of unclaimed inmates in mass pits during the Famine (Burns, 1938–1939). As a result, the workhouse's stigma hindered the institution from being perceived as a medical institution akin to the voluntary hospitals.

Workhouse administration

At the national level, the Local Government Board (LGB) oversaw the operation of the Poor Law, but the Boards of Guardians served as the local authority for the individual Poor Law Unions. The Board of Guardians was a professional administrative body elected from within the Poor Law Union's boundaries. The Guardians were responsible for employing and supervising workhouse officials, including the medical officers, while overseeing daily administration (Crossman, 2013b). Electoral reforms under the Local Government (Ireland) Act of 1898 made the Board of Guardians more representative of the local area by abolishing practices that benefited landlords, such as the appointment of *ex-officio* guardians and plural voting (Roche, 1982). In urban unions, merchants, manufacturers and individuals in the service industry were elected to the Board. In 1911, half of the SDU's Board of Guardians was comprised of individuals working in the service industry, including grocers, wine merchants, chemists and hairdressers (Cousins, 2011).

In 1913, the SDU Board of Guardians comprised 73 elected guardians and 25 co-opted members including medical officers, chaplains, relieving officers and the master (*Thom's Official Directory*, 1913). The Board of Guardians was under the leadership of John Scully, a Catholic grocer. The *Irish Worker*, a left-leaning newspaper associated with labour unions, chastised the Board of Guardians for being recruited from the upper and middle classes, who were likely to believe that poverty was a crime caused by moral degradation rather than economic circumstances. As the Guardians were detached from the realities of poverty, the paper accused them of being unsympathetic towards the inmates and ignorant of daily life in the workhouse ('Euchan', 1912).

In 1913, the SDU employed two resident and four visiting medical officers (*Thom's Official Directory*, 1913). The SDU's medical officers were just as qualified as their voluntary hospital counterparts. To be eligible to serve as a visiting medical officer, the Guardians decreed that the prospective candidate must have been licensed for at least five years, hold a medical degree or be a fellow of the Royal College of Surgeons in Ireland in addition to possessing at least one year of experience as a resident surgeon or physician in a general voluntary hospital (*An Claidheamh Soluis*, 1913a). Through these requirements, the Guardians sought to ensure that visiting medical officers would be sufficiently experienced and reliable to offer the best care and accurately diagnose a myriad of ailments while offering the same level of expertise as in a voluntary hospital. It also indicated to the public that workhouse inmates would receive a similar calibre of physicians as if they were admitted to a voluntary hospital.

As the workhouse system was funded by the Poor Rates, Guardians had to satisfy the ratepayers' interests, which were keeping costs down as much as possible. Writing under a pseudonym in the *Weekly Irish Times* in 1907, Jerry Cassidy asserted that 'the duties of a Poor Law Guardian are two-fold, to the poor, and to ratepayers, who support them' (Cassidy, 1907). For instance, in 1913, the Board of Works notified the SDU Board of Guardians that their request for a £5,500 loan to make improvements to the workhouse was denied because 'loans could not be made in view of the high rates prevailing in the Dublin area' (*Evening Herald*, 1913a). Due to existing high rates, the Guardians could not further raise the rates to finance the renovations (*Evening Herald*, 1913a). The ratepayers were conscious of the Guardians' spending and could request an audit of the accounts. John Bohan, a general labourer, attended the SDU Board of Guardians meeting on 28 January 1913 as a ratepayer to submit a written objection for the Local Government Auditor regarding the Guardians purchasing an organ for £15. As the organ was purchased from a Guardian's pawnshop and did not follow the protocol for purchasing an item over £10, Bohan requested an investigation into the manner (*Freeman's Journal*, 1913). Bohan's objection to the organ exemplifies the ratepayers' awareness of the Board's activities and willingness to challenge any improper spending. Additionally, the ratepayers elected the Guardians, so it was crucial for the Guardians to act on behalf of the ratepayers' interests in order to maintain their own power.

Contribution to mortality

The SDU administrators played a pivotal role in shaping the overall functioning of the institution. Decisions surrounding the daily administration of the workhouse indirectly contributed to institutional mortality by influencing the quality of care and level of sanitation. The Guardians' practices were motivated by satisfying the ratepayers by reducing expenditure rather than out of consideration for the inmates' health. As a result, these economic decisions put medically vulnerable inmates in a precarious situation.

Understaffing

Decisions regarding staffing levels and the competency of staff influenced the institution's mortality rate. In September 1895, Catherine Wood was commissioned by the *British Medical Journal* (*BMJ*) to inspect the conditions of several Irish workhouse infirmaries based on the Journal's assertion that the infirmaries were overlooked by the Guardians and in urgent need of reform. This inspection followed the *BMJ*'s investigation of provincial English workhouses, thus revealing these issues were not unique to Ireland. Wood visited the SDU's infirmary and noted a ratio of one trained nurse per 45–50 beds. In the evenings, there was one nurse stationed in the male and female wards respectively. Due to the dependence on pauper deputies, one or more attendant would be assigned to a ward in the evenings, thus placing the responsibility of nursing primarily in the hands of untrained inmates (*British Medical Journal*, 1895). Wood, who was former Lady Superintendent of London's Hospital for Sick Children and founder of the British Nurses' Association, advised the Board of Guardians to establish a training school for workhouse nurses and to increase the number of trained attendants in the infirm wards. Wood acknowledged the Guardians' reticence to implement reform for financial reasons and reassured them that 'from long experience in these matters, that, after the first outlay, the work would be done with greater economy and efficiency, and the South Dublin Union would take the position that belongs to it of right – that of the pioneer in the matter of workhouse reform' (*British Medical Journal*, 1895: 797). However, the SDU's Visiting Committee asserted that the *BMJ* purposely sought to find fault with the SDU, and had therefore exaggerated evidence that differed from the conditions of the wards. Guardian Joseph Mooney accused Wood of confusing the SDU with other workhouses she had inspected (*Evening Herald*, 1895). The *Freeman's Journal* concurred with the Guardians' dismissal of Wood's report as sensationalist and suggested that the Guardians should publicly correct any misstatements in order to protect the Guardians' dignity and the institution's reputation (*Freeman's Journal*, 1895). The Guardians thus adopted a defensive attitude towards the SDU administration and sought to discredit Wood as an inspector. The public discourse surrounding workhouse investigations demonstrated that ratepayers were cognizant of the management of the workhouse and could challenge the competency of the Guardians. Meanwhile the Guardians' efforts to delegitimize Wood's inspection indicated that the Guardians feared public criticism, which could result in them failing to be re-elected. As a result of the Guardians ignoring the recommendations, there were no improvements in either the staffing ratios nor in the competency of nurses and attendants.

Although the Local Government Act of 1898 prohibited workhouse inmates from serving as nurses and provided rigid classifications and delineated responsibilities for professional nurses, inmates were still able to serve as attendants with permission from the medical officer under a LGB order dated July 1901 (Birmingham, 1905). In 1913, the hospital buildings remained understaffed. The No.2 Hospital, for example, had an average occupancy of between 150 and 190 patients under the care of just two trained nurses during the day. The SDU employed 29 trained nurses including 19 Sisters of Mercy nurses (National Archives Ireland, 1913b). Poor Law Unions supported employing nuns as nurses, as they were inexpensive given the convent's charitable mission, and despite the LGB's failure to implement minimum training qualifications for nursing nuns (Clear, 1987). However, the SDU Guardians also continued to rely on inmate labour as a cost-effective measure to address staffing needs. By the time of LGB Inspector F.J. McCarthy's visit to the SDU in November 1913, there were 3,667 inmates in the institution. Of the total population, 716 individuals, or 19 per cent, were employed as inmate attendants. McCarthy observed that of the 159 men classified as 'able-bodied', around two-thirds of them were inmate attendants. Of the 716 inmate attendants, 415 were employed in a medical capacity, which included 258 serving in the hospital wards. Since the SDU did not maintain any register of inmate attendants, it is not possible to analyse the demographic profile, including previous occupations, which could demonstrate prior experiences of caregiving or service, of these attendants. What can however be deduced is that this use of inmate labour created a ratio of one day attendant for every seven patients and one night attendant for every 20 patients (National Archives Ireland, 1913b). Given the ratio of inmate attendants to professional nurses, patients were therefore more likely to be attended to by an unqualified inmate, especially in the evening.

The LGB authorized the Board of Guardians to hire as many qualified and trained nurses, in addition to attendants, as were deemed sufficient adequately to attend to all the patients in the medical department (Birmingham, 1905). By creating employment standards for ward attendants and a protocol for employing inmates, the LGB sought to minimize the presence of unqualified staff in medical wards and thus reduce the risk of death associated with the use of inmate labour. However, the use of inmate labour saved the Guardians money even though the maintenance of the inmates was at the expense of the ratepayers. In particular, rather than offer the inmate attendants a salary, they were compensated with a better diet than the standard able-bodied inmate, a lighter workload, and a weekly ration of tobacco (National Archives Ireland, 1913b). In contrast, the salary of a trained nurse and qualified nurse started at £52 and £45 annually plus accommodation (*An Claidheamh Soluis*, 1913b). Pointing to the in-kind nature of the incentives provided to pauper attendants, McCarthy accused the SDU Guardians and officials of encouraging these men to remain in the workhouse and receive special privileges rather than seeking external employment (National Archives Ireland, 1913b). For the Guardians, meanwhile, it was cheaper to provide extra rations to inmate attendants rather than pay and accommodate qualified individuals. The lack of restrictions on the number of employees indicated that understaffing was not inherent to the workhouse system and that Guardians were authorized to rectify the issue. However, the Guardians had to consider the impact of hiring staff on the rates, which ultimately influenced their staffing decisions.

One of the crucial duties of the workhouse nurse involved notifying the master whenever a patient's changing condition required the services of the medical officer (Departmental Committee on Workhouse Nursing, 1902). Without medical training, however, inmate attendants were unaware of various symptoms and unable to ascertain whether the medical officer should be summoned. Despite the LGB's authorization to hire trained nurses and Wood's recommendation of establishing a nursing training school at the workhouse, the Guardians' continued reliance on inmate labour therefore contributed to institutional mortality. In the aforementioned case of Ellen Walsh on 2 February 1913, the inmate attendant Anne Connolly did not recognize the severity of Walsh's burns, thus depriving her of receiving immediate care. Arguably the outcome probably would have been different had professional nurses staffed the ward instead. Nurse Margaret Hare expressed dissatisfaction in her correspondence with Visiting Medical Officer Dr Lewis Farrell regarding the staffing levels in the lunatic department and noted that 'I have been left without a night-attendant on that ward and on different other nights as well one woman is not sufficient to mind 40 refractory patients at night and this night attendant Anne Connolly has given me no satisfaction this long time' (National Archives of Ireland, 1913c: 137). Hare's comments demonstrate how the Board of Guardians' reluctance to hire qualified nurses in order to reduce the financial burden on the ratepayer resulted in overworked nurses relying upon untrained pauper attendants to monitor the wards. This institutional mismanagement in turn resulted, as exemplified by Walsh's case, in increased mortality within the workhouse.

Pigs and health

The inmates' health, and thus the likelihood of their deaths, was also jeopardized by the Guardians' economic endeavours. By the end of the 19th century, the medical profession and public health authorities were cognizant of the impact of the built and physical environment on health. In February 1913, the SDU Board of Guardians appointed a committee to investigate the Union's keeping of pigs on workhouse property for financial gain (National Archives of Ireland, 1913c). Raising pigs was considered a financially lucrative investment, in which the owner could expect a return of over 100 per cent of the piglet's original price (Adelman, 2020). There was no indication of how the profits were utilized or if they were reinvested into the workhouse. However, pigs were widely considered to be a public health nuisance. In the post-Famine period, Dublin Corporation and public health officials sought to remove animal waste from the city and to restrict manure yards to stables and dairies (Adelman, 2020). The SDU's piggery contained 134 pigs and thus produced extensive quantities of manure. As the piggery was located near the crèche, garden infirmary, and other hospital buildings, Guardian John Byrne argued that it was hazardous to children and the sick because they had weakened immune systems, so were more vulnerable to infectious disease. According to Byrne:

> There are always great complaints about the very heavy death rate of Children in the Crèche … there are over 4,000 people in the Union, and there is a great deal of sickness and deaths which the Piggery may be the cause of. There cannot be any doubt but that it must be unhealthy to the Hospitals and the other buildings around. (National Archives Ireland, 1913c: 243)

Byrne also cautioned the Guardians against supplying the piggery with food refuse and offal derived from the consumptive, skin disease, and other medical wards (National Archives Ireland, 1913c). Dublin Corporation's influential public health analyst, Sir Charles Cameron, believed consuming diseased meat resulted in sickness (Adelman, 2020). Therefore, Byrne approached the keeping of pigs as a public health concern, in which the public would be at risk from consuming diseased pork. Although there was no direct evidence of SDU inmates dying specifically because of exposure to the piggery, it was argued that the unsanitary conditions of the piggery would hinder overall health of the human inmates and therefore increase their risk of disease.

Furthermore, due to the profits generated by the pigs, the Guardians placed a greater emphasis on their wellbeing than the inmates. Figure 9.1, from the satirical *Leprechaun Cartoon Monthly* in 1912, depicts fat pigs consuming a lavish meal in the workhouse's dining hall while a tattered inmate eats a bone. Thus, the artist accused the Guardians of prioritizing the pigs over the inmates while informing the public of issues impacting inmates. In his investigation into the SDU piggery as a member of the Board's appointed committee, Byrne estimated that £1,200 (£93,806.64 today) was spent annually on feeding the pigs (National Archives of Ireland, 1913c; National Archives UK, nd). The *Irish Worker* asserted from its separate but concurrent investigation into the same subject that milk was given to the pigs and hungry inmates stole food from the piggery. In response, LGB Inspector McCarthy recommended that a railing should be installed outside the piggery to prevent access. The *Irish Worker* was highly critical of the Guardians' priorities and lack of support from the LGB and proclaimed that it was 'better to be a pig than a pauper in the Scully-controlled institution' (*Irish Worker*, 1913).

This statement appeared to be confirmed in a letter to the editor of the *Irish Worker* from September 1911 allegedly written by inmate 'Clare O'Brien' of the SDU's Female Infirmary Department on behalf of her fellow patients to describe how inmates suffered at the hands of the frugal Guardians.[3] According to O'Brien, the sick were served adulterated milk, which was milk diluted with water or sugar, as it was cheaper than pure milk. Since the milk contractor had friends on the Board, he or she was not prosecuted for violating the relevant public health mandates. O'Brien recalled being served half boiled and decaying cabbage resulting in the women complaining of diarrhoea. She directly accused the Guardians of prioritizing the ratepayers by stating:

> The Guardians, many of whom are supposed to be elected in the interest of the poor, know all this; they know the food we are getting, and they are not making an effort on our behalf. It would appear that the majority of the present Board of Guardians were elected for the purpose of putting down the rates. No doubt, they are doing it with a vengeance; but we are hungry. (O'Brien, 1911)

The fact that O'Brien specifically referenced the rates, and the fact that the Guardians were elected to keep these low, demonstrated that the inmates were cognizant of the Guardians' priorities. It also indicates that the inmates

Figure 9.1: 'Dives and Lazarus. It has been reported recently that in one of our Unions, the pigs were better fed and looked after than the paupers.'

DIVES AND LAZARUS.

It has been reported recently that in one of our Unions, the pigs were better fed and looked after than the paupers.

Source: S.H.Y. (1912); Dublin and Irish Collections, reproduced with the permission of the Dublin City Library and Archive

knew the quality of provisions and care in the workhouse, and therefore their health and lives, was dependent on institutional priorities determined by the Guardians.

Control of infectious disease

Within the institutional bounds of the workhouse, the Guardians adopted proactive measures to identify cases of infectious disease and deter its spread throughout the institution, thus seeking to reduce the mortality associated with disease. However, the proactivity merely reflected the Guardians' desire to avoid the financial costs associated with an epidemic while ensuring contagion did not permeate through society, rather than a genuine concern towards the inmates. Their attitudes towards infectious disease thus emphasized protecting society from outbreaks by swiftly identifying, isolating and treating any potential source of contagion.

Response to infectious disease

The Guardians sought to isolate infectious patients by erecting auxiliary wards. The workhouse was therefore prepared to accommodate infectious patients during periods of crisis, rather than transfer them to dedicated fever hospitals to increase the city's hospital provisions. In response to smallpox outbreaks during the 1870s, the SDU Guardians established the Kilmainham Auxiliary on the rear side of the property to function as a smallpox hospital. The wooden sheds could easily be built during epidemics and subsequently razed when the risk of contagion waned. The Kilmainham Auxiliary was located far from the able-bodied wards and other medical wards. The Guardians relied upon these auxiliary sheds to isolate infectious patients and to relieve the overcrowded fever hospitals. During the smallpox epidemic of 1871 to 1873, the Kilmainham Auxiliary furthermore employed a separate staff of medical officers and nurses in order to prevent the transfer of smallpox into the main infirmary buildings. They also prohibited visitors from entering the sheds, in order to further curb the spread of infection (National Archives of Ireland, 1871, 1872). During suspected epidemics, the LGB mandated the Boards of Guardians to make provision for medical aid and hospital accommodation for individuals suffering from the infectious disease. In February 1897, Dublin experienced an outbreak of smallpox and measles. The LGB commanded the SDU Guardians to erect a hospital that would treat sick and convalescent measles patients from both the North and South Dublin Unions. As the sheds were utilized by both Unions, each Board of Guardians was responsible for paying half of the costs (Local Government Board Annual Report, 1897). Part of the reason this responsibility of hosting the sheds fell upon the SDU was based on the availability of space, as the

North Dublin Union was located next to the House of Industry hospitals and the Richmond District Lunatic Asylum in a more congested district. Using the workhouse ambulances, the Guardians arranged for the transfer of measles and convalescent measles patients from the Cork Street Fever Hospital to the Kilmainham Auxiliary (*Irish Daily Independent*, 1897). This collaboration between the Cork Street Fever Hospital and the SDU enabled the fever hospital to make the beds occupied by convalescent patients available to new cases, while demonstrating the SDU's intent to prevent the spread of contagion to the workhouse and city.

Transferring inmates

The workhouse officials also prevented institutional mortality by partnering with other medical institutions in order to ensure inmates received proper care. Guardians transferred infectious patients to fever hospitals. For instance, although the workhouses were legally mandated to transfer all fever patients to an appropriate institution, workhouse officials also paid to transfer inmates to specialist institutions if necessary. As these institutions were exclusively reserved for fever and infectious disease cases, they were better equipped than the workhouse hospitals to treat and segregate infectious patients outside periods of crisis. Workhouse sheds only functioned as isolation wards when epidemics put pressure on fever hospitals. In 1885, the SDU entered an agreement with the nearby Cork Street Fever Hospital regarding the admission of workhouse inmates, devising a daily fixed rate of two shillings per inmate depending on the number of total patients at Cork Street (Dublin Hospitals Commission, 1887). In his testimony to the Dublin Hospitals Commission in 1887, North Dublin Union physician, Dr Joseph E. Kenny, reiterated that workhouses were equipped to perform amputations and other routine surgical operations. He advocated for the expansion of specialist medical departments in the workhouse to be of further assistance to the poor (Dublin Hospitals Commission, 1887). By providing medical services that were considered on par with the general hospitals, the workhouse demonstrated its legitimacy as a medical institution. However, if an inmate required treatment that was outside the scope of the workhouse infirmary's capabilities, the union would pay for them to receive treatment at another institution (Crossman, 2013b). For instance, the SDU Guardians approved Dr Dunne's request for a child to be sent to the Orthopaedic Hospital for treatment, as it was not an appropriate case for the workhouse infirmary (National Archives Ireland, 1913c). Guardians also sent inmates to general hospitals such as Sir Patrick Dun's Hospital and the Meath Hospital if necessary. Guardians also transferred inmates to the Richmond District Lunatic Asylum if they were perceived as unruly or would benefit from being in an asylum. As the medical and ward staff in the workhouse lunatic department were not trained in managing and treating lunacy, the workhouse was unsuitable for severe cases of mental illness (*British Medical Journal*, 1895). The transfer and covering the cost of maintenance indicated that the workhouse actively sought to prevent mortality by ensuring inmates received adequate medical attention. For the parsimonious Boards of Guardians, covering the cost of treatment at a specialist hospital would have been cheaper than employing a specialist visiting medical officer. Since the average length of stay in the Meath Hospital, for instance, was 33 days, the cost of paying two shillings per inmate daily would have been cheaper than hiring specialist staff and equipment (*Annual Report of the Meath Hospital*, 1914). Considering that the average weekly cost per inmate in the SDU in 1913 was four shillings, nine pence, sending inmates to specialist institutions would have reduced the burden on the ratepayers by potentially curing a sick pauper and thus preventing the need for long-term workhouse admission and a subsequent death in the workhouse (LGB Annual Report, 1914).

Conclusion

The Board of Guardians and officials' priorities and consideration for the ratepayers shaped the nature and extent of institutional mortality within Dublin's workhouses during this period. The Guardians' financially frugal measures benefited the ratepayers, as they were the group that elected the Guardians and held them accountable. Workhouse administration adopted proactive measures to reduce institutional mortality when it was seen as beneficial to the ratepayers. Guardians were the most pre-emptive regarding their treatment of infectious disease. By rapidly isolating contagious patients or paying to transfer inmates to fever hospitals, the Guardians avoided the costs of erecting auxiliary wards for infectious patients and closing wards for sanitation. This approach saved ratepayers money by preventing the expenses associated with the construction, maintenance and staffing of the auxiliary wards. Additionally, the Guardians were able to protect the community from disease outbreaks by swiftly transferring infectious patients, identifying the source of infection, and creating makeshift infectious disease wards if or when necessary.

However, workhouse officials and administration contributed to institutional mortality when an issue, such as the staffing of medical wards with unqualified inmate attendants, was inconsequential to the ratepayers or would diminish the public's trust in the institution. The Guardians fervently sought to discredit the *BMJ*'s investigation of the SDU and rejected all suggested reforms in order to maintain the impression of the workhouse as a reputable and well-managed institution.

By making the workhouse the default institution for Dublin's sick and dying poor, the Guardians' priorities of satisfying the ratepayers' interests and reducing expenditure influenced the health and wellbeing of this vulnerable group. The workhouse was initially designed to administer poor relief rather than function as a hospital, so was unequipped for this group of inmates. As a result, the inmates were caught between the Guardians' conflict of protecting the institution's reputation and securing good standards of care. Although the workhouse system was abolished in the 1920s, the issues raised in this chapter are still pertinent in modern institutions. The treatment of the SDU inmates by the Guardians poses questions into the provision of medical care for the poor and other marginalized groups. It probes further inquiry into the health of occupants residing in nonmedical institutions. Foucault posited that medicalization resulted in physicians observing the patient in relation to symptoms, thus ignoring the patient's identity and individuality (Foucault, 2003). This depersonalization contributed to the commodification of the bodies of the poor as they were exploited to benefit the medical profession. Richardson noted that the demand for organ donation in Britain in the late 1990s resulted in physicians harvesting organs from the deceased without the family's consent (Richardson, 2001). These arguments were similar to practices in the SDU, in which the depersonalization of working-class inmates facilitated the Guardians in making decisions that benefited ratepayers.

Notes

[1] In order to maintain historic authenticity, the original terms utilized by the Irish Poor Law in describing workhouse wards, occupants and administration will be used throughout the chapter.

[2] During the Famine, the workhouses were overcrowded and associated with high mortality rates. For an overview of the experience of workhouse inmates during the Famine, consult Póirtéir (1992), Kinealy (1997) and Guinnane and Ó Gráda (2002).

[3] There was no archival evidence surrounding O'Brien's existence, thus questioning whether the woman created a pseudonym to avoid retaliation or if it was written by the *Irish Worker* (National Archives of Ireland, 1911).

References

Adelman, J. (2020) *Civilised by Beasts: Animals and Urban Change in Nineteenth-Century Dublin.* Manchester: Manchester University Press.

An Claidheamh Soluis (1913a), 'South Dublin Union. Election of a Visiting Medical Officer,' 14 June 1913, p 10.

An Claidheamh Soluis (1913b) 'South Dublin Union. Election of a Nurse,' 31 May 1913, p 10.

Annual Report of the Meath Hospital and County Dublin Infirmary, Heytesbury Street, Dublin, for the Year ended March 31st, 1914. One Hundred and Sixtieth Year (1914) Dublin: George F. Healy and Co.

Birmingham, C.L. (1905) *Handbook of Irish Sanitary Law Together with Abstracts of the Various Statutes, Orders and Regulations Affecting the Administration of Workhouse Infirmaries and Poor Law Dispensary Districts also Appendix and Comprehensive Index.* Dublin: Browne and Nolan, Limited.

Breathnach, C. (2022) *Ordinary Lives, Death, and Social Class: Dublin City Coroner's Court, 1876–1902*. Oxford: Oxford University Press.

British Medical Journal (1895) 'Reports on the nursing and administration of Irish workhouses and infirmaries. I. South Dublin Union', 2(1813): 795–797.

Burns, K. (1938–1939) 'Bad times', *Cill na dTor, Dún Mánmhaí*, The Schools' Collection, volume 0305, National Folklore Collection, University College Dublin, pp 129–130.

Cameron, C.A. (1914) *Report Upon the State of Public Health and the Sanitary Work Performed in Dublin During the Year 1913*. Dublin: Sealy, Bryers, and Walker.

Cassell, R.D. (1997) *Medical Charities, Medical Politics: The Irish Dispensary System and the Poor Law, 1836–1872*. Suffolk: Boydell Press.

Cassidy, J. (1907) 'Food for the dissecting knife: how the anatomical schools are supplied with dead bodies', *Weekly Irish Times*, 13 April, p 16.

Clark, D. (2016) *To Comfort Always: A History of Palliative Medicine Since the Nineteenth Century*. Oxford: Oxford University Press.

Clark, M.J. (2010) 'General practice and coroners' practice: medico-legal work and the Irish medical profession, c. 1830–1890', in Cox, C. and Luddy, M. (eds) *Cultures of Care in Irish Medical History, 1750–1970*. Basingstoke: Palgrave Macmillan, pp 37–56.

Clear, C. (1987) *Nuns in Nineteenth-Century Ireland*. Dublin: Gill and Macmillan.

Cousins, M. (2011) *Poor Relief in Ireland, 1851–1914*. Bern: Peter Lang.

Crossman, V. (2013a) 'Workhouse medicine in Ireland: a preliminary analysis, 1850–1914', in Reinarz, J. and Schwarz, L. (eds) *Medicine in the Workhouse*. Rochester: University of Rochester Press, pp 123–139.

Crossman, V. (2013b) *Poverty and the Poor Law in Ireland, 1850–1914*. Liverpool: Liverpool University Press.

Crowther, M.A. (1981) *The Workhouse System 1834–1929: The History of an English Social Institution*. London: Batsford Academic and Educational

Departmental Committee on Workhouse Nursing (1902) *Minutes of Evidence Taken Before the Departmental Committee Appointed by the President of the Local Government Board to Enquire into the Nursing of the Sick Poor in Workhouses; Together with Appendix and Index to Evidence. Part II. Cd. 1367*. London: Wyman & Sons, Limited.

Driver, F. (1993) *Power and Pauperism: The Workhouse System*. Cambridge: Cambridge University Press.

Dublin Hospitals Commission (1887) *Report of the Committee of Inquiry, 1887, Together with Minutes of Evidence and Appendices*, 1 [C. 5042], H.C. 1887.

'Euchan' (1912) 'A pleasant Sunday afternoon: a visit to the South Dublin Union', *Irish Worker*, 16 November, p 1.

Evening Herald (1895) 'South Dublin Union', 3 October, p 3.

Evening Herald (1913a) 'Rates in Dublin area too high', 17 September, p 5.

Evening Herald (1913b) 'Old woman's death', 4 February, p 6.

Foucault, M. (2003) *The Birth of the Clinic: An Archaeology of Medical Perception.* Translated by A.M. Sheridan. Abingdon: Routledge.

Freeman's Journal (1895) 'The South Dublin Union', 4 October, p 4.

Freeman's Journal (1913) 'South Union audit: purchase of an organ', 29 January, p 4.

Geary, L.M. (2004) *Medicine and Charity in Ireland 1718–1851.* Dublin: University College Dublin Press.

Gilleard, C. (2017) *Old Age in Nineteenth-Century Ireland: Ageing Under the Union.* London: Palgrave Pilot.

Gray, P. (2009) *The Making of the Irish Poor Law, 1815–43.* Manchester: Manchester University Press.

Guinnane, T.W. and Ó Gráda, C. (2002) 'Mortality in the North Dublin Union during the Great Famine', *The Economic History Review,* 55(3): 487–506.

Irish Daily Independent (1897) 'South Dublin Union', 5 February, p 7.

Irish Worker (1913) 'More whitewashing', 24 May, p 2.

Kinealy, C. (1997) *A Death-Dealing Famine: The Great Hunger in Ireland.* London: Pluto Press.

Local Government Board (1897) *Annual Report, 25th Report Under 'The Local Government Board (Ireland) Act', 36 and 36 VIC c. 8599 with Appendices.* Dublin: Alexander Thom and Co.

Lucey, D.S. (2015) *The End of the Irish Poor Law? Welfare and Healthcare Reform in Revolutionary and Independent Ireland.* Manchester: Manchester University Press.

Mooney, T.A. (1887) *Compendium of the Irish Poor Law; And General Manual for Poor Law Guardians and Their Officers.* Dublin: Alex. Thom and Co.

National Archives of Ireland (1871) *South Dublin Union Poor Law Guardians' Minute Books.* Board of Guardians Minutes, BG/79/A/24, January 1871 – December 1871.

National Archives of Ireland (1872) *South Dublin Union Poor Law Guardians' Minute Books.* Board of Guardians Minutes, BG/79/A/25, January 1872 – December 1872.

National Archives of Ireland (1911) *South Dublin Union Poor Law Guardians' Minute Books.* Board of Guardians Minutes, BG/A69.

National Archives of Ireland (1913a) *South Dublin Union Deadhouse Records.* National Archives of Ireland, BG/79★2/1.

National Archives of Ireland (1913b) *South Dublin Union Poor Law Guardians' Minute Books.* Board of Guardians Minutes, BG/A74, July 1913 to December 1913.

National Archives of Ireland (1913c) *South Dublin Union Poor Law Guardians' Minute Books.* Board of Guardians Minutes, BG/A73, January 1913 to June 1913.

National Archives UK (nd) 'Currency converter: 1270–2017', *The National Archives*. Available at: www.nationalarchives.gov.uk/currency-converter/ [accessed 9 January 2024].

O'Brien, C. (1911) 'Correspondence', *Irish Worker*, 23 September, p 2.

O'Brien, T. and Clark, D. (2005) 'A national plan for palliative care: the Irish experience', in Ling, J. and O'Sioráin, L. (eds) *Palliative Care in Ireland*. Maidenhead: Open University Press, pp 3–18.

Póirtéir, C. (ed) (1992) *The Great Irish Famine*. Dublin: Mercier Press.

Richardson, R. (2001) *Death, Dissection, and the Destitute* (2nd edn). Chicago: University of Chicago Press.

Roche, D. (1982) *Local Government in Ireland*. Dublin: Institute of Public Administration.

S.H.Y. (1912) 'Dives and Lazarus', *Leprechaun Cartoon Monthly* (Dublin), p 179.

Thom's Official Directory of the United Kingdom of Great Britain and Ireland for the Year 1913 (1913) Dublin: Alexander Thom and Sons.

Thom's Official Directory of the United Kingdom of Great Britain and Ireland for the Year 1914 (1914) Dublin: Alexander Thom and Sons.

Weekly Irish Times (1886) 'The distress in Dublin,' 20 March, p 5.

Weisz, G. (2014) *Chronic Disease in the Twentieth Century: A History*. Baltimore: Johns Hopkins University Press.

10

Tenets and Tensions: A Critical Exploration of the Death Positive Movement

Anna Wilde

Introduction

The early decades of the 21st century have seen a flurry of organizations and activities aimed at encouraging death talk (Koksvik, 2020), such as death cafés, started in England in 2011 by Jon Underwood (Death Cafe, nd), and Death over Dinner, begun in 2014 in America by Michael Hebb (Hebb, 2018). Such initiatives began around the same time that *Ask a Mortician* presenter (and practising mortician) Caitlin Doughty started the Order of the Good Death and coined the term 'death positive' (Doughty, 2013). The creation of this term proved to be something of a watershed moment as, while other names had previously been used for social movements with similar ideologies, such as the Happy Death Movement (Lofland, 2019: 55) and the Death Awareness Movement (Walter, 2020: 112), the very incongruity of the idea of death being positive, plus Doughty's own striking image and persona on social media, were enough to capture the zeitgeist and raise awareness and popularity of death positivity, especially among a younger generation (Varghese, 2022).

Broadly speaking, death positivity asserts that within contemporary industrialized and post-material societies there exists a taboo when it comes to discussing death, leading to widespread death phobia and denial. The central purpose of the Movement is to demystify death and encourage openness and acceptance, and a key proponent of this ethos is the Order of the Good Death. The Order presents a particular viewpoint on death positivity, which – as this chapter will show – promotes a somewhat stylized version of death and dying; a version that perpetuates the view that death can be discreet and dignified, pain and fear-free. From interviews with those engaged with dying and bereaved people, who self-identify as 'death positive', it is uncertain whether such a version reflects reality, when so much of dying is outside of one's own control.

One thing is sure: the Order has been very successful in promoting death positivity and its message has spread globally, fostered by the parallel rise of social media, death cafés and people who call themselves 'death positive' (Leland, 2018). The question of whether it represents or reflects the views of the wider community and death positive supporters – what I call a wider Death Positive Movement – is examined in this chapter, supported by interviews held with 24 people who work with the dying, dead or bereaved. It explores the extent to which being 'death positive' means different things to different people, and whether these tally with the manifesto of the Order of the Good Death. In examining the principles of the Order, the chapter considers whether it is positioning itself as a 'new institution of death and dying' by seeking to replace what it considers to be established norms with its own agenda.

The Order of the Good Death and its tenets

Based in the United States, the Order of the Good Death is focused on promoting its belief that there is a better way to approach dying which encourages openness in planning for, talking about and acknowledging death (The Order of the Good Death nd a). The call for a more open discussion about death is advertised across all the Order's material, including the videos and books of Caitlin Doughty, its leader, all of which are highly successful. With over 1.9 million subscribers, Doughty's YouTube channel, *Ask a Mortician* (Doughty, nd), has viewing figures of between 125,000 and 3.5 million per video, and her three death-related books have been translated into a number of languages.

The Order has a manifesto that sets out a cultural and political agenda that critiques the way death is treated (especially in the United States) and wants to see change. The Order has eight tenets on its website, as follows:

- I believe that by hiding death and dying behind closed doors we do more harm than good to our society.
- I believe that the culture of silence around death should be broken through discussion, gatherings, art, innovation, and scholarship.
- I believe that talking about and engaging with my inevitable death is not morbid, but displays a natural curiosity about the human condition.
- I believe that the dead body is not dangerous, and that everyone should be empowered (should they wish to be) to be involved in care for their own dead.

147

- I believe that the laws that govern death, dying and end-of-life care should ensure that a person's wishes are honored, regardless of sexual, gender, racial or religious identity.
- I believe that my death should be handled in a way that does not do great harm to the environment.
- I believe that my family and friends should know my end-of-life wishes, and that I should have the necessary paperwork to back-up those wishes.
- I believe that my open, honest advocacy around death can make a difference, and can change culture. (The Order of the Good Death, nd a)

The Order further suggests that '[t]he way our society handles death and dying is broken in many ways' (The Order of the Good Death, nd b). Although the society referred to here is that of the United States and some of the statistics quoted are clearly specific to the United States, there is undoubtedly global reach and resonance for the Order, given Doughty's very high profile as an international author and motivational speaker, where the message of death positivity has travelled with her (Kelly, 2017).

The Order asserts that the ways in which death and dying are broken are as follows:

> Environmental – The modern funeral industry distances us from natural processes and poisons the earth.
>
> Financial – The $20 billion funeral industrial complex turns bereaved individuals' grief into corporate profits.
>
> Ritual – The technicians who vanish the dead behind closed doors can rob families of the experience of mourning.
>
> Access – The ability to obtain a good death differs drastically across race, gender, and socioeconomic lines. (The Order of the Good Death, nd b)

To substantiate the first point, environmental concerns, the Order points to the funeral industry performing what the Order sees as environmentally damaging procedures, such as the embalming of corpses, the waste produced in manufacturing elaborate caskets which are then buried, and by the harmful emissions created by cremation (The Order of the Good Death, nd d). In response, it promotes greener alternatives such as natural burial, resomation (often termed 'water cremation') and human composting. To the second point, financial, the Order highlights the costs of death and dying: 'Turning death into a financial transaction leads to "care" that is profit-centered rather than human-centered, with the corpse itself becoming a commodity' (The Order of the Good Death, nd b). Speaking to the third point, ritual, the Order suggests that home deathcare and simpler funerals, without expensive caskets or procedures, should replace situations where funeral directors 'ha[ve] robbed the family of valuable hands-on engagement and ritual' (The

Order of the Good Death, nd b). Finally, the issue of access to a 'good death' lies at the heart of the Order's message, whereby it asks 'How do we even begin to tackle the good death when we live in a culture that hides our dead behind closed doors and insists that speaking openly about death makes you morbid?' (The Order of the Good Death, nd b). The answer to this rhetorical question lies in the eight tenets, or 'creed', which extrapolates the Order's view of the harm caused by these 'closed doors'.

Overall, the Order objects to the dominance of the traditional funeral industry (noted elsewhere by Walter, 2017), which it sees as wishing to control the aftermath of death and the associated post-mortem procedures. In terms of discourse and terminology, the emotive language used in the tenets and concerns such as 'the technicians who *vanish the dead* behind closed doors can *rob* families of the experience of mourning' (my emphasis) implies that these activities can happen *counter to* the wishes of the relatives and friends; the technicians do not merely remove and care for the dead, they make them disappear. Similarly, the words 'robbed' and 'rob' suggests that something that was once possessed – for example, 'the experience of mourning' – has, according to the Order, been knowingly taken away, and to the detriment of grieving friends and relatives. Such provocative language supports Koksvik's suggestion that '[a]s self-proclaimed revolutionaries, death-positive advocates often adopt a distinctly oppositional tone through which their activities are positioned not simply as worthwhile but as noble, possessing a moral high ground' (2020: 962). This is exemplified in the four concerns outlined earlier, which, when read in conjunction with the Order's tenets (all of which begin 'I believe …'), encourage the reader to view the Order's work as something of a crusade or mission, positioning the Order as an alternative source of authority on the 'better' way to die, and one that is rejecting the traditional pathways of post-mortem care. Doughty's career as a mortician, which means she is an insider within the deathcare industry, is vital here, bestowing on the Order her legitimacy and credibility, echoing Armstrong and Bernstein's suggestion that 'challengers are often members, customers, or clients of the institutions they challenge' (2008: 85). This insider knowledge of the deathcare industry confers upon Doughty considerable influence as the leader of the Order and of its foundation as a new social movement, with the funeral industry as one of its targets. The question is whether, in challenging the established and traditional institutions of deathcare (the enemy) the Order is becoming something of an institution itself (Lofland, 2019: 69) and what this represents, or even risks.

Methodology

It was my interest in the authority, position and promotion of the Order within the Death Positive Movement that led to the study on which this chapter draws. In exploring attitudes towards the movement, I interviewed 24 death practitioners (funerary celebrants, embalmers, mortuary technicians, death doulas and hospice chaplains) who worked with the dying, dead or recently bereaved. Twenty were female, two were non-binary and two were male, and their ages ranged from 30 to 65. The participants' countries of origin were Canada, the United States, Australia, the United Kingdom and Israel. They were recruited via social media and self-identified as being death positive, although use of the word 'positive' within 'death positive' was flagged as inappropriate by approximately a quarter of participants, who felt that it was insensitive towards the recently bereaved who might interpret it as pressure to feel positive when death had occurred.

Interviews were semi-structured, to allow participants to guide the conversation. They lasted on average for one hour and were undertaken via Zoom, with automated transcription which was then edited manually, and coded through thematic analysis (Braun and Clarke, 2022). Through the analysis I compared and contrasted the tenets of the Order as stated on its website (The Order of the Good Death, nd b) and a selection of videos from Doughty's YouTube channel (Doughty, nd), alongside participants' comments on what being death positive meant, how they practised it, and what they saw being promoted online. As will be explored next in this chapter, the interviews demonstrated that among this cohort, there was a wide variety of opinions as to what being 'death positive' means, and no consensus as to whether the Order's viewpoint represented the views of those involved in the care of the dying or promoting death positivity in general.

The research was given ethical approach by the University of Birmingham[1] and all participants gave informed, written consent for their inclusion in this study, with confidentiality assured. All participant notable features have been removed in this chapter to protect participants' identity.

The good death

As readers of this edited collection will likely know, there is a considerable literature available on what constitutes a good death, and what it means 'to die well'. Within the Order's tenets and webpages the overall message is that a good death should be discussed beforehand, with financial and other matters taken care of, and it should take place at home with the dying person surrounded by friends and family. Following the death, the body of the deceased might be kept at home, washed and dressed by those close to them, until the time comes for it to be moved to its final resting place. A method of environmentally friendly body disposal, such as human composting, alkaline hydrolysis (water cremation) or natural burial of the unembalmed corpse are all advised by the Order as death positive ways of dealing with the remains (The Order of the Good Death, nd a, nd b).

Although the Order promotes its own version of the 'good death' it is far from the first to consider a 'better' way to die. In scholarly literature, Cottrell and Duggleby (2016) have done one of the most comprehensive analyses of the good death to date, examining 39 publications on the good death released between 1992 and 2014. Their findings show these publications described perceptions of a good death to be very similar to that promoted by the Order:

> Though subtle variations exist, the Western revivalist good death ideal is expressed throughout the literature as a peaceful and dignified death, free from pain and other distressing physical symptoms. Death is timely. It occurs in old age and follows a predictable course. It occurs at home, with the dying individual surrounded by family members. The dying individual is aware of and accepts their impending death, has made appropriate legal and financial preparations, and, ideally, has planned their dying experience through an advance directive. (Cottrell and Duggleby, 2016: 687)

In their discussion, however, the authors also found that 'a strong cultural script for the dying, as well as for those who care for the dying ... created a certain socially sanctioned way to die or to care for the dying' (Cottrell and Duggleby, 2016: 688). Such pressure to die in a socially sanctioned way, they cautioned, could be problematic, not least because – similar to birth and the reality of a baby's delivery – death does not always fit a prescribed or desired blueprint. Not only that 'failing' to die in the 'right' way can create further problems, noted by participants, who pointed out that the idealized death can mean that even in dying, people are still expected to conform, to live up to *others'* expectations. As one participant commented:

> I also think it puts some pressure on people to have a good death like, a good death for who? I feel like it's for the people watching and witnessing. ... I know this isn't what it means, but this is what I hear. Like, can you die nicely? Like, so we can all have fond memories of how you sort of drifted away, and it was beautiful and stuff. ... And some people don't want to accept it, and don't, and just want to say that, you know what? Life's really unfair and horrible. Like, all the way to the end. (Participant 1)

Reflecting the unpredictability of dying it was recognized by the majority of participants that while all deaths were individual, the dying person did not always have either choice or control over what could or would happen: 'I think when we talk about the good death, it's, it's putting us too much into the future and, and into a hope of a reality that we have and trying to give ourselves control over something we have no control over' (Participant 2).

As noted already, the illusion of control over unpredictable life events is reflected in events at the other end of life and the relatively recent trend for birth plans. Developed in the 1980s, these plans are devised for the purpose of helping the pregnant person feel they are in control. However, as Bell et al (2022: 1) suggest, this sense of control comes via negotiation with the care providers (that is, the midwife or medical personnel) and that such 'institutionally designed birth plans do not necessarily expose women to all options, but only the institution's preferred choices, thus limiting women's ability to make fully informed decisions'. Given the lessons learned from birth plans and meeting institutional aims (alongside what happened with the withdrawal of the Liverpool Care Pathway in the UK [see Seymour and Clarke (2018)]), the Order's proposal for death plans which reflect its tenets needs to be cautioned. This was recognized by a participant who made the point that planning one's death hypothetically was very different to actually experiencing dying first-hand:

> I think it's a really individual thing, I think. What you might think of personally as a good death, it would differ from person to person. And, and I certainly think that as an element of maybe what you perceive to be a good death, when you then come to it, may be not as good as you thought. (Participant 3)

The value of a death plan is therefore subject to question, as contrary to the Order's suggestion of a plan being liberatory, it may function as something that is constricting; where and when the reality of unpredictable death intrudes on the ideal plan, wishes can be negated and abandoned, and feelings of failure can result. Such a sense of failure does not correspond neatly with the positivity inherent in the Death Positive Movement, nor the Order's tenets.

Talking and taboo

Although the name death positivity may have been coined by Doughty, it borrows from a number of other death movements, one of which is the Happy Death Movement, as discussed by Lofland in her classic book, *The Craft of Dying* (2019 [1978]). The Happy Death Movement had similar ideals to the Order, including the trope of taboo and denial – both of which form a large part of the ethos of the Order. Since the publication of *The Craft of Dying*, but especially over the last 10–15 years, the proliferation of death cafés, death positive libraries, online annual death festivals, such as Lifting the Lid and Good Grief Festival, and other death-related initiatives demonstrate that, in contrast to theories of death taboo or denial, there are many people worldwide who *do* wish to talk about death, even if they have not heard the term 'death positive' before. Participants in these events can be death workers such as death doulas, funeral celebrants and grief and bereavement specialists, hosts of death cafés and others involved in death education – but they may also be general laypeople, sharing their fears or coming to terms with grief and bereavement.

While such an exponential growth in death talk is encouraging, is talking about death always a good thing? And is talking even enough? In her critique of the Happy Death Movement, the emphasis on talking about death is described by Lofland as 'expressivity' (2019 [1978]: 87), where dying people are required to engage with their authentic feelings: 'It is important to stress, however, that expressivity calls not simply for talk but *for talk about one's varying emotional states, which talk "authentically" expresses those states.* Talk that is "mere" intellectualizing is proscribed' (Lofland, 2019 [1978]: 95).

This is a critical point: the difference between authentic emotional communication about dying and more intellectually driven talk, a point that has been raised by many prominent academics (see Kellehear, 1984; Walter, 1991; Jacobsen, 2020) who have argued that death denial and taboo is largely overstated by those who wish to perpetuate the idea for their own purposes. Writing over 30 years ago, Walter felt that 'the onus is on the tabooists to show that norms against talking of death in certain situations are specially and uniquely worthy of the label "taboo". This they have not done' (1991: 296) and it is not clear – at least from the perspective of the participants in this study – whether they have done so yet. To examine this further I asked interview participants if, in their experience, they thought that death taboo still existed in their own country, and approximately two-thirds thought that it did not. Those who worked predominantly with the elderly at end of life suggested that, if there was a reluctance to talk about death, it was mainly among older people:

And there are a lot of seniors, the traditionalist generation. Uh, many of whom find that impolite to talk about … you don't talk about death … so many social mores, and you know, even, even with a close family member, her adult children one day were [there], you know, while she was [dying], 'Mom, you know this, this person in our family has just died and it started us thinking about what your wishes might be' – [shocked intonation, speaking as Mom] 'Oh NO!' (Participant 4)

Others made the point that talking about and watching death-related TV programmes was one thing, but when it came down to discussing one's own death, it became more problematic:

It doesn't necessarily feel like the taboo is around the D words, like I know people still don't like talking about death and things, but then death's in a lot of other things that we're good at, you know it's all over the TV, it's in books and stuff we're good at, actually, people are really interested in death in other areas. It's only when it's close to home, when it's your own that's different, isn't it? (Participant 1)

A disjuncture between hypothetical and idealized ideas about a good (or at least preferred) way of death, and the reality of facing one's own death in the near future is arguably a central problem for the Death Positive Movement overall, and – as far as I can see – not reflected in the Order's tenets, where they promote talking about death as a form of individual self-improvement and growth. The idea that this 'work' must be undertaken and publicly performed for the purpose of individual growth is explored further by Koksvik (2020), who discusses death positivity as a project of self-development that must be *witnessed* by others: '[it] must not be silent or unseen ... it must be displayed and *known to others*' (2020: 953, emphasis added). This is echoed by the Order's emphasis on the duty of the death positive person to encourage their friends and associates of the value of talking about death: '[T]alking about death with the people closest to you can be challenging. The first time (heck, the first few times!) you approach them, their response may be brittle and closed off. But don't give up' (The Order of the Good Death, nd c).

Such persuasive zeal about the value of talking is often portrayed by Doughty herself in her videos on death positivity, for example:

Step one is the most important of all the steps, and that's to BELIEVE that talking about death is the right thing to do. Pick up your sword of righteousness ... and go into battle, facing down your mortality. If you don't have the strength of your convictions, or just don't think it's that important to talk about, the conversation is over before it even starts. (Doughty, 2015, original emphasis)

In these videos, Doughty's language is often reminiscent of Koksvik's description of 'possessing a moral high ground' (2020: 962); Doughty talks about 'belief', 'the right thing to do' and 'righteousness', all of which suggest that her mission is to *convince* the viewer that there is a correct – or at least better – way to approach death and dying (namely the way laid out by the Order's tenets), and there is little room for reluctance, resistance, passivity, uncertainty or half-heartedness. The underpinnings of such passionate beliefs in new social movements such as the Order has been queried by Walter: '[M]ovements promoting new and, in their view, psychologically healthier and more natural ways to die, funeralize and grieve ... have been driven more by passion, belief and hard-won evidence than by careful evaluation of the evidence ... [which] is either absent or queries such practices and claims' (Walter, 2017: 1, 3).

No one could doubt the Order's conviction of its beliefs and Doughty, as a mortician and funeral director herself, has had much experience of dealing with death; but the evidence upon which the tenets are built is not clear – particularly when it comes to the value of death talk – and a fervent commitment to its own views of the correct set of actions and behaviours arguably creates a new dogma, a new desire to set out the way of death.

Caitlin Doughty/*Ask a Mortician*

This may be overstating the influence of the Order, however. Out of the 24 interview participants, two had never heard of Doughty or the Order; and the extent to which others knew of them was varied, as was the association between the term death positive and the Order. Those that were aware of Doughty felt that she was a recognized and recognizable figurehead, which death positive followers coalesced around. Not all agreed that numbers of followers was enough to amount to a new social movement or new institution of/for death: 'I'm not sure that I understand exactly what her overall aim is. … To me, it's not explicit community building as such. It's still very much an individual, like go and watch the channel on your own or go and do this on your own' (Participant 5).

Having said that, a number of participants were effusive with their praise both for Doughty's style and her work in making the issue of death more visible. They enjoyed her communication style and ability to engage viewers, apparent in nearly all of Doughty's '*Ask a Mortician*' videos, of which there are nearly 300 on her YouTube channel. Such an approach, Bennett-Carpenter (2021) suggests, utilizes sensation, and emotional appeal to allow viewers to experience the world in a simulated way, where truths – such as the fact that death is inevitable – can be received positively and result in transformative action. Doughty's documentary-style videos, served up in bite-sized chunks of usually around 10–20 minutes, accord with this simulation theory by utilizing both instruction and emotional language and feeling to appeal to her audience, usually in a comic style, often involving her dressed up in costume, with the films themselves containing special effects, jokes and music. Such humour and style are part of a wider trend towards the 'tivolization' of death, originally identified and defined by Jacobsen (2020): '[The] otherwise inconspicuous normality of certain events or themes transformed or even exaggerated into a playful, carnivalesque, commercialized, entertainment-based, self-propelling, unserious, and often rather superficial kind of spectacle' (Jacobsen, 2020: 27).

This process of tivolization can clearly be seen within Doughty's work, no matter how sensitive the topic of the video might be. She refers to her viewers as 'deathlings', a playful 'pet-name' reminiscent of the way some popstars refer to their fans. There are also opportunities for the audience to spend money: on the Order's website there is an online store where 'merch' can be purchased, in the form of T-shirts, hoodies, mugs, bags and badges (The Order of the Good Death, 2022). The items sold within the store are sometimes referred to by the Order as part of its 'advocacy', carrying the message within a 'playful and carnivalesque' (to borrow from Jacobsen) style: that is, mainly black, with coffins and dancing skeleton motifs, with slogans such as 'Future Corpse', alongside the Order's branding.

There was a mixed reception to this tivolizing from participants. While some had no problem, others were less sure about the impact of what they called 'toxic positivity':

> She's [Doughty's] a natural, and I love watching a lot of her things and she's coming at it from a different perspective. I guess, um, in the States it's very different to over here [UK]. For what I've noticed is this what I would feel toxic positivity, um, coming out of a lot of it where people are forcing people to be jolly and happy when they actually aren't even have been allowed to grieve properly. (Participant 7)

An emphasis on positivity is not unique to the Order or the Death Positive Movement overall, as in recent years it has become popular at funerals or wakes to hold a personalized celebration of life of the deceased (Caswell, 2011), but this participant expressed a concern that such an emphasis on positivity or celebration risked overshadowing the distress of grief (although Doughty is at pains to explain that this is not how death positivity should be interpreted). Such overshadowing, it has been argued, risks delegitimizing the impact of death, and losing sight of the need after death for acknowledgement of suffering and involvement from others: 'As humans, don't we need others to authenticate our losses? To recognize them as losses rather than to pass over them in silence? Don't we need, in other words, a dialogue of mournings?' (Leader, 2009: 85).

Leader goes on to argue that various anthropological studies have found that where the sadness of death, grief and mourning are suppressed, physical symptoms in the bereaved can surface, often around the anniversary of the death of the deceased. The multiplicity of the 'dialogue of mournings' that Leader refers to, in recognizing that death can be very painful and distressing, is therefore *just as essential* as talking positively about death and celebrating life. But, within the videos of Doughty and the Order's tenets, there is very little said about the potential agony, stress and hurt of death and loss. One specific video, *Helping a Friend through Grief* (Doughty, 2018), does cover the subject but along with jokes and humour. For example, close to the beginning of the video, Doughty acknowledges that death phobia and grief phobia are intertwined and continues in a joking voice: 'But I'm the corpse girl – won't anyone think of the corpses?' (Doughty, 2018).

The use of humour like this felt jarring to one participant, who made the point that care was needed around people dying or suffering from grief and bereavement:

> I'm not the type of person that's likes a lot of humour. Because I realized that it's, it's such a sensitive topic. And when whatever you know, post online, especially when it's something that goes public, there's always someone who will have a story, and it may be really triggers them or really upsets them or even insults them ... so I try to be really mindful about that. (Participant 8)

Another participant agreed, feeling that the humour in the videos did not reflect their experience of dealing with the dying and bereaved:

> [I]t's the attitude of sensationalism, drama, um, facial expression and mock shock horror that I find is so far removed from what you're dealing with when you're with families in a mortuary setting ... some, some of the, the, um, the information that she's actually produced is really useful and really nice. It's just the delivery that I find very, very, very difficult to cope with. (Participant 6)

Evidently, there is still much to debate regarding death positivity and its public depiction and presentation.

Conclusion

The responses explored in this chapter demonstrate the ambivalence towards one of the key figureheads and ethos in the Death Positive Movement by people who identify as 'death positive' themselves. While some of the participants recognized the value of Doughty, her videos, and the Order more broadly, there was an unease at the tivolization of death, and some identified a dissonance where dealing with death 'positively' did not always equate to dealing with death 'sensitively'. What became evident in interviews was that, for many participants, the tivolization of death by Doughty and the Order did not correspond with their own experience of working with the dying and bereaved, where compassion and sensitivity were required, along with recognition of their pain. As a result, there was disagreement as to whether they represented or reflected the Death Positive Movement more broadly, and whether their work constituted a liberation or constraining of a 'new' approach to death.

The work done by the Order to demystify death has resonated with many worldwide as confirmed by the numbers of followers on social media on their various channels. Doughty has built a personal brand by promoting death positivity via her books, YouTube channel and by speaking appearances, promoting the Order's vision of how death should be approached. However, the data in this chapter shows that the methods and media that are used to convey the death positive message are not, as the interviews indicate, universally supported even among those who declare themselves to be death positive and who work within the sphere of death.

There was a further dissonance for participants between authentic emotional talk about dying, and a more intellectual public performance of being seen to engage with death. Concerns were raised by participants by the use of the word 'positive' and its propensity for being misunderstood. Similarly, some felt that a toxic positivity could minimize the reality and pain of dying, grief and loss. Talking about death with those approaching end of life was not always appropriate or desired; indeed, some of the older people who participants worked with refused to engage with the subject completely. Personal choice within death and dying were highlighted as important by participants, and if that choice involved *no* discussion at all, it was – they felt – valid and appropriate for the person concerned.

In sum, this chapter goes some way towards understanding the Order of the Good Death and its cultural and social significance in promoting its version of death positivity. It demonstrates that although the wider Death Positive Movement is comprised of a range of people with differing views and experiences, there are risks within the movement in creating an institutionalization of positivity that places additional burden and pressure on dying people. There is – as yet – no consensus as to whether the Death Positive Movement constitutes a new cultural (and arguably institutionalized) approach to death and dying.

Note

[1] Reference Number: ERN_21-0968.

References

Armstrong, E.A. and Bernstein, M. (2008) 'Culture, power, and institutions: a multi-institutional politics approach to social movements', *Sociological Theory*, 26(1): 74–99.

Bell, C.H., Muggleton, S. and Davis, D.L. (2022) 'Birth plans: a systematic, integrative review into their purpose, process, and impact', *Midwifery*, 111: 103388.

Bennett-Carpenter, B. (2021) 'Death and documentaries: heuristics for the real in an age of simulation', in Wang, W.M., Jernigan, D.K. and Murphy, N. (eds) *The Routledge Companion to Death and Literature*. London: Routledge, pp 121–131.

Braun, V. and Clarke, V. (2022) *Thematic Analysis: A Practical Guide*. London: SAGE.

Caswell, G. (2011) 'Personalisation in Scottish funerals: individualised ritual or relational process?', *Mortality*, 16(3): 242–258. doi: 10.1080/13576275.2011.586124

Cottrell, L. and Duggleby, W. (2016) 'The "good death": an integrative literature review', *Palliative and Supportive Care*, 14(6): 686–712.

Death Cafe (nd) *What is Death Cafe?* Available at: https://deathcafe.com/what/ [accessed 18 January 2024].

Doughty, C. (nd) *Ask a Mortician*. Available at: https://www.youtube.com/c/AskAMortician [accessed 11 November 2022].

Doughty, C. (2013) Tweet. Available at: https://twitter.com/thegooddeath/status/328636776367415296?lang=en-GB [accessed 30 November 2022].

Doughty, C. (2015) *Talking to Your Parents About Death*. Available at: https://www.youtube.com/watch?v=4DZumsrUejI [accessed 15 December 2022].

Doughty, C. (2018) *Helping a Friend through Grief*. Available at: https://www.youtube.com/watch?v=lGbI7zn2UV0 [accessed 30 November 2022].

Hebb, M. (2018) *Let's Talk about Death (over Dinner): The Essential Guide to Life's Most Important Conversation*. United Kingdom: Orion Publishing Group, Limited.

Jacobsen, M.H. (2020) 'Thoughts for the times on the death taboo: trivialization, tivolization and re-domestication in the age of spectacular death', in Teodorescu, A. and Jacobsen, M.H. (eds) *Death in Popular Culture*. London: Routledge, pp 15–37.

Kellehear, A. (1984) 'Are we a "death-denying" society? A sociological review', *Social Science and Medicine*, 18(9): 713–721.

Kelly, K. (2017) 'Welcome the reaper: Caitlin Doughty and the "death-positivity" movement'. Available at: https://www.theguardian.com/books/2017/oct/27/caitlin-doughty-death-positivity [accessed 19 January 2024].

Koksvik, G.H. (2020) 'Neoliberalism, individual responsibilization and the death positivity movement', *International Journal of Cultural Studies*, 23(6): 951–967.

Leader, D. (2009) *The New Black: Mourning, Melancholia and Depression*. Minneapolis: Greywolf Press.

Leland, J. (2018) 'The positive death movement comes to life'. Available at: https://www.nytimes.com/2018/06/22/nyregion/the-positive-death-movement-comes-to-life.html [accessed 18 January 2024].

Lofland, L. (2019 [1978]) *The Craft of Dying: The Modern Face of Death* (40th anniversary edn). Cambridge, MA: Massachusetts Institute of Technology.

The Order of the Good Death (nd a) *Death Positive Movement*. Available at: https://www.orderofthegooddeath.com/death-positive-movement/ [accessed 3 January 2022].

The Order of the Good Death (nd b) *Welcome to the Future of Death*. Available at: https://www.orderofthegooddeath.com/ [accessed 3 January 2022].

The Order of the Good Death (nd c) *5 Ways to Affect Death Positive Change*. Available at: https://www.orderofthegooddeath.com/five-ways-to-affect-death-positive-change [accessed 11 January 2023].

The Order of the Good Death (nd d) *Everything You Need To Get Started*. Available at: https://www.orderofthegooddeath.com/start-here/ [accessed 17 November 2022].

The Order of the Good Death (2022) *The Order of the Good Death Store*. Available at: https://the-order-of-the-good-death.myshopify.com/ [accessed 17 November 2022].

Seymour, J. and Clark, D. (2018) 'The Liverpool care pathway for the dying patient: a critical analysis of its rise, demise and legacy in England', *Wellcome Open Research*, 3: 3–15.

Varghese, R. (2022) *Death Be Not Proud: Gen Z's Attitudes Surrounding Death and Dying*. Available at: https://www.talkdeath.com/death-be-not-proud-gen-zs-attitudes-surrounding-death-and-dying/ [accessed 18 January 2024].

Walter, T. (1991) 'Modern death: taboo or not taboo?', *Sociology*, 25: 293–310.

Walter, T. (2017) *What Death Means Now: Thinking Critically about Dying and Grieving*. Bristol: Policy Press.

Walter, T. (2020) *Death in the Modern World*. London: SAGE.

11

Representations of Immortality and Institutions in 21st-Century Popular Culture

Devaleena Kundu and Bethan Michael-Fox

Introduction

According to Reed and Penfold-Mounce (2015: 136), engagement with death and the dead through popular culture can be a productive mechanism to reflect on and engage with 'sweeping sociological themes', such as mortality and immortality. Popular cultural texts have the capacity to spark the 'thanatological imaginations' of their varied audiences, Penfold-Mounce (2019) goes on to argue, and in the context of playful entertainment can offer meaningful opportunities to negotiate existential and practical concerns about death, dying and the dead in a safe space (Michael-Fox, 2020). Here, in this chapter, we are concerned with how popular cultural texts can offer a space to negotiate the meanings and implications of potential routes to immortality. Immortality, as something no one has to date experienced, is beyond direct experience. As Clarke (2006: 154) has argued, 'in the absence of personal experience' people often 'rely on various media, among other things, for information, attitudes, beliefs and feelings about death and its meanings'. We argue in this chapter that, given this, popular cultural texts[1] can function to both inform and reflect sociocultural concerns about death and the potential for immortality. Considering one film documentary – *Freeze Me* (2006), two television series – *Torchwood: Miracle Day* (2011) and *Upload* (2020–) – and one narrative fiction novel – *Death at Intervals* (Saramago, 2008), we show how a range of popular cultural narratives produced between 2005 and 2020 effectively function as spaces through which to negotiate shifting 'real life' anxieties about the medical and political institutionalization of death in the early 21st century. These texts, we argue, produce an accessible space through which audiences can explore relationships between death, capitalism and necropolitics. While the routes to immortality in the texts we examine are varied, we show how powerful and elite institutions are positioned as central in all of these cultural representations of immortality on screen and in literature. In offering spaces through which to explore themes of mortality and immortality, these texts draw attention to the problematic notions of institutional involvement within the processes of life and death with institutions that feature in these four texts often taking on a shadowy form with nefarious motivations and ties to economic and social privilege.

Certainly, interest in immortality is growing, with scholars within and beyond death studies beginning to examine recent developments relating to immortality from different perspectives. For example, Cohen (2023) has outlined the preponderance of new religious communities focused on radical longevity and immortality in the 21st century and explored their potential motivations and features. And, elsewhere, Hurtado Hurtado (2022) has emphasized that the many ways in which individuals, groups of people and societies might seek to transcend death and achieve immortality can be interpreted through a 'plurality of frameworks'. In this chapter, rather than focusing on communities concerned with achieving immortality, we focus on popular cultural texts produced in the 21st century that represent and explore forms of immortality. As Kundu (2020) has argued, humanity has had a long-standing preoccupation with the idea of corporeal immortality, and this concern proliferates across – and is reflected in – popular culture. Kundu (2020, 2023) has additionally explored how the very pursuit of immortality functions as an act of transgression in literary representations, crossing the culturally, medically and socially inscribed boundary between life and death which is tied so closely to a range of institutions – religious, medical and legal among others. Yet a fascination with immortality is in some ways antithetical to an increasingly institutionalized Death Positive Movement (see Chapter 10, this volume), given that fantasies of immortality are premised on the idea of avoiding death altogether. As we will demonstrate in this chapter, what the texts we have selected here demonstrate individually and as a whole is the ways in which popular cultural representations of immortality are tightly bound with representations of institutions and the institutionalization of death. Twitchin has emphasized that while death will affect everyone, its highly social condition means it will impact us all 'unequally' (2023: 186). Here we will show that a concern with inequality within representations of immortality, and the role that institutions and institutionalization play in this, are at the fore of each of these texts. Questions about whether institutions can be trusted and about the roles they play in deciding what life and death are, as well as who gets to live and die, come to the fore across the range of popular cultural examples discussed in this chapter, demonstrating how popular cultural texts can function as spaces through which to negotiate sociocultural concerns about mortality.

In selecting 21st-century popular texts concerned with immortality for analysis we were spoiled for choice due to how numerous they are across different genres and media. In light of this, we chose those texts that examined a form of corporeal immortality in which the living self continues and maintains their unique selfhood, excluding examples that included an element of monstrosity – where immortality was a form of zombieism or vampirism, for example. Instead, we opted to focus on texts where verisimilitude and realism were a central feature.

Ultimately the choice of the four texts forms an assemblage drawn from our own experiences and from our own interdisciplinary and 'intellectual promiscuity' (Butler, 2006: x). Butler (2006) notes that such a promiscuity is characterized by a tendency to read together texts that were never intended to be read together, including both cultural texts and the work of intellectuals and academics. As Ahmed (2010: 19) has made clear, the personal 'archives' of our research 'are assembled out of encounters, taking form as a memory trace of where we have been'. In working together, our own personal and experiential archives have combined and we have selected together four texts that we feel reflect broader sociocultural concerns about immortality and the role of institutions in the management of death. With our backgrounds in the academic discipline of English literature, we are both concerned with how 'works are not mysteriously inspired' (Eagleton, 1976: 6) or explicable in terms of the individual psychology of those who produced them, but a reflection of dominant ways of seeing the world that can reflect the 'ideology of an age'. While the texts we have chosen originate from the United Kingdom, United States and Portugal, representing only a small proportion of the world and of the immensity of popular cultural texts that proliferate globally, their international success and spread means they provide an interesting sample for analysis that while inevitably partial, remains valuable. Each text is considered in terms of its representations of immortality and institutions in order of date, before conclusions are drawn about the similarities across the four texts.

Freeze Me (2006)

This 45-minute documentary gives context to the other texts examined in this chapter, and represents a fascination with cryogenic freezing as a route to immortality visible in a broad range of cultural texts from popular comedy *Austin Powers* (1997) to crime series such as *Castle* (2011) and myriad other popular examples. For several organizations involved with immortality research, one of the primary objectives is life extension. *Freeze*

Me depicts how the modern perception of immortality is an 'expression of prolongevitism taken to its limit' (Overall, 2005: 126). The documentary focuses on Alcor, a cryonics organization base in Scottsdale, Arizona, as one of two institutions in the United States (the other being the Cryonics Institute in Clinton town, Michigan) that preserves bodies indefinitely in the hope that science will make it possible to resuscitate them in the future. The process of cryopreservation at Alcor takes two forms: one could either preserve the entire body, or just the severed head because the individual undergoing the process would desire a new (often younger) body. Common across both options is that, for most individuals, signing up for cryonics is rooted primarily in the slim possibility that it could work and the desire to be revived in the future (Romain, 2010). The entire process involves a significant amount of money and several individuals, interviewed as part of the documentary, express their willingness to invest in the possibility of living forever. For example entrepreneur Terry Katz, who signed up for a full-body preservation at Alcor cryonics, is seeking an extension of humankind's quest towards prolongevity. He considers his payment towards the cryopreservation services to be an investment that would potentially allow him to witness the future and be part of it. Individuals like Terry would rather pay towards cryopreserving themselves – the cost of which is approximately ten times that of an average funeral (Mullock and Romanis, 2023) – than towards traditional forms of life insurance. This level of investment is not unusual; as Romain (2010) highlights, those seeking cryopreservation are required to enter into a contract with a cryonics institution and pay a substantial amount ranging between $28,000 and $150,000 for the storage and preservation of their bodies. Beyond the United States, KrioRus, the first cryonics institute to be set up in Eurasia, charges between $10,000 and $30,000 (Bernstein, 2015), with the amount usually determined based on whether the entire body or merely the brain/head is being preserved. Hence, for those on a budget, preserving the brain proves to be a feasible alternative, although as Bernstein (2015) notes, orthodox cryonicists deem the preservation of the brain to be ideologically much more advanced a step. However, many perceive investments towards such life extension to be misguided, misplaced and speculative given that by extraordinarily stretching the human life span cryonics merely creates a semblance of physical immortality, leading to a false sense of hope that the bodies preserved will be reanimated sometime in the future (Woods, 2016; Arnold, 2020). Despite such ideological differences, cryonics facilities aimed at death-defiance and extreme life extension are being set up in various parts of the globe, indicating a growing interest in the field.

At the time of filming the documentary in 2006, the Cryonics Institute and Alcor together had approximately 147 people cryonically preserved and nearly 1,000 people who had signed up for the services post their legal death. A little more than a decade later the numbers are significantly higher. Cohen (2020) records that as of 2020 Alcor has over 1,300 members and 181 patients while the Cryonics Institute has over 1,700 members and 196 patients. Wilson (2021) notes that the global encounter with death during the COVID-19 pandemic between 2020 and 2022 has prompted further interest in the field of cryopreservation. Crucially, while cryonicists claim that in opting for cryopreservation individuals are investing in their futures, it is a future that is yet to be imagined. Romain (2010: 200) writes that '[c]ryonicists strategically use loopholes within the state regulation of bodies and lives to secure and sanctify their project'. Within the documentary, what is perhaps shocking is the revelation that the cryonics institute is not legally required to have medically trained professionals associated with it in order to run. In the absence of medically trained personnel, there is even less guarantee that the measures undertaken to preserve the bodies will prove successful. Huge financial investment coupled with zero assurance of success are reasons why many have deemed cryonics exploitative, with the human body becoming a commodity in the process, an object that can be exchanged for money within a techno-capitalist market that is increasingly engulfing human interactions (Romain, 2010; Farman, 2020; Hurtado Hurtado, 2022). Cryonics is, it is claimed, almost predatory for it exploits a fundamental vulnerability faced by humankind – the erasure of one's identity in death (Arnold, 2020). This is reflected in how within the cryonics community 'dead bodies' are not labelled 'dead'; instead, they are referred to as 'patients', an act that sustains the notion of (ongoing) personhood. The speculations and hopes surrounding an unknown future revival thus, it is argued by Hillenbrink and Wareham (2024), not only hinder the process of mourning but may prevent a true sense of emotional closure after someone has died. In contrast, those in favour of cryonics believe the hope of reviving the dead helps with grief and closure since the body is readied for the future instead of being disposed of (Mullock and Romanis, 2023).

In sum, this documentary and many others like it represent the popular cultural fascination with cryonics as a route to immortality. The text also shows how institutions come to be represented in relation to immortality in popular culture, with their representation being tied to questions about finance, ethics, trust and integrity.

Death at Intervals (2008)

'The fundamental question for sociologists', Howarth observes, is '[h]ow is it possible for societies to continue in the face of mortality?' (2007: 15). For the characters in the novel *Death at Intervals* by Portuguese novelist José Saramago the question is rephrased as 'How is it possible for societies to continue in the face of deathlessness?' By subjecting a section of humankind to 'the brink of death which is permanently being denied to [them]' (Saramago, 2008: 18), in his novel Saramago generates a new category of 'living cadavers', the modern-day methuselahs. Suspended between life and death, they do not necessarily require medical technology for prolonging longevity; nor would a withdrawal of medical care end their lives. They are not quite dead. In such a state of exception 'to kill' is a necessity and the sovereign power steps in to exercise control over who lives and who dies in an attempt to restore natural order. Although in *Death at Intervals* Saramago does not treat the body as a biopolitical site, it is nonetheless hinted at, with the interminable withering away of the body leaving behind ghostly apparitions of former selves. Unable to provide for themselves or their families, the 'living cadavers' are deemed unproductive and parasitic members of the society. Here, in this text, the government not only approves of 'social deaths' for citizens above the age of 80 but it also sanctions homicide 'to slow down the mounting numbers of the terminally dying' (Saramago, 2008: 78). It is the ultimate form of control as sovereignty of the government is determined by its exercise of the right to kill or allow its citizens to live (Mbembe, 2003: 66). Social thinkers contend that this very essence of the right of life and death is actually the right to kill. Achille Mbembe (2003: 66) begins his essay 'Necropolitics' by stating that 'the ultimate expression of sovereignty resides, to a large degree, in the power and the capacity to dictate who may live and who must die'. However, by locating death *outside* of human authority and control – deathlessness in the narrative is a result of death's decision to go on a holiday – Saramago deprives humankind of its endeavours to defy it. Humans can neither make changes nor reverse the circumstances they find themselves in. The quest for immortality loses its relevance, in the novel at least, the moment it is imposed rather than achieved. Besides, in this text it is not the 'immortality' that humankind had wished for. Devoid of corporeal imperishability, this version of immortality is merely deathlessness; an absence of death effecting an infinitely stretched out longevity.

As a result, although initially deathlessness is welcomed as the fulfilment of 'humanity's greatest dream' (Saramago, 2008: 5), once the cumulative disarray of the social order surfaces, Saramago's population recognizes it as a bane rather than a boon. An absence of death, therefore, not only generates a new state of being but also redefines humankind's perception of immortality; the state of deathlessness stimulates emotions of love and fear, responses that are similar to humankind's response to a corpse. On witnessing a corpse, Malinowski and Redfield (1948: 30) remarks, survivors are faced with complex emotions: 'love of the dead and loathing of the corpse, passionate attachment to the personality still lingering about the body and a shattering fear of the gruesome thing that has been left over, these two elements seem to mingle and play into each other'. Likewise, deathlessness elicits the love of eternal life vis-à-vis the horror of incapacitation. Interestingly, here, the fear of annihilation is overtaken by the fear of 'physical invalidity'. The narrative thus presents a site of conflict; it manifests the strife between life and death, raising philosophical and existential questions about the desirability of immortality in different forms as well as exploring state institutional involvement in decisions about life and death.

Since death in any form is impossible within the geographical limits of Saramago's fictional country, the event of death is turned into a covert business with the government liaising with the mafia to allow its citizens to trespass into adjacent countries and get rid of their 'dead-weights'. By zeroing in on the ramifications of deathlessness, the novel renders corporeal immortality dystopic, and it is governments and social institutions that, as in many dystopian fictions, are portrayed as powerful deciders of life and death. Arguably Saramago's text is a commentary on the politics of the death industry and, in examining this novel already, Kundu (2019) has highlighted how its narrative functions to question whether the 'death industry' is a requirement for the management of death, whether it functions as a safeguarding mechanism, or whether, in the context of an urban environment, the proto-industrialization of death becomes a logical advancement to sustain order. Whatever the function of the narrative, institutions are positioned here in relation to immortality as powerful; often nameless and faceless decision-making bodies function to exert control often in the name of a social good, while having highly economic motivations including the maintenance of the status quo to enable the very power of those institutions that is being exerted in deciding how to 'manage' immortality and death.

Torchwood: Miracle Day (2011)

The third text in this chapter is the British/US televisual collaboration *Torchwood: Miracle Day*, an offshoot of the popular series *Doctor Who*. The series positions a moment when death has been eradicated globally – people have simply stopped dying. In this notion of death 'stopping', the series shares much in common with Saramago's novel, with the consequences of no death explored in a series saturated with references to the Second World War. The anxieties of an age when medical interventions are able to extend life in new ways are at the fore, and the historical focus on the Second World War is representative of the significant cultural impact of a war that introduced radically new technologies of death, not limited to but perhaps best symbolized by the atomic bomb.

Luckhurst (2016) has argued for the capacity of popular cultural representations to function as effective social critiques – in particular he has argued that the living dead of zombie horror fictions can be read as a form of social realism with their own necropolitics, a term coined by

Mbembe (2003) to examine how social and political powers can dictate life and death. In Luckhurst's (2016) theorization, hordes of the undead can be read metaphorically as global populations who represent workers deemed disposable in a profit-driven capitalist culture. *Torchwood: Miracle Day* is perhaps the most explicitly political of the four examples in this chapter in its social realism via its engagement with images highly reminiscent of concentration or internment camps (which, while heavily associated with the Second World War, are by no means restricted to any point in history – they continue to exist in various forms across the globe today). The camps in the series are run by military and government institutions and in the series emerge as a way to manage the 'not dead'. Because death has stopped globally, the population continues to multiply, and without the daily release valve of death to prevent issues of scarcity and humanitarian disasters associated with overpopulation, the camps are justified as necessary by governments across the world.

A central concern in the series relates to the capacity for corruption when decisions relating to the ontological categories of life and death are placed in the hands of the state or an institution. To manage the rapidly increasing population life is divided into four categories: category three is the 'healthy'; category two is made up of those whose death was prevented by Miracle Day and who will recover to full health; category one is those who have no consciousness, or who suffer a debilitating disease that prevents them from being 'useful' members of society, and who are therefore deemed 'as good as dead'; and category zero, effectively the death penalty for anyone 'healthy' and well but deemed suitable for incineration for moral reasons. Those designated category one or zero are burned in 'overflow' camps explicitly described as concentration camps in the series. Designation to categories becomes subject to both human error and intentional subterfuge, and the debates that the series provokes clearly relate to those associated with thanatological themes from genocide to assisted dying and the notion of what constitutes a valuable or useful life. As Testoni and Arnau (2023) have examined in a case study about biopolitics and an assisted death in Switzerland, which involved an institution aiding the death of an individual that it later transpires was 'healthy', anxieties abound in the 21st century about the ethics, risks, morality, practicalities, legalities and accountability of institutions in the management of death. What *Torchwood: Miracle Day* does is both negotiate these within an imaginative popular cultural fiction, and situate them specifically in relation to the Second World War and the broader legacies of the 20th century. The series ends with the words: 'World War II, what the hell did you do to me?' Although 'World War II' is the nickname of Captain Jack Harkness, the series' central character, the layered meaning is evident in signalling significant sociocultural concerns evident across so much of early 21st-century popular culture about guilt, responsibility, accountability and technology, and their relationship to the dead, which have been effectively examined in terms of their sustained relationship to postmodernism, trauma and the catastrophes of the 1940s by Crosthwaite (2009).

Further, in relation to institutions and immortality in the series it emerges in *Torchwood: Miracle Day* that the event of death stopping is the consequence of a conspiracy by a shadowy and powerful elite – the Families – for their own gain both in terms of ensuring their own immortality but also their own financial and socially elite status in the new world order. In this, the extension of global inequality from life and death into immortality is explored, as the series imagines how deeply ingrained social and economic inequalities might play out in a potential circumstance of immortality – as Jameson (2003) has suggested, it is easier to imagine the end of the world than to imagine the end of capitalism. The series positions institutions in two main ways, both largely negative. First, as powerful decision-makers that decide on life and death, wherein individuals must negotiate their own decision-making powers and capacity for agency in a way that is reminiscent of debates about the tensions between individual responsibility and state totalitarianism perhaps best encapsulated in the work of Arendt (1951, 1964). Second, institutions are difficult to pin down, elite, hidden and shadowy organizations that function to facilitate the ongoing privileges of the wealthy.

Upload (2020–)

In the context of *Upload*, a comedy drama set in 2033, a digital afterlife into which people can be uploaded has been designed and come into practice. The series is heavily concerned with digital inequality, as at first the capacity to upload to a digital afterlife is limited only to wealthy elites – even within the costly world of *Upload*, it is possible for people to be downgraded to the '2gig plan', in which even thinking can exhaust your data usage leaving you frozen until the new month of data kicks in. Efforts to create an accessible digital afterlife form a central narrative arc in the series, where a backdrop of government legislation and policy making reflect the complexity of institutional involvement within the processes of life and death both in terms of governance and finance. The series' representation of a controversial, sometimes stigma-laden and complex new set of circumstances surrounding life and death offers a light and entertaining way to engage with real-life concerns such as those explored in Winnington's chapter in this collection (Chapter 3), which explores the introduction of the End of Life Choice Act (2019) in Aotearoa New Zealand.

For example, one of the complexities of *Upload* and the need for involvement from institutions (medical, legal, government/policy making) is that in order to upload, the decision must be made *before* death has occurred (people's heads are literally sucked off with a machine while they are still alive and uploaded in a very visceral decapitation process that sits in tension with the cleanliness of the digital afterlife of those uploaded experience). This means that those who upload effectively decide to end their lives. This is reminiscent of Cohen (2023),who has examined the complexity and ethics of the potential for 'cryothenasia' (a play on euthanasia) as a means for people to choose to die in order to be cryogenically frozen. Unlike medically assisted dying, in 'cryothenasia' or the circumstances outlined in the series *Upload*, there is the promise of future life – immortality in a different form. However, the existence of the uploaded worlds relies on the living, who must maintain them. As such it is often low-paid workers whose labour sustains the immortal afterlives of wealthy elites within *Upload*. The series thus raises questions about what constitutes life, as within *Upload* people must negotiate what it is to live *without* death. As Han (2021: 60) has argued, this creates something of a limbo, neither dead nor alive: 'The pain-free life of permanent happiness is not a human life. … If you seek to remove all pain, you will also have to abolish death. But life without death and pain is not human life; it is undead life.'

Such questions about what constitutes life and death are largely existential and the *Upload* series explores many pertinent sociocultural concerns about technology, social media and the notion of the 'good life', presented in images of a sanitized and perfect world, and the ethics and consequences of artificial intelligence. However, the series also functions effectively to relate such concerns to practical questions around the roles of technology companies, governments, legislatures and religious and social institutions in managing life, death and the afterlife.

In this series, the notion of corruption among financial institutions in particular comes to the fore as it is revealed that the central character's death (and upload into the afterlife) was part of a conspiracy for financial gain: a group of wealthy and powerful individuals orchestrated the murder of Nathan Brown in order to take his work (code for an affordable afterlife) and utilize it for their own profit and gain. Similar to *Torchwood: Miracle Day*, institutions emerge in the series as shadowy, corrupt and underhand organizations that are difficult to identify, working in the background in a way that impacts the lives of many, here bringing into place the option for a mass-market, new, affordable digital afterlife – but ultimately doing so for their own financial gain, not for any benevolent reason. Institutions are further positioned as competing within the series, as religious institutions and social movements who stand against the notion of a digital afterlife come into conflict with financial and technological institutions who champion it. Overall, institutions within this series are represented as stifling but essential to the functioning of everyday life – large corporations manage everything from the printing of digital food to digital dating apps, with everything rated and reviewed in an imagined world in which concerns about the role of digital technology in everyday life are at the fore. All interactions are managed by algorithms and encounters rated from one to five stars in an imagined future in which the attention economy of social media (see Chapter 12, this volume) has become the institutionalized framework of all experience.

While in some ways the representation of institutions in *Upload* is quite neutral, it represents a society in which financial and technology focused institutions manage and dictate the minutiae of every moment of people's lives. While many of the characters appear to have individual choice and agency in a highly consumerist society, the series suggests that much of the choice experienced by individuals is merely an illusion, with an elite and powerful group working in the background to maximize their own profit and maintain their status. Like in *Torchwood: Miracle Day*, the notion that life, death and immortality are all largely controlled by a range of institutions that shape individual experience is at the fore, reflecting central debates about structure and agency that emerged in the social theory of the late 20th century and exemplified in the work of Giddens (1979). In this series, institutions are portrayed as key structuring factors in people's lives, deaths and afterlives, sometimes in visible and transparent ways, and sometimes in more evasive and nefarious ones. This reflects too, perhaps, the shift towards diminishing trust in traditional institutions and their authority outlined in the late modern theory of Bauman (2007).

Conclusion

Each text examined in this chapter represents popular engagement in the 21st century that reflects the shift towards 'spectacular death' outlined by Jacobsen (2016), with their representations of (im)mortality characterized by the mediatization, commercialization and re-ritualization of death. Each text explores immortality as a speculative idea tied to technological, cultural and social changes, positing it as achievable, perhaps even likely, in the near future. What all four texts have in common is a concern with the many ethical, moral, emotional and practical complexities of immortality, and how they might be shaped and informed by institutions that seem to be above or beyond individual agency and control. Each one explores the potential for extreme inequality in the possibility and processes of immortality. As Michael-Fox et al (2023: 5) have argued, 'death is often difficult because it occurs at the nexus of myriad forms of social inequality that function as mechanisms of systemic marginalisation'. The same is true in the context of immortality in all of these selected texts, in which economic, geographical and social privilege function to make available and shape experience. Hurtado Hurtado (2022: 16) has examined how, in a study of a range of potential options for immortality, its achievement 'may be available only to the wealthy and influential, thus deepening inequalities between social groups and potentially creating new forms of discrimination'. This is certainly a central feature of each of these texts, though most pronounced in *Upload*, with its very concerted focus on economic inequality extending into its representations of immortality.

One of the challenges of these texts is that they conceptualize institutional involvement in immortality as shadowy and problematic, often nefarious at worst and utilitarian at best, as complex practicalities must be negotiated at an institutional level. Sumiala (2022: 58) has pointed out that what is socially constituted as a 'bad death' is far 'more likely to become a public event in hybrid media'. This perhaps extends to representations of immortality, with these texts emphasizing enduring themes of fears about institutionalization and its risks. Yet this runs the risk of producing among audiences the notion that institutionalization and any institutional involvement in the processes of immortality (or death) is itself inherently 'bad'. Popular cultural representations can function as a form of 'death education', a concept discussed by Wheatley (2023), and may inform audiences' understandings across the lifecourse. While Norwood (2018: 462) has suggested that television portrayals in particular may have the potential to give the impression of 'the most unlikely forms of death' as 'daily routine', it is important not to assume that all popular cultural representations of death are problematic, detrimental or frivolous in their representations of death. Popular cultural representations have instead the capacity both to inform and to provoke the 'thanatological imagination' (Penfold-Mounce, 2019), leading in this context to consideration of the challenging ethical, moral and emotional complexities of potential forms of immortality.

While each text has the potential to inform audiences' understandings, these examples and the many others like them emerging across popular culture also reflect a broader social and cultural zeitgeist. Informing each of them is an underlying social and cultural concern about what Moerman and van der Laan define in Chapter 2 as a need for 'necroaccountability'. Moerman and van der Laan characterize this as an accountable relationship to the dead involving various institutions, regulatory bodies and intermediates, each with responsibilities, which they may either enact or discharge. In the four examples examined here, there is a sense of overwhelming complexity in terms of identifying what institutions and power structures are at play, and their responsibilities, as people seek to come to terms with a new reality – the possibility of immortality. This reflects the speed of technological change that has characterized the late 20th and early 21st centuries, forming the backdrop to all of these popular cultural examples. As both the opportunities afforded and anxieties provoked by new technologies emerge, concerns about how those will be managed, legislated and controlled by amorphous and powerful institutions in the context of immortality feature in each text. At times, this means that the concept of the institution – far-reaching, broad and ill-defined – becomes shadowy and potentially nefarious in its motivations, running the risk of reinforcing the notion that institutional involvement in death is inherently 'bad'.

Note

1 Within literary and cultural studies, the term 'text' refers to any work that contains linguistic and semantic codes allowing for meaning making. The term entails understanding the conditions of production as well as reception of a given work of art.

References

Ahmed, S. (2010) *The Promise of Happiness*. Durham, NC: Duke University Press.

Arendt, H. (1951) *The Origins of Totalitarianism*. New York: Harcourt Brace Jovanovich. Third edition with new prefaces, 1973.

Arendt, H. (1964) 'Personal responsibility under dictatorship', *The Listener*, pp 185–205.

Arnold, B.B. (2020) 'Thawing out personhood: Australian law and cryonics', *Canberra Law Review*, 17(1): 43–60.

Bauman, Z. (2007) *Liquid Times: Living in an Age of Uncertainty*. Cambridge: Polity.

Bernstein, A. (2015) 'Freeze, die, come to life: the many paths to immortality in post-Soviet Russia', *American Ethnologist*, 42(4): 766–781.

Butler, J. (2006) *Gender Trouble* (2nd edn). New York and London: Routledge.

Clarke, J.N. (2006) 'Death under control: the portrayal of death in mass print English language magazines in Canada', *Omega*, 52(2): 153–167.

Cohen, J. (2020) 'Frozen bodies and future imaginaries: assisted dying, cryonics, and a good death', *Religions*, 11(11): 584.

Cohen, J. (2023) Interview on *The Death Studies Podcast* hosted by Michael-Fox, B. and Visser, R. Published 1 April 2023. Available at: www.thedeat hstudiespodcast.com [accessed 20 October 2024].

Crosthwaite, P. (2009) *Trauma, Postmodernism, and the Aftermath of World War II*. Basingstoke: Palgrave Macmillan.

Eagleton, T. (1976) *Marxism and Literary Criticism*. Berkeley: University of California Press.

Farman, A. (2020) *On Not Dying: Secular Immortality in the Age of Technoscience*. Minneapolis: University of Minnesota Press.

Giddens, A. (1979) *Central Problems in Social Theory*. London: Red Globe Press.

Han, B. (2021) *The Palliative Society: Pain Today*. Translated by D. Steuer. Cambridge: Polity Press.

Hillenbrink, R. and Wareham, C.S. (2024) 'Mourning the frozen: considering the relational implications of cryonics', *Journal of Media Ethics*, 50: 388–391.

Howarth, G. (2007) *Death and Dying: A Sociological Introduction*. Cambridge: Polity Press.

Hurtado Hurtado, J. (2022) 'Envisioning postmortal futures: six archetypes on future societal approaches to seeking immortality', *Mortality*, 29(1): 18–36.

Jacobsen, M.H. (2016) 'Spectacular death: proposing a new fifth phase to Philippe Ariès's admirable history of death', *Humanities*, 5(19): 1–20.

Jameson, F. (2003) 'Future city', *New Left Review*, 21: 65–79.

Kundu, D. (2019) 'Transacting death: José Saramago's death at intervals and the politics of the death industry', *Thanatos*, 8(2): 203–216.

Kundu, D. (2020) *Interminable Living: Reflections on the Dynamics of Arrested Immortality*. Doctoral thesis, The English and Foreign Languages University, Hyderabad, India.

Kundu, D. (2023) 'Negotiating transgression, deathlessness, and senescence in Mary Shelley's *The Mortal Immortal*', *Victoriographies*, 13(2): 174–191.

Luckhurst, R. (2016) *Zombies: A Cultural History*. London: Reaktion Books.

Malinowski, B. and Redfield, R. (1948) *Magic, Science and Religion: And Other Essays*. Glencoe, IL: The Free Press.

Mbembe, A. (2003) 'Necropolitics'. Translated by L. Meintjes. *Public Culture*, 15(1): 11–40.

Michael-Fox, B. (2020) 'Dead chatty: the rise of the articulate undead in popular culture', in Coward-Gibbs, M. (ed) *Death, Culture and Leisure: Playing Dead*. Bingley: Emerald, pp 111–124.

Michael-Fox, B. Coleclough, S. and Visser, R. (2023) 'Introduction to difficult death, dying and the dead in media and culture', in Coleclough, S., Michael-Fox, B. and Visser, R. (eds) *Difficult Death, Dying and the Dead in Media and Culture*. Cham: Palgrave Macmillan, pp 1–22.

Mullock, A. and Romanis, E.C. (2023) 'Cryopreservation and current legal problems: seeking and selling immortality', *Journal of Law and the Biosciences*, 10(2): np.

Norwood, F. (2018) 'The new normal: mediated death and assisted dying in the United States', in Robben, A.C.G.M. (ed) *A Companion to the Anthropology of Death*. Hoboken: John Wiley and Sons, pp 461–476.

Overall, C. (2005) *Aging, Death, and Human Longevity: A Philosophical Inquiry*. Berkeley, Los Angeles and London: University of California Press.

Penfold-Mounce, R. (2019) 'Mortality and culture: do death matters matter?', in Holmberg, T., Jonsson, A. and Palm, F. (eds) *Death Matters: Cultural Sociology of Mortal Life*. Cham: Palgrave Macmillan, pp 265–279.

Reed, D. and Penfold-Mounce, R. (2015) 'Zombies and the sociological imagination: *The Walking Dead* as social-science fiction', in Hubner, L., Leaning, M. and Manning, P. (eds) *The Zombie Renaissance in Popular Culture*. Basingstoke: Palgrave Macmillan, pp 136–137.

Romain, T. (2010) 'Extreme life extension: investing in cryonics for the long, long term', *Medical Anthropology*, 29(2): 194–215.

Saramago, J. (2008) *Death at Intervals*. London: Vintage.

Sumiala, J. (2022) *Mediated Death*. Cambridge and Medford, MA: Polity Press.

Testoni, I. and Arnau, L. (2023) 'Journey to Switzerland as a state of exception: a *"homo sacer"* Italian experience', *Mortality*, 29(4): 728–746.

Twitchin, M. (2023) '"There is Nothing like a Dead Man to Demand" (Antonin Artaud,' in Coleclough, S., Michael-Fox, B. and Visser Existence, R. (eds) *Difficult Death, Dying and the Dead in Media and Culture*. Cham: Palgrave Macmillan.

Wheatley, H. (2023) Interview on *The Death Studies Podcast* hosted by Michael-Fox, B. and Visser, R. Published 1 March 2023. Available at: www.thedeathstudiespodcast.com [accessed 20 October 2024].

Wilson, P. (2021) 'The cryonics industry would like to give you the past year, and many more, back', *The New York Times*, 26 June. Available at: https://www.nytimes.com/2021/06/26/style/cryonics-freezing-bodies.html [accessed 18 January 2024].

Woods, S. (2016) 'Questions you should ask yourself before getting cryogenically frozen', *The Conversation*, 21 November. Available at: https://theconversation.com/questions-you-should-ask-yourself-before-getting-cryogenically-frozen-69064 [accessed 16 February 2024].

12

'I Was So Lost … And Who Brought You Back? Me.': Deathstyle Gurus and the New Institutional Logics of Mourning on Instagram

Johanna Sumiala and Linda Pentikäinen

Introduction

In recent years, researchers have witnessed a shift in grief management.[1] One important feature is a shift from religious and medical institutions that traditionally have managed death and grief in society into more individually centred, experience-based grief management carried out by individuals in diverse digital platforms (Arnold et al, 2018). Consequently, grief today is managed more and more typically as a vernacular and individualized procedure (see, for example, Walter, 2002; Arnold et al, 2018). One important element of social media grief management is the 'grief specialists' who perform the task of mourning for others and from whose experiences others can learn (see also Jacobsen, 2021). Not surprisingly, an ever-increasing number of grief specialists can now be found on social media platforms, including Instagram. As Stephanie Baker and Chris Rojek (2020) demonstrate, today, many people turn to the internet when they feel the need for other people. Losing a loved one marks such a circumstance.

This chapter aims to look beyond 'the individualized grief management thesis' where people are argued to 'do death and grief' in their 'own way' (Walter, 2002) and approach grief and its management as not only an individualized matter but also a profoundly digitalized practice adapted to the institutional logics of commercial social media and the related attention economy. So, instead of simply arguing for the deinstitutionalization of grief management in digital society (see Sumiala and Jacobsen, 2024), we take a position where people's grief management activities are discussed in a broader context of the operation mode of social media. Further, we emphasize analysing 'grief specialists' as 'deathstyle gurus', a concept we have developed from Baker and Rojek's (2020) theory of 'lifestyle gurus' and their work on social media.

In brief, we define deathstyle gurus as Instagram content producers who are typically self-educated and whose expertise is based predominantly on their own experiences. These gurus perform the task of mourning on social media by posting messages about their grief and longing and sharing information on how to find meaning and cope with such a situation. As gurus, they have a number of followers who regularly visit their accounts and engage with each guru's mourning and coaching activities. In addition, they are skilful in adapting their communicative logics to the attention economy and related commercial logics of the platform they are using. This type of *vernacular hybridity* (Howard, 2008a, 2008b), the use of individualized, vernacular and social media-adapted institutional conventions, practices and discourses, we argue, is typical for grief gurus (see Abidin, 2018; Baker and Rojek, 2020).

Our empirical analysis is based on a digital ethnographic study conducted on Instagram in 2023. In this process, an ethnographer follows an algorithmic flow and how it shapes and reshapes the content offered by the platform (Hine, 2015; Pink, 2021). Consequently, we followed grief-based content and content producers on Instagram and used hashtags such as #griefjourney, #thisisgrief, #griefsupport and #widowshelpingwidows to navigate 'the messy' field of Instagram (see also Postill and Pink, 2012). As a part of our fieldwork, we took notes and screenshots and saved videos. Our fieldwork on Instagram lasted about 12 months, and during the course of this research, two active Instagrammers – *Spilledmilkmamma* and *Heatherquisel*[2] – appeared particularly interesting. Based on their popularity, the number of followers, the public nature of these accounts and the commercial activity of these actors, we began to think about their grief work in the framework of a deathstyle guru.

A note of ethical reflection is appropriate here. A qualitative digital ethnographic study must consider the ethical implications of presenting results collected in online social environments, particularly when studying people in vulnerable positions or those at risk of experiencing harm by the study (see, for example, Markham, 2018). In this work, we rely on a distinction between commercialized and non-commercialized social media accounts. Both *Spilledmilkmamma* and *Heatherquisel* can be categorized as social media professionals (compared to many ordinary social media users with public accounts) whose aim is to gain attention and publicity to strengthen their status as popular Instagrammers. We thus argue that their social media posts constitute products from a commercial entity that can be publicly addressed and discussed without a means of fabrication (Markham, 2012). Nonetheless, we have chosen not to publish the first or last names of our studied content producers nor other names that would reveal the personhood of the subject in these posts. Further, we only refer to information that is openly and publicly available for any Instagram user interested in this content.

The chapter is structured as follows. First, we discuss social media platforms as social institutions and Instagram gurus as distinct actors within them. Second, we turn to our empirical case of the two Instagrammers we call deathstyle gurus and analyse:

1. how they are building and maintaining their status as individual grief specialists;
2. how they utilize social media platforms to manage grief and engage with their audience; and
3. how these practices are embedded in the social institutional logics of Instagram.

In conclusion, we bring the different threads of the analysis together and reflect on how Instagram as a social institution may shape grief and its management in digital society. We also reveal how deathstyle gurus as new institutional actors on Instagram may endorse the instrumentalization and commodification of human vulnerability and pain, platforming their vernacular and hybrid activities.

Platforms as social institutions

In line with Zygmunt Bauman (2007), we argue that a characteristic of late modern society is diminishing trust in the authority of traditional institutions. This trend has only been intensified through the increase of internet-based, horizontal and networked communication (Papacharissi, 2019) in society, and it also affects where people turn when they face the loss of life (Jacobsen, 2021). As many scholars of digital death have shown, individuals now have many alternatives to choose from and to identify with when it comes to managing death and grief (Jacobsen, 2021; Sumiala, 2021).

However, even if people have become more sceptical towards traditional authorities and related institutions and their structures (Furedi, 2013) and more interested in finding their own individual way in death and grief-related matters, the need to seek support and validation for one's individual choices from some collective instance has not disappeared. Thus, we may consider social media platforms as *social institutions* that serve this purpose. As argued by Kneese (2023), these digital platforms were not originally designed to serve such a purpose. Nevertheless, after social media users as mourners began to appropriate them, platforms have begun to better adapt to these needs and curate services accordingly.

Similarly, Art Silverblatt (2004) clarifies that 'a social institution provides a support system for individuals as they struggle to become members of a larger social network'. As *social institutions*, social media platforms offer people the possibility of feeling a sense of belonging and a community in which they can participate. Through these institutions, people are able to strengthen their social bonds and confirm aspects of their identity by taking part in the issues they find important. Being part of a social media platform can offer individuals a sense of identity, which Silverblatt (2004) terms as one of the key meanings of social institutions. To understand how these platforms function the way they do as social institutions, we need to look more closely at how they are structured.

As a platform, social media can best be approached as a digital surface or a structure that enables communication and interaction among many people simultaneously (see, for example, Meikle, 2016). Social media platforms rely on sharing, communicating, building networks and uploading content from their users. This type of 'culture of connectivity', as van Dijck (2013: 5) calls it, has further created so-called affective networks (see, for example, Papacharissi, 2019) and a 'ring of authentic co-existence' (Baker and Rojek, 2020) where personal and intimate information can be shared with a larger audience and, consequently, establish and maintain a sense of belonging and community within this social institution. Platforms also shape the ways content creators act within them. By knowing the rates of likes, shares, saves and comments, algorithms can further create content that sparks the most interest (and thus, consists of economic potential). Then, followers further shape the type of content circulating on social media and thus give visibility to certain actors on those platforms. As a result, platforms with their algorithms gain a new type of control over what is produced and circulated and under what conditions such content is produced and shared by the audience (Gillespie, 2010, 2018).

Notably, platforms are also structured as powerful and global economic agents. They are privately owned corporations created to make a profit. As commercial platforms, they are driven by the attention economy and its related logic of communicative capitalism (Kneese, 2023; see also Dean, 2005), where the product is 'us' who produce content and networks as part of our daily social media activities for the benefit of the platform to sell this data to its customers and advertisers. To make a profit, platforms use algorithms that guide the interests of the users when navigating social media.

The making of a guru on Instagram

In line with many other social media platforms, Instagram is a deeply commercialized social institution – it is driven by an advertising logic and algorithms that offer its users content based on their interests. While Instagram has recently adopted more discursive and argumentative features (see, for example, Schreiber, 2023), it is still strongly based on visuality and certain aesthetics – both commodified features – that make it highly suitable for advertising products and services highlighting wellness, beauty and youth (Baker and Rojek, 2020).

One of the key features of Instagram is the ability to share stories about one's personal life. Such affordance contains the potential to provide various frames for communication that create a so-called *platform vernacular* (Gibbs et al, 2015). A way to perform platform vernacular is to post and share everyday life issues triggered by some mundane incident. Such content may give visibility to content creators, but it may also help others who follow such posts and who are in a similar situation. This dynamic leads to a condition where individuals present their mundane everyday selves to the audience to trigger engagement and gain attention. Consequently, they can turn themselves into a marketable resource. Thus, sharing one's own life on Instagram may turn into a *goal-directed activity* with the hope of gaining not only more followers but also micro-celebrity status, whether as an influencer or a guru (see, for example, Senft, 2008; Khamis et al, 2017; Abidin, 2018).

Typical of all these categories (micro-celebrity, influencer or guru) is that they have the potential to attract attention and, thus, have marketable value. This type of self-branding can be monetized and turned into a profit (Baker and Rojek, 2020). Therefore, such actors are constantly trying to gain attention and seek more followers by sharing more content that is already recognized as popular (Van Krieken, 2020). One important method in seeking, maintaining and managing attention is sharing affective and emotion-arousing material about one's private life and thus building a sense of authenticity and trust between the Instagrammer and their audience and followers. While micro-celebrities, influencers and gurus may share many similarities in their Instagram style of activity, we wish to analyse the work of gurus as grief specialists. Baker and Rojek (2020) define lifestyle gurus in the following manner: 'Lifestyle gurus typically portray themselves as offering practical, non-nonsense advice on life issues.' Four goals are of specific value: acceptance, approval, social impact and self-validation. We argue that all these goals can also be identified in the work of deathstyle gurus. First, deathstyle gurus provide advice on how to attain recognition as a grieving person (typically a widow) in the virtual community of Instagram. Second, they help their audience seek approval for grief work. Third, they wish to make a social impact by inviting their audience and followers to see their grief as a 'journey' towards a better life. Fourth, they help their audience and followers gain a new type of self-validation as a mourner. By performing their grief tasks and accepting their journey, they can find a new sense of positive self-worth (see also Baker and Rojek, 2020; Harju and Pentikäinen, forthcoming).

Moreover, Instagram gurus as deathstyle gurus are expected to be 'authentic'. Such an image of authenticity can be achieved by skilfully managing self-disclosure (Baker and Rojek, 2020) and sharing personal and intimate experiences, such as loss and grief. This communicative practice is also supposed to provide peer support for the audience and followers, inviting greater engagement with the guru and their Instagram account. Consequently, deathstyle gurus and their audience and followers together contribute to building a platform economy of affect, attention and engagement (see, for example, Abidin, 2018; Baker and Rojek, 2020) – all means to facilitate peer-to-peer marketing on Instagram. Abidin (2018) highlights the importance of being a 'real' person with 'real problems'. Instagram deathstyle gurus use social media platforms to share their feelings, thoughts, ideas and advice towards a better life after losing a loved one. They offer solutions from a peer position. The advice from Instagram deathstyle gurus can cover basically anything from weight loss to mental health care, fashion to skincare and overall wellbeing. A deathstyle guru's performed authenticity gives an image of one seeking help from a friend. However, as Baker and Rojek (2020) point out, an Instagram guru's authenticity is typically performed and driven by competition and commerce. A similar pattern, we argue, can also be recognized in the Instagram activity of deathstyle gurus.

Furthermore, in line with other social media platforms, Instagram's algorithms favour dramatic content. Death, grief and mourning trigger strong emotions and reactions in the guru as well as in their audience. This type of highly affective and intimate content may attract deeper involvement from followers, a relationship that materializes in likes, shares and comments (Baker and Rojek, 2020). As an outcome, Instagram deathstyle gurus can become 'trusted companions' (Baker and Rojek, 2020) of their followers (see also Senft, 2008; Baker and Rojek, 2020).

Next, we will take a closer look at *Spilledmilkmamma* and *Heatherquisel*, two Instagrammers, and their activities and public performances of grief on Instagram. Our interest lies in these grief gurus' ways of building the visual vernacular mode of communication (Gibbs et al, 2015) on Instagram and how they utilize the social media platform in their grief management and audience engagement. This approach offers an understanding of vernacular hybridity (Howard, 2008a, 2008b) as it shows how social media as an institution is profoundly present in the individualized management of grief on this platform. We look in particular at:

1. how the two deathstyle gurus are building and maintaining their status as individual grief specialists;
2. how they utilize social media platforms in their grief management and how they interact with their audience and followers in this process; and

3. how these practices are embedded in the social institutional logics of Instagram.

Analysing deathstyle gurus' grief work on Instagram

Both *Spilledmilkmamma* and *Heatherquisel* have public accounts on Instagram, so while one does not have to register to follow them, one needs to have an account. On their accounts, they both claim the status of a widow and refer to the loss of their husband in their biography (a brief description of the account owner). Hence, the personal loss experienced becomes a key part of their publicly created self-image on Instagram. Both Instagram accounts have commercials attached to their daily stories, and both gurus actively promote diverse wellness products to help them cope with their loss. Thus, there is an explicit monetary profit associated with the Instagram activity of these deathstyle gurus.

Spilledmilkmamma started to post about her loss a week after losing her husband, and *Heatherquisel* tells her audience that she began posting about her grief two years after her loss. Both *Spilledmilkmamma* and *Heatherquisel* were married to their partners, and they had children together. In their posts, they both refer to their current position as a single mother, a role that has explicit value in their Instagram content as deathstyle gurus. Notably, *Spilledmilkmamma* and *Heatherquisel* were active on social media before the loss of their husbands. *Spilledmilkmamma*'s initial plan was to create an account offering content about motherhood with two children under the age of two. *Heatherquisel*'s account was focused on inspirational lifestyle content prior to her loss.

Nevertheless, the number of *Spilledmilkmamma*'s and *Heatherquisel*'s followers has grown tremendously after they began to post on mourning and grief. For example, *Spilledmilkmamma* reached 10,000 four months after losing her husband, and she now, about two years later, has 175,000. *Heatherquisel* now has 92,100 followers, a number that only increased in 2023 with 8,000 more followers. On Instagram, a guru's value can be measured against the high engagement rates of the followers.

To characterize their daily Instagram activities, *Spilledmilkmamma* adds new mourning content every day. She posts weekly (sometimes several) commercials with different brands. She refers to the help she gets from the product or service for the negative changes grief has caused to her looks or wellbeing. Her content focuses explicitly on lifestyle and fashion, and she frequently posts about her children, re-posts the content created by other widows or shares quotes focusing on mourning. She has recently remarried, and some of her latest content also includes elements of their new life together.

Heatherquisel's content relies more explicitly than *Spilledmilkmamma*'s on grief-based advice, and she also calls herself a widow coach. Her main guru Instagram activities are posted on weekdays, and she articulates the importance of spending time on weekends with her children. *Heatherquisel* focuses on interacting with her followers by addressing and sharing their questions about grief on her account, networking with her followers in her daily story section (short videos which stay online 24 hours from the moment they are posted). In addition to sharing her experiences, *Heatherquisel* also addresses topics like parenthood or her diet. Furthermore, she promotes her weekly *Widows Wednesday*, a private group discussion, where she promises to give more detailed advice and share more intimate discussions on mourning and grief with other widows. In a nutshell, both *Spilledmilkmamma* and *Heatherquisel* use multiple Instagram tools to add videos, images and text-based content to their accounts. They also actively post reels that include 15 second videos with audio and multiple effects.

Performing authenticity

When we look at how these two deathstyle gurus are building and maintaining their status as grief specialists, the question of affective communication associated with authenticity becomes of key relevance. This aspect of their online identities helps them to create the sense that they are trustworthy companions in peer interactions with their followers. Both *Spilledmilkmamma* and *Heatherquisel* maintain a communicative style that is consistent with what can be called *emotional labour* (see, for example, Hochschild, 1983; Senft, 2008; Marwick, 2013), helping gurus to appear reliable and relatable in the eyes of their audience and followers. Gurus need to present themselves as *trusted companions*, following Baker and Rojek (2020). An essential element in this communication strategy is revealing their emotional struggles as widows and single parents to the audience.

To give one example, *Spilledmilkmamma* writes about her feelings intimately on National Grief Awareness Day:

> It's #nationalgriefawarenessday and how appropriate that my body feels so heavy today. I've talked many times before on how physical grief is, but I bet you didn't think it lasts as long as it does. I still get sick almost every morning. I try hard to eat most days but it's difficult. I get easily exhausted after social events and my back feels like it's constantly full of rocks. Some days walking to the kitchen feels like I'm walking through mud. ... My body never lets me forget. (30 August 2022)

In this post, *Spilledmilkmamma* is sharing her vulnerability and revealing painful emotions. Emotional labour includes manufacturing the public self by revealing vulnerable information about oneself (Marwick, 2013).

For example, both *Spilledmilkmamma* and *Heatherquisel* post short video clips of themselves crying and openly showing the pain they are feeling. However, as gurus, they also need to present themselves as consistent, positive and motivated – worthy of listening to and able to educate (Baker and Rojek, 2020). An example of resilience in the face of grief is a reel of *Spilledmilkmamma* crying with a wine bottle on the terrace of her house, but then the image changes to her as a smiling person. The audio and the text on the reel state, 'I was so lost … and who brought you back? Me. I think you are the only person that can bring you back.' The caption next to this reel states: 'Don't give up 🤛 ⚓ #yougotthis #griefjourney #widowjourney #grieftruths #mentalhealthawareness #dontgiveup' (20 February 2023). Her post on National Grief Awareness Day ends with a positive note:

> But grief's a bitch and doesn't end.
> We learn to live around it.
> Deal with triggers better.
> It becomes a part of us instead of the whole.
> My hope this past year has been to educate just a little bit on what trauma and grief can do to a person. Because to be honest, I had no clue.
> I can tell you this…
> • it's gets better
> • you will genuinely laugh again
> • you will have more good days than bad
> • you will love again and have purpose again
> Keep going. ❤
> You are stronger than you realize.
> #griefawareness #grieftruths #widowtruths #griefjourney
> #nationalgriefawarenessweek (30 August 2022)

Self-disclosure is an integral part of presenting oneself as authentic (Marwick, 2013; Baker and Rojek, 2020). By showing painful emotions and sharing vulnerable stories openly, *Spilledmilkmamma* and *Heatherquisel* increase the trust in the eyes of their followers and communicate that they are just like anyone else. What makes them distinct is their desire to guide others through a painful process of mourning and grief they have themselves experienced (and still do). For example, in her biography, *Heatherquisel* describes being 'Your best widow friend and widow coach'. Highlighting friendship can be perceived to be a way of building the feeling of intimacy between the guru and their audience (Baker and Rojek, 2020). Presenting themselves as authentic peers, the deathstyle gurus communicate that they are to be trusted and that their lives are worth following. In this sense, *Heatherquisel* performs intimacy and authenticity by frequently featuring herself doing household chores like cleaning, cooking and doing laundry while talking and giving advice to her followers about grief. This approach shows her encouraging her followers to continue their mundane lives while grieving.

In this medium, however, friendship is never one-directional. Hence, both *Spilledmilkmamma* and *Heatherquisel* ask their followers to share their thoughts in the comments section – such activity can also be perceived to increase engagement in their accounts. *Heatherquisel* interacts with her followers by involving them in discussions which may seem intimate and equal. She frequently asks her followers to talk about the person they have lost or if they felt similarly to her after the loss of their husbands. Interaction with the audience can be argued to strengthen the followers' feeling of closeness in the Instagram community of mourners.

An example from one of *Spilledmilkmamma's* videos demonstrates how she addresses her followers in a tone of encouragement based on her own experiences:

> Coming out of the grief hole (as I call it) especially as a parent of young ones is close to impossible. It takes incredible strength that no one but yourself can do. The holidays are extremely draining and your body needs and wants to sleep and rest and to just turn off. But that's not an option for a lot of us. So if you overcame over more day. One more holiday. One more broken sentimental object. ... If you cleaned today or if you just fed your kids and turned on movies all day. If you showered or brushed your teeth. ... Gosh you did it. Because you don't know until you know ... but I made it one more day. One more holiday. One month. One more year 🤜 #widowjourney #griefeducation#wewillsurvive #itsamarathonnotasprint #widowedmom #toddlermom #wegotthis #widowhoodsisterhood #holidayseason (2 January 2023)

This caption is accompanied by the video of her cleaning the kitchen and, at times, crying and holding her face. The text on top of the reel states:

> Grief is not linear. Not even in a 15 minute period. Coming out of the grief hole is harder than anyone realises unless you're in it ... I started making this video to show that I was doing it ... but another wineglass broke. After 2 of my wedding ornaments broke that morning. And I know they are just things. But sometimes ... right when you feel you are coming back ... one trigger will bring you back down. And that's ok. We keep going. We have to. (2 January 2023)

She has also added an audio – Blü Eyes, 'Healing Hurts' – to this video, which further highlights its emotional spirit. *Spilledmilkmamma* here shares her thoughts about the nature of grief and shows how it changes over time. For deathstyle gurus, it is important to also show resilience and development in their journey to make their experience and advice accountable.

Commodifying influence

To study how the two deathstyle gurus utilize social media platforms in their grief management and how they interact with their followers, we must examine the ways in which their communication is adapted to the communicative logic of Instagram as a commercial platform. As discussed, on Instagram, users are able to write a short biography of themselves, where they can describe who they are and indicate how they want to be portrayed. This biography plays a central role when creating a public self-image and attracting the interest of followers. *Spilledmilkmamma*, for example, describes herself as a 'young widow, new bride and mama'. Her self-description provides important information about her situation and reveals how she wants to be seen by her followers. In the biography, she has added a link to her own webpage, where she tells her story of becoming a widow. She also markets products on her website, which she curates and produces, that she finds helpful for grieving people. These include headbands and a book about grief for children. There is also a link where one finds things *Spilledmilkmamma* is wearing in her Instagram posts. She also provides a discount code for her followers.

Furthermore, *Spilledmilkmamma*'s daily content draws on commercialized cooperation with different brands that focus mainly on style, clothes, makeup and hair products. She mentions the effects of grief on her looks and advertises products and services helping to solve this problem. In an Instagram story made in summer 2023 (screenshot taken 13 July 2023), *Spilledmilkmamma* talks about the beauty treatments she has recently undergone. She thanks, for example, services like lipsbywhit, glowbylo and spasydellat for helping her to recover from the negative effects grief has caused her. In the video, she states that 'grief makes you lose collagen … so they just literally brought me back to life'.

Fashion and clothing styles consist of a large percentage of her content. For example, in an image where *Spilledmilkmamma* is standing in an airport wearing a sweater and shorts with images of lemons, it states, 'When life gives you lemons 🍋… hop on a plane with your girlfriends 🦋💫✨' (4 May 2023). She has tagged the clothing brand's Instagram account in the picture for followers to access if they want to order a similar outfit. With 'lemons', she seems to be referring to the death of her husband 1.5 years earlier and her life with small children since then.

As mentioned, *Heatherquisel* refers to herself as a widow coach, which she also states in her biography. Through her biography, one can order the *Widow*

Survival Guide she wrote. *Heatherquisel* also asks her followers to send her a direct message if they are interested in ordering other products she promotes.

The commercial interests driving the lifestyle advice can sometimes be more implicit (Baker and Rojek, 2020), and this is also the case for many of *Heatherquisel*'s services. For example, she focuses on self-care and advice, but that also involves commodified cooperation with products helping to maintain her complete wellbeing:

> // THE BODY KEEPS SCORE. My favorite essential oils for triggering a reset + power down of the body are: ◊ Balance ◊ Serenity ◊ Adaptiv. All three of these blends come in my grief starter collection 🌿 ● Also, super-grounding oils like Vetiver, Frankincense, and Cedarwood are some of my favorites for bringing stillness to a racing mind, 🧘 and Ylang Ylang and Magnolia (the floral MVP's) help to release the heavy burdens you carry on your shoulders and ease irritation you have with the world around you. (6 November 2022)

It is a typical feature of Instagram gurus to advise their followers, often based on their own experiences and knowledge gained from the setbacks they have experienced in life (Baker and Rojek, 2020: 59). *Heatherquisel*, for example, focuses on highlighting her expertise in the area of loss through losing her husband and the father of her children. This significant event in her life has classified her as attention-worthy (Abidin, 2018), and she has been able to turn her private life experiences into her profession. As a deathstyle guru, she further gains credibility on top of the lived experience:

> // IT CHANGED EVERYTHING
> In 2020, I was using essential oils heavily to deal with the grief and big grief-y hurdles of Year 2 without Harry,[3] and by 2021, I had this really strong pull to SHARE all of it with other widows and grieving hearts.
> I wanted to help, and I had these tools to help process and heal big grief + emotions...
> But I was still grieving, myself.
> 🙏I just wanted to help you, and I wanted to show you it could be done in the brokenness and confusion of it all.
> ⚜ Thank you for being such a huge part of my healing since then, and thank you for trusting me.
> Has your career changed, too?
> #startingover #lossofalovedone #copingwithgrief #thisisgrief #selfdiscoveryjourney #rebuildyourself #rebuildyourlife (17 September 2022)

This example is accompanied by a video of her giving a speech in front of a large audience, framing her professional status. *Heatherquisel* highlights the fact that while still in a state of mourning, she felt that her experiences were something she had to share. She explains to her audience how her activities are based on her will to help people in the same situation as she was.

Grief management as a commodity of platformed institutions

The ethnographic description of the grief management of the two deathstyle gurus makes it explicit that their style of performing grief on Instagram is not only an individual practice but an effort closely adapted to the social institutional logic of Instagram. Both gurus actively produce emotional labour (see also Marwick, 2013) in their public grief work. By posting about their personal grief, loss and struggles as widows and single mothers, both *Spilledmilkmamma* and *Heatherquisel* open their intimate, emotional lives to the Instagram public.

Through their communicative work, these gurus perform authenticity by addressing their pain and appealing to their followers as 'trustworthy' companions, inviting others to feel connected to the digital community of mourners. *Spilledmilkmamma* and *Heatherquisel* also enhance a sense of 'widow solidarity' by actively interacting with their followers and requesting that they share their stories of loss. *Heatherquisel* sees herself as a widow coach, and *Spilledmilkmamma*'s communication style consists of elements employed regularly by social media influencers (Khamis et al, 2017). They both provide advice and guidance for their followers by responding to their questions and offering curated digital spaces for private discussions as well as a possibility to share intimate feelings of loss and bereavement.

All these activities offered by *Spilledmilkmamma* and *Heatherquisel* are also tightly tied into the commercial logic of the attention economy characteristic of Instagram. Their daily activities can be interpreted as attempts to arouse interest and increase visibility (see also Kneese, 2023) among their audience and invite more followers to their accounts. From this perspective, both deathstyle gurus actively work to commodify their influence as grief specialists. They have developed a self-brand and a public image that can be (and factually is!) marketed to develop economic gain (Marwick, 2013; Senft, 2013) and to increase their cultural and attention capital (see, for example, Krieken, 2020) on Instagram.

Thus, their performance of grief work helps them to monetize their self-brand and attract advertising. Both gurus materialize their value through personally curated recommendations and active advertising and selling different types of wellness products (such as cosmetics, clothes and accessories) marketed to help mourners cope with their situation and feel better while still suffering from their loss. These commercialized relationships between the guru and their followers (as customers) are based on the emotional labour carried out by the gurus, enabling their commercial success as deathstyle gurus with a considerable audience (Baker and Rojek, 2020).

Conclusion

In sum, this chapter aimed to look beyond 'the individualised grief management thesis' where people in contemporary, digital society 'do grief' in their own individualized way. Instead, we argue that people's grief management activities – here on Instagram – must be analysed in a broader context of the operation mode of these digital platforms. In our ethnographic analysis, we demonstrated how the studied deathstyle gurus utilize platform vernacular (Gibbs et al, 2015) to perform their grief tasks for others. This use of an individualized, vernacular and peer-related style of communication, building upon claims of authenticity, is connected to the attention economy and the related commodified logic of Instagram as a social institution. This condition, we argue, creates a new type of vernacular hybridity (Howard, 2008a, 2008b) around grief and its management in today's digital society. As a vernacular, it is centred around grief gurus' personal experiences and their communication by using Instagram's typical affordances, and as a hybrid, it is well adapted to the institutionalized commercial and attention-driven logic of this platform.

Drawing this discussion to a close, inhabitants of digital society may have lost their trust in traditional institutions and their authorities' ability to guide us through grief. However, the need to find and follow role models and to seek guidance on what to do in these life-disturbing situations caused by death has not disappeared. In digital society, social media has become one obvious site to seek guidance and consolation. As a social institution, Instagram carries the promise of collective support, a sense of belonging and an identity for those looking for ways to assuage their grief and pain (see Silverblatt, 2004). Managed by these gurus – grief experts by experience, Instagram as an institution appears to be leaning towards a vernacular, individualized and personal approach to grief management.

In this chapter, we have attempted to demonstrate how such individualized mourning practices may not be best understood simply as deinstitutionalized social activities but as practices profoundly adapted to the institutional and commodified logic of Instagram (Sumiala and Jacobsen, 2024). Deathstyle gurus play a vital role in this cultural process as they shape grief and its management in the present-day digital society. From this perspective, grief management on Instagram appears first and foremost as a monetized interaction of communicative capitalism (see also Sumiala, 2021). In this condition, not only grief and mourning but also mourners themselves become instrumentalized items and goods to be sold to the platforms according to their business model.

Notes

[1] We acknowledge that in some discussions (see, for example, Mulemi, 2017), grief and mourning are applied to characterize different bereavement activities (grief referring to more intimate and private experiences and mourning to the more public exercise of bereavement). However, for the sake of simplicity, we use grief and mourning synonymously in this chapter.

[2] For the sake of consistency, we use *Heatherquisel* instead of *heatherquisel* as a style of spelling in the article.

[3] Name fabricated by the authors of this chapter.

References

Abidin, C. (2018) *Internet Celebrity: Understanding Fame Online*. Leeds, UK: Emerald Publishing Limited.

Arnold, M., Gibbs, M., Kohn, T., Meese, J. and Nansen, B. (2018) *Death and Digital Media*. Abingdon and New York: Routledge.

Baker, S.A. and Rojek, C. (2020) *Lifestyle Gurus: Constructing Authority and Influence Online*. Cambridge: Polity Press.

Bauman, Z. (2007) *Liquid Times: Living in an Age of Uncertainty*. Cambridge: Polity Press.

Dean, J. (2005) 'Communicative capitalism: circulation and the foreclosure of politics', *Cultural Politics*, 1(1): 51–74.

Furedi, F. (2013) *Authority: A Sociological History*. Cambridge: Cambridge University Press.

Gibbs, M., Meese, J., Arnold, M., Nansen, B. and Carter, M. (2015) '#Funeral and Instagram: death, social media, and platform vernacular', *Information, Communication and Society*, 18(3): 255–268.

Gillespie, T. (2010) 'The politics of "platforms"', *New Media and Society*, 12(3): 347–364.

Gillespie, T. (2018) *Custodians of the Internet: Platforms, Content Moderation, and the Hidden Decisions that Shape Social Media*. London: Yale University Press.

Harju, A.A. and Pentikäinen, L. (forthcoming) 'Re-writing the "grief journey" - capitalising on grief through resilience', *Nordic Journal of Media Studies*, 7.

Hine, C. (2015) *Ethnography for the Internet: Embedded, Embodied and Everyday*. London: Routledge.

Hochschild, A. (1983) *The Managed Heart: Commercialization of Human Feeling*. Berkeley: University of California Press.

Howard, R.G. (2008a) 'The vernacular web of participatory media', *Critical Studies in Media Communication*, 25(5): 490–513.

Howard, R.G. (2008b) 'Electronic hybridity: the persistent processes of the vernacular web', *Journal of American Folklore*, 121(480): 192–218.

Jacobsen, M.H. (ed) (2021) *The Age of Spectacular Death*. London: Routledge.

Khamis, S., Ang, L. and Welling, R. (2017) 'Self-branding, "micro-celebrity" and the rise of social media influencers', *Celebrity Studies*, 8(2): 191–208.

Kneese, T. (2023) *Death Glitch: How Techno-Solutionism Fails Us in This Life and Beyond*. New Haven: Yale University Press.

Markham, A.N. (2012) 'Fabrication as ethical practice: qualitative inquiry in ambiguous internet contexts', *Information, Communication and Society*, 15(3): 334–353.

Markham, A.N. (2018) 'Afterword: ethics as impact – moving from error-avoidance and concept-driven models to a future-oriented approach', *Social Media + Society*, 4(3): 1–11.

Marwick, A.E. (2013) *Status Update: Celebrity, Publicity, and Branding in the Social Media Age*. New Haven: Yale University Press.

Meikle, G. (2016) *Social Media: Communication, Sharing and Visibility*. London: Routledge.

Mulemi, B.A. (2017) 'Mourning and grieving', in Leeming, D. (ed) *Encyclopaedia of Psychology and Religion*. Berlin: Springer, pp 1–5.

Papacharissi, Z. (ed) (2019) *A Networked Self and Birth, Life, Death*. New York: Routledge.

Pink, S. (2021) *Doing Visual Ethnography* (4th edn). London: SAGE.

Postill, J. and Pink, S. (2012) 'Social media ethnography: the digital researcher in a messy web', *Media International Australia*, 145(1): 123–134.

Schreiber, M. (2023) 'Text on Instagram as emerging genre: a framework for analyzing discursive communication on a visual platform', *Studies in Communication Sciences*, 24(1): 141–157. https://doi.org/10.24434/j.scoms.2024.01.3882

Senft, T.M. (2008) *Camgirls: Celebrity and Community in the Age of Social Networks*. New York: Peter Lang.

Senft, T.M. (2013) 'Microcelebrity and the branded self', in Hartley, J., Burgess, J. and Bruns, A. (eds) *A Companion to New Media Dynamics*. Hoboken: John Wiley and Sons, pp 346–354.

Silverblatt, A. (2004) 'Media as social institution', *American Behavioral Scientist*, 48(1): 35–41.

Sumiala, J. (2021) *Mediated Death*. Cambridge: Polity Press.

Sumiala, J. and Jacobsen, M.H. (2024) 'Digital death and spectacular death', *Social Sciences*, 13(2): 1–11.

van Dijck, J. (2013) *The Culture of Connectivity: A Critical History of Social Media*. New York: Oxford University Press.

Van Krieken, R. (2020) 'Economy of attention and attention capital', in Ritzer, G. and Rojek, C. (eds) *The Blackwell Encyclopaedia of Sociology*. Hoboken: John Wiley and Sons, pp 1–4.

Walter, T. (2002) *The Revival of Death*. London: Routledge.

Afterword

Kate Woodthorpe, Helen Frisby and Bethan Michael-Fox

This collection has been a pleasure to put together, and we hope that you have enjoyed reading it. Collectively, the chapters show that institutions and processes of institutionalization are the product of complex and ever-changing forces, contexts, people and perspectives. Never fixed and always in flux, institutions and the processes within them are constantly evolving. Their role and potential is enormous, creating and sustaining norms of behaviour, turning everyday practice into standards, and manifesting identities. Their reach and influence on the end of life and its aftermath is immense, and can include the law and markets (Chapters 2 and 3), state service providers (Chapters 1, 4, 5, 6), issues of performance (Chapters 6, 7, 11 and 12), the implementation of ideas (Chapters 8 and 10) and can facilitate death itself (Chapter 9). Simultaneously contradictory and consistent, as the chapters in this book have shown they can make material and tangible the invisible on the one hand, and conceal and obscure on the other. They can make death more equitable while at the same time more political and unfair. There is nothing static or inevitable when it comes to institutions.

Within this ever-changing landscape, a common theme throughout the chapters in this book has been the significance and dynamics of knowledge(s). As the chapters show, particular forms of knowledge, holders of knowledge and locations of knowledge have been – and continue to be – privileged over others. This can include the establishment of places, policies or practices, the implementation of law, or the (re)presentation of ideas and opinions. Prioritizing and privileging some knowledge(s) over others is not a value-free 'neutral' decision and, instead, needs to be understood for what it is: the expression and outcome of power.

Readers will not be surprised that knowledge and power are central to institutions and institutionalizing processes, as they have been intrinsically connected in some of the most well-known theories about how places, organizations and landscapes shape behaviour and exercise authority, and not least in terms of death. Medicalization, professionalization and psychologization have all been covered extensively in relation to the end of life across disciplines, along with the role of 'structures' such as ethnicity, belief, governments, healthcare, and so on. Within this, a consistent key question has been the agency of individuals and their relationships to bigger systems, be they familial, political, governmental, religious or economic. Given this, at the outset of creating this book we expected power – and surveillance as a form of or practice in power – to feature more heavily in the chapters, given how in death studies to date the organization (and institutionalization) of the dying and bereaved, and its consequences, has been a dominant theme. We also anticipated more on sequestration, and the extent to which institutions make evident or conceal particular peoples and practices, or the way in which efforts to improve services have historically succumbed to quantifiable measurements that have been their downfall. What we did not foresee were the more subtle features of institutions and institutionalizing processes documented in these chapters, which show institutions' humanity, vulnerabilities and weaknesses, and the degree of choice and even creativity of those navigating them. We did not further fully anticipate the entanglement of culture and power, which is at the heart of almost most, if not every, chapter in this book. Certainly, despite this book belonging to Bristol University Press' *Death and Culture* series, we did not predict that the nuances of culture would have *such* an influence over the way in which death is managed, experienced, interpreted, governed, measured, evaluated, commodified, gamified, positioned and (re)presented. As each chapter has shown, whether it is on the historical parading of children in funerals, or the implementation of contemporary legislation, or the commodification of grief online, behaviour, process and governance needs to be understood through a cultural lens, to be able to understand behaviours and actions, critically assess social norms and acceptance and contestation, and societal responses. Such is the value, we think, of bringing together a wide array of disciplines and contexts to explore the topic, and authors from around the world, in being able to see the influence of culture and cultural difference on death, dying and bereavement.

We thus end the book with a call to arms for the study of death and dying to continue to be as interdisciplinary and global as possible. As editors, we are based in the United Kingdom and span sociology, history and English, and have learnt much from both the chapter authors and each other, in terms of theoretical perspectives, writing styles and convention, and what constitutes evidence. We have sought to keep our editorial input to a minimum to enable the differing disciplinary voices and conventions to emerge. We recognize, however, that there are gaps in this book, both in terms of disciplines and in nationalities, that would have helped create a more inclusive and global conversation. As a truly interdisciplinary field, death studies thrives on that inclusivity and if anyone takes up the mantle to create a second volume of this book we would recommend the inclusion of perspectives from geography, politics, criminology, climate sciences, psychology and more, and from authors based in the Global South. That they would have something to say about institutions and institutionalization is a given, such is the universality of the topic.

The importance of keeping these interdisciplinary conversations open and of not working in silos is critical in an increasingly pressured global academic sector. We trust that this collection and contribution to the *Death and Culture* series has illustrated the potential for examining the intersection of death and dying with major societal practices, trends, histories, landscapes, markets and social movements, of which culture is at the core.

Index

References to figures appear in *italic* type; those in **bold** type refer to tables. References to endnotes show both the page number and the note number (153n3).